CORPORATE **Explorer** Fieldbook

INTRODUCTION BY MICHAEL TUSHMAN

ANDREW BINNS
EUGENE IVANOV

CORPORATE **Explorer** Fieldbook

How to Build New Ventures in Established Companies

WILEY

Published by John Wiley & Sons, Inc., Hoboken, New Jersey.
Published simultaneously in Canada.

For general information on our other products and services or for technical support, please contact our Customer Care Department within the United States at (800) 762-2974, outside the United States at (317) 572-3993 or fax (317) 572-4002.

Wiley also publishes its books in a variety of electronic formats. Some content that appears in print may not be available in electronic formats. For more information about Wiley products, visit our web site at www.wiley.com.

Library of Congress Cataloging-in-Publication Data

Names: Binns, Andrew (Managing principal), editor. | Ivanov, Eugene (Innovation advisor), editor.
Title: Corporate explorer fieldbook : how to build new ventures in established companies / edited by Andrew Binns and Eugene Ivanov.
Description: Hoboken, New Jersey : Wiley, [2023] | Includes bibliographical references and index.
Identifiers: LCCN 2023010333 (print) | LCCN 2023010334 (ebook) | ISBN 9781394159222 (paperback) | ISBN 9781394159246 (adobe pdf) | ISBN 9781394159239 (epub)
Subjects: LCSH: Technological innovations. | Creative ability in business. | Corporations.
Classification: LCC T173.8 .C695 2023 (print) | LCC T173.8 (ebook) | DDC 303.48/3–dc23/eng/20230314
LC record available at https://lccn.loc.gov/2023010333
LC ebook record available at https://lccn.loc.gov/2023010334

ISBN: 9781394159222 (Paperback)
ISBN: 9781394159239 (ePub)
ISBN: 9781394159246 (ePDF)

Cover Design: Paul McCarthy

SKY10051231_071723

In memory of Melissa Annette Ellis
—Andy

In memory of Tatjana Ivanova and Leonid Ivanov
—Eugene

CONTENTS

PREFACE AND ACKNOWLEDGMENTS

THE REAL WORK for an author starts after the book is published. Since *Corporate Explorer: How Corporations Beat Startups at the Innovation Game* (co-authored with Professors Charles O'Reilly and Michael Tushman)[1] was published in spring of 2021, Andy Binns has been on the road. He has spoken with hundreds, if not thousands, of innovation practitioners who run innovation programs within large corporations in different industries all around the world.

They were inspired by the real-life stories of leaders who built new businesses inside large corporates, such as IBM, RELX, UNIQA, and Analog Devices. They recognized themselves not as entrepreneurs, but as *Corporate Explorers*, a distinct role inside corporations that may not attract the same attention as their startup brethren, but still generate extraordinary results.

In May 2022, our friends at Robert Bosch GmbH convened a conference, Corporate Startup Fusion, bringing together a wide range of innovation practitioners from across Europe. What was clear from presentations, discussions, and conversations was how much insight and experience about corporate exploration existed inside corporations. There is no question that management gurus and academics make an important contribution — through concepts, methodologies, and canvases – but in many ways practitioners are far ahead of them. Business school professors talk; these people do.

This realization was the seed for this book. A kitbag full of practical, time-tested methods and tools applicable to every step of the new venture-building process, written by and for the Corporate Explorers themselves. It covers much of the same territory as the previous book, but goes deeper, presenting even more details on *how* to define ambition and hunting zones for a corporation; *how* to ideate, incubate, and scale new ventures; and *how* to build and implement an ambidextrous organization.

Each large company is different, so it's next to impossible to invent methods and techniques that would work the same way everywhere, every time. Reflecting this point, *Corporate Explorer Fieldbook* is not a textbook or recipe. It's not a collection of *answers*; rather, it's a library of *questions*. We want every Corporate Explorer to start a new project — or a new phase of the ongoing project – with a set of questions that would guide their activity. The answers will be different for every Corporate Explorer – depending on the industry they operate in or the nature of their project – but asking these questions will make their job more effective and, eventually, more successful.

Corporate Explorer Fieldbook has two pillars. One of them is the foundational research performed by Professors Charles O'Reilly of Stanford and Michael Tuchman of Harvard. For years, Charles and Michael have been describing structures and tools that allow large firms to *explore*, that is, to create new ventures while fully exploiting all the assets provided by the core business. Central to this process is their concept of ambidextrous organization, an organizational type that makes disruptive innovation in large companies possible. Charles and Michael's contribution also includes their painstaking description of the three major disciplines of innovation: ideating, incubating, and scaling.

All our authors have been tremendously responsive and collaborative to work with, which is a great experience for us. Thanks to Andreas Brandstetter, Narendra Laljani, Tony Ulwick, George Glackin, Kaihan Krippendorff, Bea Schofield, Simon Hill, Uwe Kirschner, Michael Nichols, Vanessa Ceia, Sara Carvalho, John Greco, Erich Kruschitz, Richard Robertson, Alex Pett, Kristin von Donop, Michael Tushman, Charles O'Reilly, Sarah Spoto, and Yaniv Garty for their excellent contributions. However, we must reserve special thanks to our colleagues, Christine Griffin and Vincent Ducret, who have been tireless in their efforts to bring our vision to fruition, working on many chapters, reviewing drafts, and acting as thought partners.

The other pillar is Change Logic, a firm Andy, Charles, and Michael co-founded in 2007 together with Peter Finkelstein. Change Logic has worked with some of the most innovative firms in the world, and through this work, sharpened our understanding of what Corporate Explorers need to carry in their toolboxes to be successful. Some of our former and current clients have become friends; a few of them showed their friendship by agreeing to contribute to this book as authors. Our Change Logic team has been a constant source of ideas and support – even those who have not contributed a chapter. This book is very much a team effort. Thanks to Aaron Leopold, Nishi Gupta, Alina Cowden, and Sara Orlando. We also thank the many Corporate Explorers we have met over the years. They are the inspiration for our work and originators of so much that we are sharing with our readers.

Most of all we thank Mike Tushman and Charles O'Reilly for their inspiration and guidance. They have touched all the contributors to this book in different ways, through their research, writing, and teaching. This book is another example of how they multiply that impact through patient mentorship and support to the many others who seek to carry their work forward.

—Andy Binns and Eugene Ivanov, Massachusetts, USA, February 2023

CORPORATE EXPLORATION: INSIGHTS FROM THE FIELD

Michael Tushman

AS AN UNDERGRADUATE in electrical engineering at Northeastern University, I participated in its co-op program for which the school is rightly famous. It gave me not only intensive classroom time, but also hands-on work experience. My co-op assignment for four years was with the firm General Radio, at that time a leader in automatic test equipment, and already a 50-year-old company. During my time at General Radio, HP and Tektronics initiated several major technological advances in test equipment design and production. General Radio had no answer for these competitive provocations, which precipitated a crisis for the company. After a shift in strategy, structure, and culture, General Radio reemerged as GenRad, a different company, quite unlike the one that I had joined. As a budding electrical engineer, I had experienced my first example of reactive punctuated change.

General Radio had to experience a crisis before it could adapt to the market. I was profoundly puzzled that a company with all the resources of a successful enterprise and staffed with brilliant engineers should struggle, so hard and so unsuccessfully, to shape its fate. This experience led me to three critical questions that have shaped my subsequent career as a scholar of innovation and change and as an advisor to firms at technological junctures. Why is it that successful firms like General Radio frequently fail at the moments of industry transition? What can they do to be more dynamic and adaptable at these critical points? And how do they execute these changes?

The "why" question is well understood. This is the story of organizational inertia. The more successful a company gets, the more well-honed it becomes at delivering more of the same. Of course, this generates lots of long-term value and is a rich source of innovation at the core business. However, it welds the organization – its structures, processes, people, and culture – to the job of optimizing its existing business. Great for delivering results today, but when the world changes, it leaves them vulnerable to what my colleague Don Sull describes as "the dynamics of standing still." Organizational renewal has been the core of my work since that searing experience at General Radio.

The "what to do" question led me, my students, and my colleague Charles O'Reilly to the concept of the "ambidextrous organization." Structural ambidexterity creates a formal separation inside the company between two tasks, the one of optimizing the core business and the one of exploring into new domains. The notion of structural ambidexterity has taken some time to catch on as an approach. I remember vividly colleagues at Columbia Business School and Harvard Business School telling me that it was "a lovely idea, but could never work in practice." Better for incumbents either to spin out this exploration work or to leave it to entrepreneurs. Then, I had the privilege of pragmatically exploring these ideas with IBM in the late 1990s and early 2000s. Under the leadership of Lou Gerstner and Sam Palmisano, IBM created a string of emerging business opportunities that applied the ambidextrous approach with great success, yielding a quarter of the company's profits by 2010. Working with Charles O'Reilly and Bruce Harreld (IBM strategy head and then HBS colleague), we explored factors that discriminated between more versus less successful examples of core and explore at the business-unit and corporate levels at IBM. IBM subsequently suffered a tough decade, but it has survived several industry transitions, while rivals, such as EMC, Sun Microsystems, HP, and CSC, all struggled and were eventually acquired or restructured.

However, there was still a gap. While we knew that structural ambidexterity was one solution to the innovator's dilemma, it required much from the senior leadership team. Paradox, contradiction in the face of historically rooted inertia, often held incumbents hostage to their pasts. Charles and I became interested in the issue of how to execute ambidexterity. From my position in the classroom at Harvard Business School and boardrooms with Change Logic, a consulting business that I co-founded with Andrew Binns and Charles, we have learned much about how to execute ambidexterity and associated punctuated organizational change. Through Change Logic's work with a range of firms, we have developed a point of view on both the "what" and the "how" of strategic organizational renewal. The number of firms applying the ambidextrous solution is substantial. I now have research- and practice-based responses to my car-pool friends from General Radio so many years ago!

While our initial books explored the "what" of structural ambidexterity, what was missing was a deep dive into the "how." How do firms explore into emerging areas so that they can lead more of critical transitions, rather than finding themselves the victims of disruption? This is the work of Corporate Explorers. They ideate, incubate, and scale new ventures, so that incumbent firms could use these ventures to navigate through times of high uncertainty. Our 2022 book, *Corporate Explorers: How Corporations Beat Startups at the Innovation Game,*[1] told stories of multiple leaders who had the commitment and personal passion to lead these new ventures.

This new book goes a step further by having practitioners themselves explain how they achieve such extraordinary results. It combines the insights of innovation managers, company executives, strategic advisors, and scholars to present a comprehensive guide to the work of Corporate Explorers. That's why the book is titled *Corporate Explorer Fieldbook*.

Corporate Explorer Fieldbook follows a similar structure to the previous one. It has three main sections: Strategic Ambition, Innovation Disciplines, and Explore Organization and Leadership.

Strategic Ambition refers to the need of providing an overarching vision that elicits compelling emotional purpose and guiding strategic rationale for exploration.

Chapter 1 describes how to turn high-level corporate statements into an empowering Strategy Manifesto that helps align senior leaders on the ambition and then communicate this ambition to their organizations. This chapter is co-authored by Andrew Binns and his client for many years, Andreas Brandstetter, CEO of UNIQA Insurance Group and President of the General Assembly of Insurance Europe.

Chapter 2, written by Andrew Binns, takes one step forward by describing how firms can select Hunting Zones for their exploratory efforts. This helps align the energy and inventiveness of the Corporate Explorer with the strategic intentions described in the Manifesto.

The next two chapters offer two different lenses on the same question: How to select the starting point of exploration? Chapter 3 by Narendra Laljani argues for an outside-in market learning as an antidote to the toxic assumptions that develop within successful incumbent firms and blind them to the shifts in customer behavior. In Chapter 4, Tony Ulwick describes how to define markets from the customer's viewpoint, by using the concept of jobs-to-be-done.

Chapter 5 brings these threads together by focusing on how Corporate Explorers win support for exploration. George Glackin outlines how Corporate Explorers first decide which opportunity to pursue and then develop an opportunity story that explains to investors why a new venture deserves funding.

The second section, Innovation Disciplines, comprises a series of chapters on ideating, incubating, and scaling new ventures. These are the essential practices that a Corporate Explorer needs to apply to convert an idea into a revenue generating business.

In Chapter 6, Kaihan Krippendorff presents his methodology for ideating from within the companies, explaining how to liberate the insights of the company's employees. Chapter 7 turns to ideation from the outside, as Simon Hill and Bea Schofield describe how the challenge-driven-innovation methodology can be used to tap on the intellectual power of external crowds.

The next six chapters take deep dives into the topic of incubating new ventures. These are practices that seem relatively straightforward from the outside but are difficult in real life as they run counter to the culture of delivering predictable results from the core business. That makes the lessons from Bosch, General Motors, and P&G of such great value.

Chapter 8 frames the challenge of incubation as one of business model maturity. Uwe Kirschner and Michael Nichols describe a methodology, developed at Robert Bosch GmbH, for assessing when a venture has matured sufficiently to justify further investment.

Vanessa Ceia and Sara Carvalho leverage the lessons learned at Bosch to present, in Chapter 9, some practical tools to be used in the process of customer discovery.

In Chapter 10, George Glackin teaches how Corporate Explorers can develop a value proposition that would persuade both their colleagues and upper management to support the development and launch of the new venture.

In Chapter 11, Sara Spoto and Vincent Ducret introduce us to the art and science of business experimentation, a process of testing a Corporate Explorer's instincts and assumptions against the sets of on-the-ground data demonstrating that an idea is worth pursuing (or not).

The next two chapters specifically deal with the process of scaling new ventures.

It's not often that a Corporate Explorer has all the means at their disposal to scale a new venture. However, these means can be acquired through "ecosystems" composed of other market players. To address this important point, Christine Griffin and John Greco outline, in Chapter 12, steps Corporate Explorers need to take to develop their ecosystem playbooks, based on work that they did together at Analog Devices.

To make scaling of a new venture a disciplined, data-driven process, Corporate Explorers need success metrics. Developing these metrics isn't easy, and in Chapter 13, Ellie Amirnasr and Charles Vaillant describe three metrics, developed at MANN+HUMMEL, that measure a new venture's progress toward success.

The final section of the book, Explore Organization and Leadership, addresses the organizational aspects of new venture creation and touches upon an all-important topic of leadership.

In Chapter 14, my friend and colleague, Charles O'Reilly, and I explain the concept of ambidextrous organization. This is a decision for the Corporate Explorer, or more likely for their senior sponsor and perhaps even for the CEO, to make about how best to structure the organization for success. Some innovations can succeed from inside the core business; others are appropriate to spin out in a venture studio or some other vehicle. However, the strategically important ones that can go faster by leveraging the firm's existing assets need an ambidextrous approach.

Once the decision to create an ambidextrous organization has been made, it's time to begin building an exploratory unit, and in Chapter 15, Christine Griffin and Erich Kruschitz describe practical steps to realizing this goal, using the example of SanusX, an explore venture launched by the Austrian insurance firm, UNIQA.

Richard Robertson reminds us, in Chapter 16, of the importance of the strategic diversity of innovation teams. We each have preferences that align us with different roles in the growth of a new venture: some are natural explorers; others bring structure and apply discipline. There is no right profile; the task is to match the composition of the team to the current stage of the venture development.

In *Corporate Explorer,* we talked about the risk of "silent killers" of innovation, borrowing a term coined by my colleague, Mike Beer.[2] These are largely the same forces of organizational inertia that I experienced so vividly at General Radio. In Chapter 17, Alex Pett discusses how to have high-stakes conversations with senior team members, who may be ducking the important issues facing a new venture. Alex also describes how Corporate Explorers can learn to create and maintain constructive tension.

However, "silent killers" are only overcome by enrolling many other people in the work of transformation. This is what we call a leadership movement. In Chapter 18, using the example of their work with Intel Israel, Yaniv Garty and Kristin von Donop describe how to build this movement and use it to overcome resistance that often emerges as the venture starts to grow.

Finally, in Chapter 19, Charles O'Reilly describes the key levers for overcoming silent killers by transforming organizational culture, illustrating this approach with excellent examples of Microsoft's transformation under Satya Nadella.

We could have added a dozen more chapters and still not fully encompassed the issues facing the Corporate Explorer. Even so, this is a comprehensive guide that will serve as an invaluable resource to leaders starting the journey toward building a new venture from inside an existing corporation. We are not offering a prescription from the classroom or a special formula of a management guru. There is no magic bullet for overcoming the very real challenges that confront innovators when they try to move large, successful organizations into new technologies and/or markets. It is painstaking, hard work that carries the day, not application of the latest theory or framework. That this book is based on the lived experience of practitioners gives it an authenticity and value that should be attractive to anyone starting their journey as a Corporate Explorer.

SECTION I

STRATEGIC AMBITION

CHAPTER 1

Strategy Manifesto: Answering the Big "Why"

Andrew Binns and Andreas Brandstetter

A PROBLEM WITH STRATEGY PLANS

Strategy plans often fail at the most basic level. They rarely talk about the big challenges companies face or present a point of view about how to win. Instead of articulating a plan for growing beyond today's business, they often focus on sustaining performance in the present or the near-term future. When they do talk about the future, it is in vague and aspirational terms that fall short of real commitment. The plan may list possible areas for growth. It may estimate the size of the growth opportunity or, even worse, predict a "hockey stick" trajectory for future revenues when these opportunities are realized. Even when there is a strategy plan with a clear point of view about how to explore and win in emerging markets, that can get lost in a tsunami of PowerPoint slides.

Such plans leave Corporate Explorers confused. A Corporate Explorer is no clearer about the company's aspirations, the impact it wants to have on the world, or where it sees the biggest opportunity for future growth. This makes any aspiring Corporate Explorer wonder: are senior managers committed to innovation? If I spend time developing a proposal, will they want to listen? Should I take my idea to outside funders? The alternative is for the senior team to make a clear statement of the company's strategic ambition in a clearly written strategy manifesto. The manifesto is a document of three to five pages of text that explains the firm's strategic ambition, the implications for the core business strategy, and the opportunity to explore beyond the core. When done well, it is a statement that every member of the senior team can stand behind and explain to their teams. It is the North Star, providing an organization with a clear answer to the "big why" question that informs all other growth and transformation efforts.

The strategy manifesto also gives aspiring innovators a "license to explore." This is an invitation to managers and employees to develop ideas for how to solve important customer problems within the boundaries defined by the firm's strategic ambitions and hunting zones. It says, "this is what we want to achieve, and we are open to ideas on how we get there." The strategy manifesto does not replace the detailed analytic work of a strategy plan. It just makes explicit the choices that the company is making with its strategy and provides the rationale for those decisions.

This chapter describes the components of the strategy manifesto, how to create and use it, and what to do if you are a Corporate Explorer in an organization without a clear manifesto. We also include an Application Case Study of how UNIQA Insurance in Vienna developed a strategy manifesto and what role it played in the company's explore business strategy.

COMPONENTS OF A STRATEGY MANIFESTO

A strategy manifesto needs to tell a story that engages its reader and avoids ambiguity. Here is a format that we recommend with suggested word count (Figure 1.1). We provide some examples that are drawn from real strategy manifestos used by companies across many different industries—automotive, semiconductor, and health care—to provide context for how to apply the format.

Context (250–300 words)

The purpose of this section is to acknowledge the past and position the story within the shared experience of the team.

- **History.** Evoke pride by referencing a shared experience of success. For example, *"As a company, we created the* [insert descriptor] *market and have shaped its success for over 50 years. . ."*
- **Change.** Recognize the shifting reality in these markets. *"The emergence of digital natives that offer cheaper alternatives has led us to question this future and whether we can compete."*
- **Question.** Formulate an implicit or explicit "troubling" question to which this document will give the answer. *"Can we be a winner in the next generation of our markets or is defense our only game?"*
- **Answer.** Provide a succinct statement of the senior team's point of view. *"Success is possible if we pursue a strategy of optimizing our current business and exploring into the emerging market, leveraging our assets to move faster than the start-ups."*

01	**CONTEXT** (250–300 Words)	**History.** Evoke pride by referencing a shared experience of success. **Change.** Recognize the shifting reality in these markets. **Question.** Formulate an implicit or explicit "troubling" question to which this document will give the answer. **Answer.** Provide a succinct statement of the senior team's point of view.
02	**CHALLENGE** (500–600 Words)	**Market Change.** Describe shifts in customer preferences, market dynamics, competitor activity. **Innovation.** Name the most important technologies or capabilities that could disrupt your markets – opportunity and threat. **Consequences.** Make the potential positive and negative consequences as tangible as possible.
03	**AMBITION** (300–400 Words)	**Emotional hook.** Give people something to believe in that elicits an emotional connection with the company's strategy. **Logic.** Provide a rationale for the strategic decisions. **Aspiration.** Set a tangible goal that is equal to the scale of the opportunity or threat of disruption.
04	**STRATEGIC CHOICES** (250–300 Words)	**Core business objectives.** Set specific end goals for what you will achieve in two to three years. **Explore hunting zones.** Describe where you see the areas of the greatest potential for the future growth of the business. **Portfolio.** Outline how you will allocate resources across different parts of the business to achieve the ambition.
05	**EXECUTION** (250–300 Words)	**People & Culture.** Explain how employees fit in, what they can expect, and how you want them to behave. **Innovation.** Outline the process for managing the flow of ideas. **Organization.** Describe any specific organizational units that will be created to manage the growth strategy. **Capabilities.** Give specifics about how you will meet the need for additional capabilities outside the firm's traditional strengths.
06	**NEXT STEPS** (250-300 Words)	**What happens next...**

Figure 1.1 Strategy manifesto template.

Challenge (500–600 words)

This section crystalizes the key reasons compelling your company to act now, rather than defer action to another time.

- **Market Change.** Describe shifts in customer preferences, market dynamics, competitor activity. *"Customers expect more integrated solutions that are easily configurable with software . . ."*
- **Innovation.** Name the most important technologies or capabilities that could disrupt your markets. *"Electrification of vehicles is a revolution for our industry that changes the product we offer, and the capabilities required to be successful."*
- **Opportunity.** Explain why the market changes, and innovation is an opportunity for the company. *"Although there are many claiming to have the best new technologies in the market, none can rival our distribution, manufacturing, and sales capabilities. If we can match these to winning customer value propositions, then we can lead the next generation."*
- **Threat.** Explain the logic for concern about the emergence of a disruptive threat. This is often suppressed in successful organizations because it may look like disloyalty or a lack of confidence. A manifesto is an opportunity to name the threat that everyone sees. *"Tesla is ahead, we cannot pretend otherwise. They have made themselves synonymous with electric vehicles, despite what we see as inferior build quality."*
- **Consequences.** Make the potential positive and negative consequences as tangible as possible. *"In the short term, the new market is small in absolute value, representing only 5% of total sales. However, in less than a decade, we anticipate it to be worth double that of our traditional markets. We are either in a position to win an unfair share of this market or we defend an ever-shrinking market."*

Ambition (300–400 words)

This section presents a big message that inspires teams and helps guide their actions. It should be short, memorable, and provide employees with three key pieces of information.

- **Emotional hook.** Give people something to believe in that elicits an emotional connection with the company's strategy. *"We want to wage a war on cash, replacing money with digital payments"* (Mastercard).
- **Logic.** Provide a rationale for the strategic decisions – making a move into digital payments or renewable energy or whatever the opportunity might be. For example, Mastercard got to say "by converting more of the 85% of manual cash transactions to digital," thereby expanding their market from the head-to-head competition with VISA and AMEX for the other 15%.

- **Aspiration.** Set a tangible goal that is equal to the scale of the opportunity or threat of disruption. *"Only sell emission-free vehicles by 2035"* (GM); "*Improve the lives of three billion people*" (Philips Healthcare).

Strategic Choices (700–800 words)

This section articulates the "so what" of the ambition.

- **Core business objectives.** Set specific end goals for what you will achieve in two to three years. "*We will increase market share by x percentage points versus our principal competitors*"; "*We will increase gross margins by two points.*"
- **Explore hunting zones.** Describe where you see the areas of the greatest potential for the future growth of the business. These "hunting zones" tell aspiring Corporate Explorers where to focus their efforts. See the case study on UNIQA for an example.
- **Portfolio.** Outline how you will allocate resources across different parts of the business to achieve the ambition. "*We will change our approach to R&D investment so that it is focused on a small set of cross-business priorities. Some of these are in our core business. Others will be investments in our future business growth.*" This may include highlighting what you are not doing, that is, areas where you are going to withdraw investments, or others that you are deliberately choosing not to enter. "*That means we have made the tough decision to exit business x and y, and to shelve plans for entry into market z.*"

Execution (500–600 words)

Here is the section where you describe what it will take to be successful.

- **People and Culture.** Explain how employees fit in, what they can expect, and how you want them to behave. "*This is a renewal of our organization and its culture, as much as it is of our growth strategy. We aim to create opportunities for teams to demonstrate their passion for customers and demonstrate the entrepreneurial spirit to solve them.*"
- **Innovation.** Outline the process for managing the flow of ideas into incubation projects. "*We will invite employees to participate in innovation challenges to propose solutions to customer problems within our hunting zones ...*"
- **Organization.** Describe any specific organizational units that will be created to manage the growth strategy. "*We will establish a small Emerging Growth Unit responsible for supporting new ventures as they get selected for seed funding. It will collaborate actively with the business units to help our Corporate Explorers leverage the assets they need to succeed.*"

- **Capabilities.** Give specifics about how you will meet the need for additional capabilities outside the firm's traditional strengths. "*We will appoint a head of software with the remit to hire an additional 100 software engineers within the next six months to professionalize our approach . . .*"

Next steps (250–300 words)

Be clear about what happens next.

- **Leader.** Name the leaders responsible for the different aspects of the strategy.
- **Milestones.** Identify important dates in the next three months that people can watch out for.
- **Personal action.** Include some immediate actions for the readers of the manifesto. "*Register your interest in participating in the Innovation Challenge at . . .*"

CREATING A STRATEGY MANIFESTO

Manifestos are short and mostly reflect things that organizations already know, even if they have never put them in this format before. The problem is to tune out the noise of the day-to-day business and to crystallize this knowledge into a succinct articulation of what you believe needs to be done. Here are five steps to provide structure to the effort.

Step 1. Develop a point of view. Start with a point of view about the ambition: What does the organization want to achieve? This could be the "so what?" statement that comes from months of in-depth analytical strategy work or, as happens to many leaders, an instinctual statement of the potential that lies dormant in the company. This point of view should reflect the company's commitment to positively impact the world and its customers, not just a pious vision statement. A key test question here is: Could this apply to any company other than us? Is it okay if others could set the same ambition? It is *not* okay if the statement is so generic that it could apply to anyone. Another key test is the quality of the emotional response you get from those outside the team – you want people to be excited, a little surprised by the ambition, not confused or uncertain!

Step 2. Assemble facts and perspectives. The best manifestos come from a disturbing encounter with the outside world that punctuates the usual conversation inside the company. The UNIQA case (see later) describes one technique for achieving this goal. What matters is that this should not be the senior team speaking to itself in an echo chamber. You must be willing to raise troubling questions that the business needs to answer.

Step 3. Create a first draft and iterate. Someone needs to be the draft leader, who owns the document and creates a high-quality first draft. That individual should be a good writer who understands the company and its aspirations, so that the language fits the culture and mood. Like a "minimal viable product," getting an early draft out is a very good way of learning what people really think about the issues in the manifesto.

Step 4. Engage with disagreements. The problem with most PowerPoint charts is that they leave so much room for interpretation that agreements about the content of a strategy are rarely authentic. Spend time resolving the big issues so that the document reflects a shared plan for action and does not hide disagreements at the top. Writing a manifesto can be emotionally charged. When the authors first collaborated, Andreas (the CEO) was very frustrated with Andrew (the consultant) and his rewriting of the first draft. Andreas felt strong personal ownership of what he had written. It took a few days to accept the challenging feedback that the first draft was not sufficiently precise, and that the new version brought clarity.

Step 5. Adapt for different audiences. The purpose of the first draft of the manifesto is for the senior team to make sure that there are no areas of ambiguity or unresolved disagreements. Then, it can be adapted for other audiences, of which the most important is the next layer of management in the company. In larger organizations, this is where strategy execution often gets stuck. Middle managers are often focused on achieving narrow product-line goals and do not naturally think about the overall enterprise context. The manifesto helps to make the context and the company's response explicit to the "sticky middle" of the organization.

INFLUENCER APPROACH

A strategy manifesto is ideally the work of the senior team, be that at the corporate or business unit level. This is where responsibility for the explore strategy should lie, because senior managers are best placed to make the trade-offs between the short-term needs of the core business and those of investing in long-term growth.

However, the reality is most readers of this Fieldbook are not on the senior team, where they could influence the creation of a strategy manifesto. So, what can aspiring Corporate Explorers do to trigger change in their organizations, to tip the balance to the side of investing for the future?

Here are five approaches that work in large, complex organizations. They each take time – many months – and there are no guarantees of success, but ultimately, they can create the sort of bottom-up pressure that can shift action at the top of an organization.

Approach 1. Outside-in exploration. Create a sense of urgency by organizing workshops on "future market trends," "disruptive forces," or similar topics that resonate within the organization. Invite external speakers (customers, academics, or ecosystem partners) to present different perspectives on how the world is changing. Or organize "future search" or "scenario planning" workshops, where the objective is to make sense of shared experience of current trends. Use these activities to develop a shared view of the potential futures that current trends might create.

Approach 2. Use executive education. Enroll Human Resources or learning teams in helping develop a shared view of the future. Anticipating future market trends is a desired leadership attribute at many firms, so you may find willing collaborators who could help shape a conversation about how the firm is positioning itself to lead the next wave of industry growth.

Approach 3. Create a focal point for explorers. Create a club or interest group about innovation and growth; it could even be a Corporate Explorers Club. Many organizations have such groups, and they can provide a low-risk mechanism for opening conversation with managers. Handpick your members and then invite senior leaders to come to speak.

Approach 4. Draft your own manifesto. Write your own version of the company's strategic manifesto. Use a club or one of the exploration meetings described earlier to share your point of view with others, and get their reactions. It is remarkable how quickly such efforts gather momentum and help shift executive action.

Approach 5. Cultivate a sponsor. Nurture a relationship with a specific power sponsor. Do not waste energy trying to persuade an entire executive team, at least not at first. Think about who has something to gain from supporting your plan and enough influence to get it done. Then find ways of engaging them with your story: What is the customer problem, what options have you got, how is this relevant to a wider strategic context? Most importantly, what outcomes are you seeking to generate? It's not all about the idea.

APPLICATION CASE STUDY: UNIQA 3.0 STRATEGIC MANIFESTO

In 2018, I (Andreas) was searching for an answer to the question of what next for UNIQA, the European insurance company of which I have been CEO since 2011. We were coming to the end of a long-lasting strategy that we called UNIQA 2.0. This led us from the depths of the financial crisis of 2007–2008 to making UNIQA a successful, growing firm with 15 million customers, and more than 6 billion euros in revenues. Now, we were aiming to write the next chapter for growth in the company's history, UNIQA 3.0.

Our vision was to expand the relevance of UNIQA to its customers. We aimed to help our customers live "longer, safer, healthier lives." Our insurance products are incredibly important in helping our customers do this, but this is only part of the answer. We wanted

UNIQA to be even more useful to customers. One area that made sense to focus on was health and well-being, because we already owned a chain of hospitals, and, as Austria's largest provider of private health insurance, we were already part of the healthcare ecosystem. We also knew that there was a long list of customer problems to solve: from mental health to adopting a healthier lifestyle, getting access to primary care, and aging safely at home.

We created a project team combining some of our brightest talents with a group of invited experts. The outside influence was critical, because these were people from the frontline of healthcare challenges: doctors, nurses, public officials, charity workers. They helped us learn about the real challenges people faced in their daily lives, making sure we were not thinking like an insurance company, but were genuinely trying to learn where we could make the most difference. What emerged was a strategy for exploring that led to the business that today we call Mavie.

However, before we could make this strategy happen, we needed to connect the rest of the company to our strategy. We needed our explore business of healthcare to be connected to the core business of insurance, so that we could count on all colleagues to help the new growth area succeed. The group executive board (our senior team) had already been on a voyage of discovery learning about the opportunities in healthcare, so now we had to be sure that a wider leadership group was engaged. We wanted them to understand what UNIQA 3.0 meant to them, and how they could help make it succeed.

Our Strategic Manifesto was vital to our success. The first draft helped us clarify our thinking as a senior team on the rationale behind UNIQA 3.0. We used it as a forcing mechanism to make certain that, as a team, we understood the choices we were making and that we all shared a commitment to growth in both the core and explore businesses. It was hard for my colleagues and me on the senior team to reach agreement on what the core business was and what was to be explored. It sounds easy, but it raises so many fundamental questions, that tension is inevitable. These were right-versus-right conflicts. That we all had the best interests of the company, its employees, customers, and shareholders in mind did not make it any easier.

After we had gone through many iterations, it was time to engage our next hundred leaders, a mixture of direct reports to the members of the senior team and our highest potential managers from across the organization. We brought them together for a week at Harvard Business School to learn about key topics, such as innovation, customer centricity, and culture change. Every member of the group got a copy of the Strategic Manifesto, and we used this event to open a dialogue with the team about what it would take for us to be successful. Every member of the team had the opportunity to share their feedback on our strategy and recommend actions needed for us to execute.

The Strategic Manifesto ensured that, as we started the next chapter in our company's evolution, our top 100 leaders all had the same vision of what we were changing, why, and what it would take to succeed. It is not filled with perfect foresight; we have had to experiment and learn what the market will reward. The manifesto was a starting point.

As I look back on several years of tremendous success of UNIQA, I see this document as one of the bedrocks of our success. It helped us maintain the vital connection between healthcare and insurance in our business. It continues to inspire Corporate Explorers within the company to lead innovation and growth.

CHAPTER 2

Hunting Zones: Selecting Where to Explore

Andrew Binns

HUNTING ZONE

Corporate Explorers are leaders who build new ventures in established organizations. Like entrepreneurs, Corporate Explorers often start with an observation about a customer problem, something in the world that they think they can make better. It's the passion to solve this problem that fires up so many Corporate Explorers and starts them on the hard road to building a new venture.[1]

Where should an aspiring Corporate Explorer look for this inspiration? What guidance can you give if you are trying to encourage Corporate Explorers to step forward? How do you increase the odds of getting high-quality proposals? How do you get started and how do you guide the energy of other budding corporate innovators toward market opportunities that may attract support and funding from senior sponsors?

The answer is to define market areas in which there may be attractive opportunities for Corporate Explorers to pursue. These "hunting zones" provide boundaries to guide those with an innovative impulse to generate ideas and opportunities that are in line with the business strategy and are, therefore, more likely to attract investment.

BOUNDED DIVERSITY

Despite having a reputation of being top-down hierarchies, corporations often put a high value on consensus and participation. Employee involvement in idea generation is a vital part of innovation programs inside corporations. Employees bring firsthand experience of customers, products, and competitors, and see opportunities that may be hidden to executives. Indeed, many Corporate Explorers start as winners in employee idea competitions, which propels them on the journey to creating a new venture.

However, this openness to new ideas carries risks. It's relatively easy and risk-free to generate ideas; it's much harder to execute by converting them into scaled ventures. High-participation idea generation quickly leads to having more ideas than available resources. Many of these ideas would lack a strong connection to the business strategy, so killing them off quickly should be easy. Unfortunately, the democratic nature of the process and a reluctance to say "no" makes it hard instead. As a result, resources get spread thinly across many projects. People continue working with shoestring budgets and little hope of converting them into scalable ventures. You are in the innovation zoo!

A much better approach is to define some boundaries within which ideation can be given a free range. This "bounded diversity" approach invites ideas that are more likely to gain corporate support, creating a win-win situation for both idea generators and investors.

We call these boundaries a *hunting zone*. Hunting zones provide a license to explore. They describe where a business sees the best potential prospects for realizing its growth ambition; they help narrow the focus of exploration.

At Nvidia, the CEO, Jensen Huang, has shifted the company into new market areas, helping it build a new software ecosystem, alongside its traditional semiconductor business.[2] Huang set an ambition to put Nvidia at the center of Artificial Intelligence (AI) and invited his team to think creatively. "What are we great at and love doing?" "What doesn't exist today, but the world would love it if we made it?"

However, this was not an open-ended exploration; Huang defined boundaries. He had a strong sense for which industries would likely be the earliest adopters of AI, and he challenged his team to search for problems that could be solved in four specific hunting zones: gaming, autonomous vehicles, enterprise computing, and scientific computing. These were new markets for the company, which had previously sold processors to manufacturers of computers and other electronic devices. AI and autonomous vehicles are now obvious areas of growth for a technology firm, but 10 years ago, this seemed like a fantasy to many of Huang's semiconductor industry colleagues.

DEFINING HUNTING ZONES

Market selection is a well-honed strategy discipline that assesses market size, spend, demand, growth rate, and competitive intensity to make a recommendation about which markets to enter. However, defining hunting zones is not the same as market selection. We are dealing here with *exploratory* innovation, where a market is yet to emerge. There are few "facts" on which to base judgments. When Huang announced his strategy, there was no market for autonomous vehicles (it still doesn't exist today), and deep computing for scientific discovery was in its infancy. He was anticipating markets that would only emerge and that he believed his company could shape.

How can you replicate such selection and, therefore, narrow your aperture for ideation? I recommend following a four-step approach to make these judgments (Figure 2.1). It is one that we have applied multiple times with our clients, and which has helped them start on the Corporate Explorer journey:

- Step 1. Map the innovation landscape.
- Step 2. Assess the likelihood of emerging opportunities to mature.
- Step 3. Apply selection criteria.
- Step 4. Select your initial set of hunting zones.

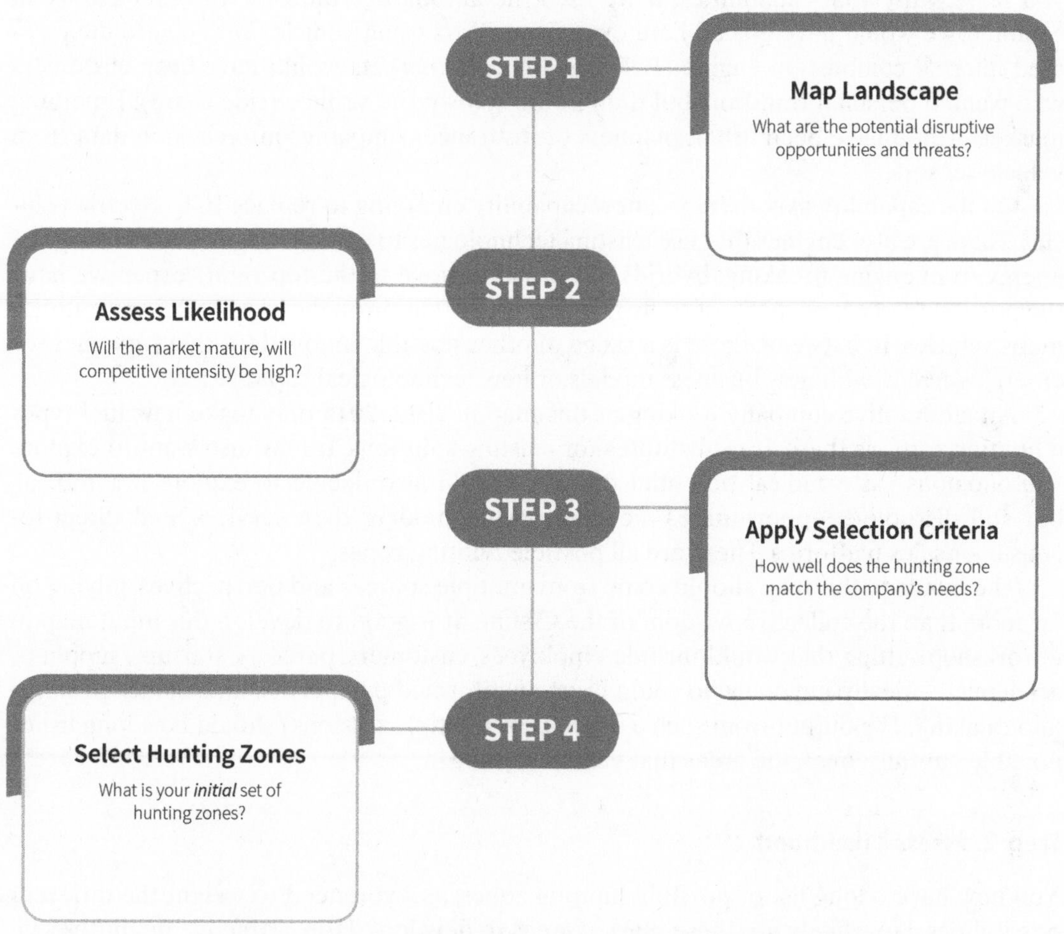

Figure 2.1 A four-step approach to hunting zone development.

I am not offering a special formula for finding hunting zones. These are judgments that will be based on instinct and vision, as well as on fact and analysis. The goal is to narrow the range of possibilities to a manageable portfolio that has a logical rationale and that you can explore with discipline. It is also just an initial set, not the final word on where to explore. It is a hypothesis, and, having done more in-depth investigation, you may drop a hunting zone and move to another one.

Step 1. Map Landscape

The first task is to define the innovation landscape. What do you know about the changing market needs and disruptive capabilities that are emerging? One way to do this is using the innovation streams map[3] (Figure 2.2).

You start by describing in the bottom-left corner your core business: what customers you serve, with what capabilities. If we used the automotive industry 10 years ago as an example, we would have placed here owner operators using vehicles with a gasoline powered internal combustion engine (ICE). In adjacent markets would have been customers who wanted personal transport but didn't want to own the vehicle (ride share). Emerging markets would have been urban planners or insurance companies interested in data from vehicle sensors.

On the capability axis, there is a new capability emerging to replace ICE: electric vehicles. There are also engines that use existing technologies to extend range by harnessing the energy from engine breaking: hybrids. Then, as we move to the top-right corner, we have the possibility of a new mode of transport that uses breakthroughs in AI to deliver autonomous vehicles. In between, there is a range of other possible innovations that serve new or emerging needs, with new business models or new technological capabilities.

An automotive company looking at this map in 2012–2015 may make new fuel types a hunting zone, as these are substitutes for existing solutions. It may also want to explore "autonomous" as a radical potential future. It could also decide to explore less radical, but still disruptive, opportunities: new ownership models, data services, and direct-to-consumer sales platforms. These are all possible hunting zones.

The inputs to this map should come from multiple sources and perspectives, relying on far more than the collective wisdom of the C-suite. It is good to develop this input map in a workshop setting that would include employees, customers, partners, startups, suppliers, academics – ideally, anyone who could bring an informed perspective and challenge status quo thinking. The output from such a session (or multiple sessions) should be a long list of possible hunting zones, the areas that you could play in.

Step 2. Assess Likelihood

You now have a long list of possible hunting zones, and you need to weight the different possibilities. How likely are these market areas to develop? How attractive might they be as a future market? There are some very sophisticated methods for anticipating future

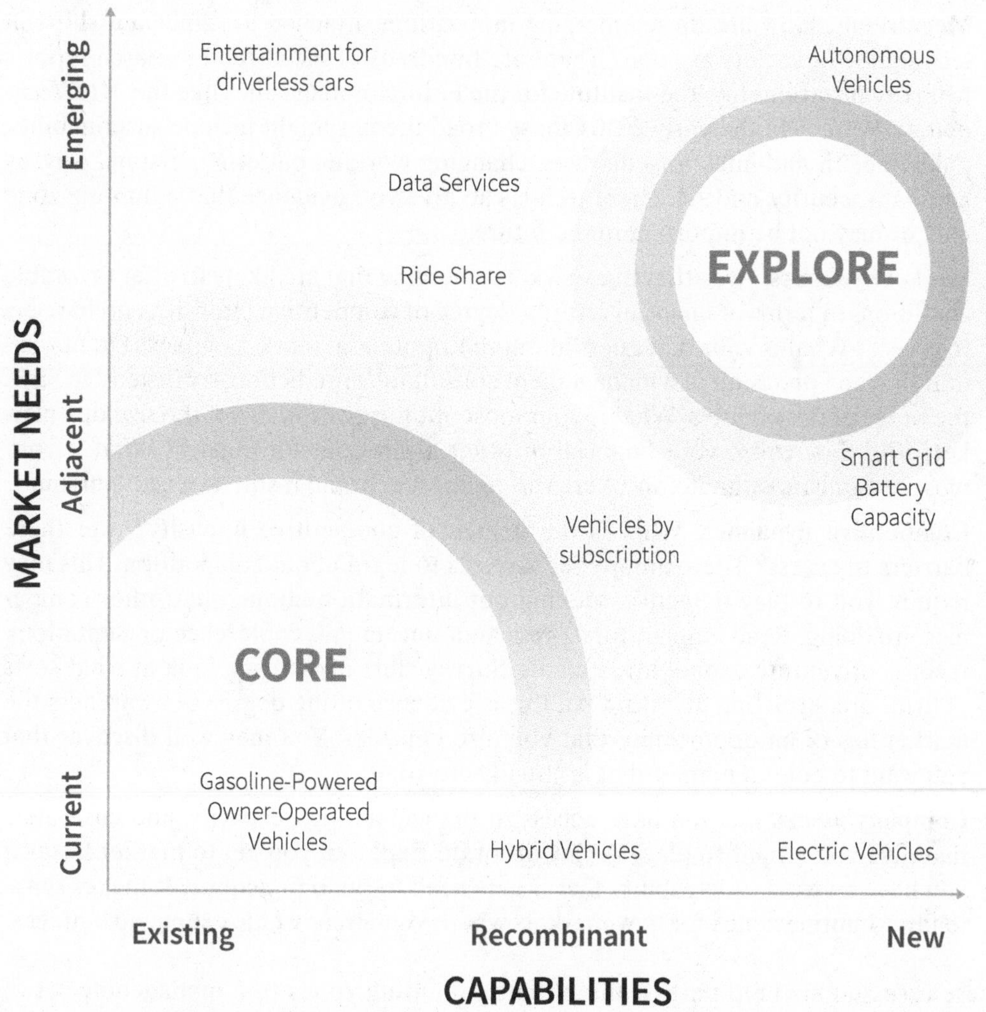

Figure 2.2 Innovation streams map (automotive industry example).

market developments, for example, scenario planning. However, there is a danger of being too confident about the quality of available data. We remember a prediction a McKinsey team made in 1982 while assessing the size of the market for cellular phones. Noting the problems with the handset's short battery life, weight, and poor coverage, the team concluded that the total market by 2000 would be 900,000 units worldwide. The actual number was 405 million.[4]

You may not be able to predict the future, but you can estimate probability. Four inputs can help you make these assessments:

1. **Megatrends.** How are these emerging innovations attached to significant shifts in technology or society at large? There are hundreds of megatrend research reports from organizations like the Institute for the Future or magazines like the *MIT Technology Review*. In the early 2020s, these broad themes might include sustainability, public health and infectious diseases, changing working patterns, personal privacy and data security, and AI. These trends can give you evidence that a hunting zone may or may not be important in the future.
2. **Market dynamics.** Are attractive markets emerging that are likely to offer favorable conditions in terms of financial returns, degree of competitive intensity, and barriers to access? What is your best guess about their potential market impact? Do not fall into the faux precision of a management consultant's prediction; try instead to scale the range of possibilities. What is your most optimistic estimate of the size of a market? Will this realize your financial or other aspirations for impact? What is your most pessimistic estimate, and were this to be true, would it still be worth pursuing?
3. **Competitive dynamics.** What is the degree of competitive intensity? Are there barriers to access? There are myriad sources to learn about competition. This may require you to play detective, seeking out information about what other companies are doing. Read competitors' press announcements, conference presentations, records of venture capital investments. Survey start-up activity; look at what sorts of firms are attracting investors. All this is evidence of the degree of awareness the market has of an opportunity that you also consider. You may well discover that you want to enter a market that is already crowded.
4. **Company assets.** Do you have access to the capabilities, capacity, and customers that give you a right to play? As a Corporate Explorer, you get to market faster if you have an asset or capability that others need to build or acquire. It makes sense to filter hunting zones for new markets where you already enjoy some advantages.

These assessments help narrow the potential hunting zones to a manageable set of options. For example, our automotive company will have found reports describing megatrends for rapid urbanization, climate change, sustainability, and a millennial generation less committed to personal car ownership. The exploration team could conclude that car ownership would be less attractive in the future and, therefore, a hunting zone focused on alternative business models would make sense. They may also decide against autonomous vehicles, because it was already a crowded space: Google set up its Waymo autonomous vehicle unit in 2009; many others were already active by 2015.

Step 3. Apply Selection Criteria

The assessment until now has mostly been outside-in – namely, using data about what is happening in the world to develop a set of options. This selection-criteria step is about matching the potential zones to a company's own needs. Is the potential hunting zone worth the effort of trying to ideate, incubate, and scale a venture? Here we need some inside-out criteria to make the final selection.

The criteria tend to be simple and represent fundamental issues. These are the sorts of issues that will lead a company to invest in potential opportunities or ignore them. Corning, for example, expects a new business to leverage the company's deep expertise in optical physics and sophisticated manufacturing, so that they can create a barrier to imitation. Similarly, in the early 2000s, IBM's emerging business opportunity program aimed to develop new ventures that would leverage cross-company capabilities (hardware, software, and consulting) to generate a new source of customer value. Intel's emerging growth program set a bar that new ideas should have the potential to scale to a billion-dollar business, leverage Intel's assets and capabilities, and disrupt or replace Intel's existing businesses.

Companies need to compile their own criteria. There are several that are worth considering (Figure 2.3):

- The company has the assets to win. It would make sense to filter hunting zones for markets where a firm enjoys some advantages, and, therefore, can get there faster.
- Evidence is available that there are customer problems to solve.
- Potential financial returns would represent a boulder, not a pebble, in terms of market size.
- There is a fit with ambition, which will help the company advance toward its overarching aspiration.
- There is a Corporate Explorer driven by commitment to pursue an opportunity; there is advocacy inside the company to support the Corporate Explorer.

Step 4. Select Hunting Zones

After you have applied the criteria, you should be left with a small set, no more than three, of potential hunting zones. Even if you have resources to do more, there is a value to staying focused and not overstretching decision-making resources over many potential zones. If you have more than three, create a backlog to come back to it in the future.

Keep in mind that this is just a starting set of hunting zones. As you investigate each zone in search of opportunities, you may learn that it is not an attractive one after all and exit. The value of the approach is that you can make this selection in a disciplined way, rather than reacting piecemeal to individual opportunities as they arise. Selecting the hunting zone gives you a launching point for exploring.

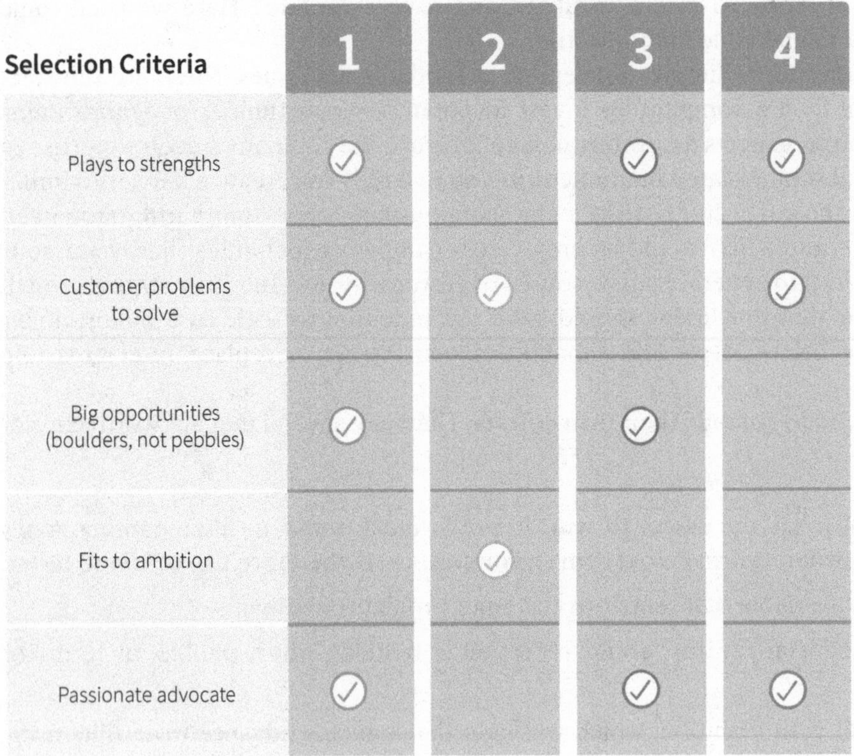

Figure 2.3 Hunting zones and selection criteria.

APPLICATION CASE STUDY: AGC

AGC is a hundred-year-old company, previously famous as the world's largest glass company. It operated in four main businesses: architectural and industrial glass, automotive glass, chemicals, and electronics (including substrates for liquid crystal display (LCD) panels). As well as the largest, it was also the most diversified glass company in the world.

In 2014, Takuya Shimamura was appointed CEO and he observed that AGC's markets were all slow-growing commodity businesses that relied on continuous improvement for revenue and profit growth. Glass business was increasingly competitive with the entry of Chinese companies, such as Fuyao, threatening to lower AGC's margins further. Shimamura faced the challenge of rebalancing the business portfolio and revitalizing the company's culture, which had become inward-looking.[5]

To begin the process, Shimamura declared his management philosophy as "AGC+," which meant changing from a material *manufacturing* company to a material *development* company. This ambition was articulated as "Vision 2025," which defined the firm's *core* and *strategic* businesses. Uncompetitive businesses in the core would close, and the rest would focus on efficiency and productivity. The strategic businesses were areas where AGC would target high growth.

AGC selected several key hunting zones: mobility (for example, the technologies and materials needed for transportation infrastructure, such as autonomous vehicles), electronics (including the materials needed for high-speed communication and semiconductors), and life sciences (such as leveraging the company's strength in fluorinated chemicals and high-quality contract manufacturing). Shimamura then set up, as separate units, three new strategic ventures and allocated resources, about $50 million per year, for the new-growth initiatives.

Concurrent with this new business development effort, Shimamura also initiated a firm-wide culture change process designed to shift the focus from reducing costs and increasing efficiency, which Shimamura's predecessor had emphasized, to a more open and innovative culture. The previous leadership had implemented a top-down, command-and-control style, in which employees were accustomed to following orders and avoiding mistakes. Because of this, some of the high-potential younger employees felt frustrated and were leaving the firm for more entrepreneurial companies.

Shimamura met with groups of younger managers to elicit their suggestions. He formed teams of 10 high-potential managers to participate in "Vision 2025" and challenged them to decide into what areas the firm should move over the coming decade. He initiated a *Gong Show* as a type of pitch event during which young researchers and engineers could propose their ideas to business leaders and top management.

AGC converted the ambition of becoming a material *development* company into a set of hunting zones, and then engaged high-potential managers to step up as Corporate Explorers. In 2022, the company reported that one-quarter of the company's profits came from these new strategic businesses, and analysts reclassified the company as a growth stock. Shimamura's strategy had reshaped the company.[6]

CHAPTER 3

Outside-In: Overcoming Toxic Assumptions with Market Insight

Narendra Laljani

WE HAVE MET THE ENEMY, AND HE IS US.[1]

Corporate Explorers use market insight to sensitize organizations to emerging opportunities and threats, so they can develop ideas for how to create new value for customers based on these insights. Unfortunately, both are easier said than done, with many traps that organizations often fall into.

From *Encyclopedia Britannica* to Kodak to the travel agency Thomas Cook, the corporate graveyard is littered with case histories of organizations that once dominated their markets but could not or did not adapt to a changing environment, even when the forces of change were clear to see. Often these organizations failed because they kept doing for too long what made them successful in the first place. In other words, they developed a success recipe, which became deeply embedded in the organization and blinded them to the signals of change. We call this the "inside-out" challenge. This reinforces the established paradigms that the Corporate Explorer must confront.

The second critical task, which we call the "outside-in" challenge, is to develop meaningful insights into customer needs. It is tempting to think that just asking customers should suffice, but we know that many remarkable innovations, from motor car to web browser to iPhone, would never have seen the light of day if customers had been asked what they wanted. Indeed, the task is to understand customers better than the customers themselves may be able to articulate. This is where we can find uncontested market space, where real opportunities for growth and building competitive advantage lie.

The common denominator in both cases is that we are limited by the patterns of thinking and behaving that have taken root in our organization. Often, the enemy is not so much the agile upstart competitor but is, in fact, within us, within our established routines and practices, and within our ability to sense, imagine, and learn.

In this chapter, we consider these two pathologies, and offer suggestions for how a Corporate Explorer may deal with them. While they are presented sequentially, they go hand in hand in real life. Deeply held assumptions and beliefs within an organization can blind us to emerging market realities. Conversely, a distinctive market insight may result in the case for letting go of an organization's traditional success recipe and open the door to transformational change. An accompanying case, "The Whole Health Strategy at Cigna Europe," offers an example of a Corporate Explorer who has achieved exactly that.

CHALLENGING TOXIC ASSUMPTIONS

All organizations have a *business model*, which typically consists of choices about market segments, value propositions, and supply chains. Strategy discussions are often dominated by considerations of growth, competitive advantage, pricing, product or service portfolio, and internal organizational structure and processes.

What is rarely understood, however, is that organizations also have a *mental model*, which is made up of unconscious, unarticulated, and unexamined assumptions and beliefs that have taken root in the organization.[2] Typically, these assumptions and beliefs are the products of past success and can be thought of as a "success recipe," which, over time, becomes "the way we do things around here." This, in turn, determines what we pay attention to and what we ignore, what we value and what we don't. This has also been described as conventions, norms, orthodoxies, paradigms, or the genetic code of an organization. The DNA metaphor is particularly helpful as it suggests a reflex response to events.

Make no mistake: DNA serves a useful purpose. This automatic and instinctive understanding by thousands of people of the "way we do things around here" is what keeps organizations ticking over. Lacking this, we would need to consult a procedure manual every few minutes, and that, of course, is not a way to run a business.

Over time, however, in a world that is constantly evolving, some of these assumptions and beliefs can become toxic. Even smart, intelligent, talented, and hard-working people can get defeated by these assumptions.

For example, in a leading British chemical company, once a household name in many parts of the world but now defunct, there was a deeply held belief that "the better molecule will win." This had been the secret of the company's success for many decades as it launched a steady stream of technologically innovative products. The company rewarded excellence in chemistry and was steeped in a culture of chemical excellence; the heroes within it were chemists. Products were sold and priced based on chemical specifications. However, there came a time when customer needs shifted from chemical specification to effects ("Can you help me make more bubbles in my shampoo?"). The organization was unable to make the transition to this new world. What was once a core competence had become a core rigidity. Paradoxically, the single biggest contributor to future failure is past success, simply because success encourages us to do more of what made us successful yesterday.

Newcomers often see these blind spots clearly, but when newcomers arrive, organizations usually unleash socialization processes that are designed to integrate these newcomers into "our way of doing things," as rapidly as possible. The faster the newcomer adjusts to the host organization's way of working, the more we congratulate the newcomer and each other on a successful recruitment: "She has settled in very nicely." In fact, a valuable opportunity to inject fresh thinking into the organization has been lost.

As if this was not problematic enough, there is an added complication, which is that entire industries also have mental models. Industry conventions are a menace, and result in most airlines believing that passenger journeys begin and end at airports, or hotels thinking that guests will steal their hangers. By contrast, innovators create value by challenging industry paradigms (think Southwest Airlines, which broke many of the rules for the airline industry).

The old mental model will always give you only variations of the old strategy. If a truly innovative and transformational strategic initiative is to gain traction within a well-established corporation, a Corporate Explorer must start with a new mental model. This requires challenging the conventional wisdom at both organizational and industry levels and starting to ask "blasphemous questions," such as:

- What are some of the "hidden" assumptions and beliefs in our industry and within our organization?
- Are any of these toxic to our future?
- If we are to create new wealth in new ways in the future, what do we need to think and do differently?

Table 3.1 provides a framework for undertaking this thinking (derived from the work of Sull, and Hamel and Prahalad[3]). This list is illustrative but not exhaustive.

In the case of *Encyclopedia Britannica*, for example, the organization became trapped in a mindset in which the dominant beliefs were that the organization was in the book-publishing business (not in the information business), that customers were corporate librarians or anxious parents (not 12-year-olds playing on a home computer), that customers purchased scholarly research-based information (not education and fun packaged together), that the best way to get the product to the customer was through a door-to-door sales force (not by creating end user "pull"), that the value associated with the product was typically $1,000–$3,000 (and not $99 associated with a rival product on a CD-ROM), and that the real competition was other publishing companies (not a software company in Seattle).

Table 3.1 Questioning existing assumptions.

	Question	Current assumption	Different view	Implications
1	What business are we in?			
2	Who are our customers?			
3	What do they buy from us?			
4	Why do they buy from us?			
5	How do they access our products and services?			
6	What is the price–performance ratio?			
7	Whom do we compete with?			
8	What is our competitive advantage?			
9	What do we need to be good at?			
10	How should we organize ourselves?			

Despite having a glorious heritage and a powerful brand, the *Encyclopedia Britannica* was blindsided by new technology and has since become and remained a pale shadow of its former self.

This exercise of identifying and challenging toxic assumptions is best undertaken by a team in which two different demographics come together: some newcomers, not yet fully conditioned by the host organization's DNA, and some industry or company veterans who know the nuts and bolts of the industry. Such a team may be inspired by the "destroy your business" initiative successfully used by GE to reshape itself from a chimney and smoke-stack business to one that embraced the opportunities offered by the internet. This was a process that required large numbers of people in teams to challenge the company's success recipe – and not when it was faltering, but at the peak of its success. The underlying thinking was to help insiders to think like outsiders.

Imagine that you no longer work for your current employer but are part of an agile entrepreneurial startup. Knowing what you do about your current employer, what are all the things you would do to destroy it and create new value in new ways? And then, how can you make the business case for successfully doing these same things within your current organization before somebody else does it to you?

GOING BEYOND CUSTOMER-LED

Great innovations are built on the back of great insights about customers, by knowing something about customers that others cannot or will not understand. Customer insights help us create compelling value, improve the customer experience, enhance the brand, and break into new markets (or redefine existing) with a competitive advantage.

The critical issue is that asking customers what they want is not good enough because customers are limited by their ability to imagine only what's possible.[4] They may not be

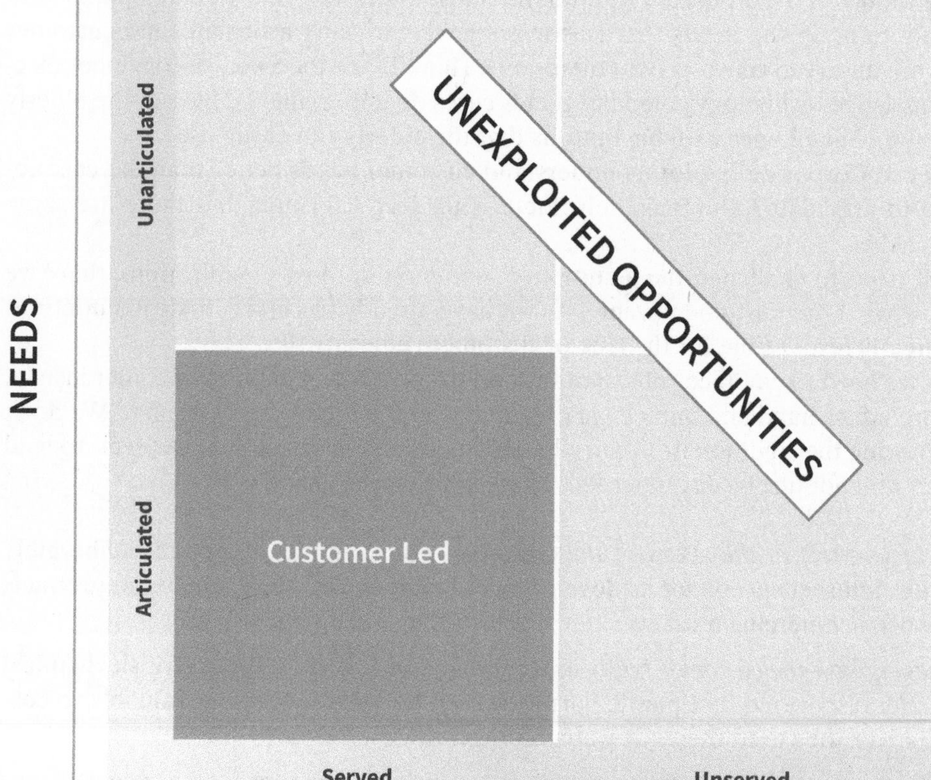

Figure 3.1 Customer needs matrix.

Source: G. Hamel and C. K. Prahalad, *Competing for the Future* (Harvard Business Review Press, 1996).

able to articulate or even recognize their own needs. In addition, we also know that people are often unreliable reporters of their own behavior and give answers they think are expected from them. This complication was eloquently summed up in a quote widely attributed to Henry Ford: "If I had asked customers what they wanted, they would have said a faster horse."

Traditional forms of market research, which tend to be "inquiry-based," are, of course, useful, but by themselves, not good enough to help Corporate Explorers. This challenge is illustrated in Figure 3.1.

Most organizations compete in the bottom-left quadrant. They know who their customers are, and they try to outperform their competitors in the efforts to meet the needs these customers have expressed. Unfortunately, this usually results in crowded markets, and a battle of attrition. For a Corporate Explorer, the most interesting and valuable opportunities are likely to be in the needs that customers have, but can't articulate, and customer groups that are unserved (the top-right quadrant). Think Doro, the Swedish consumer electronics and assistive technology company, that focuses on improving the lives of the elderly by producing mobile phones with big buttons that the elderly can easily use.

So, how can Corporate Explorers understand customer needs better than the customers are able to articulate? Unfortunately, there is no secret formula, but there are some useful approaches.

First, we need to challenge the assumption, common in most organizations, that "we already know what our customers want." As we have already discussed, toxic assumptions are often directly responsible for the lack of customer-centricity.

Second, we need to embrace "observation-based" methods of gaining customer insight, which require a first-hand and immersive experience in the life of the customer.[5] We don't call for eschewing the traditional "inquiry-based" methods; we argue that we need to lead the customer and not just be customer-led. These approaches include:

- *Putting yourself in the shoes of the customer*. For example, Facebook deliberately throttles internet speeds for its development teams so that they can design products that work in emerging markets.
- *Observing how the customer really uses products and services*. ICI, a British chemical company, discovered that plastic barrels it used for packaging were valuable to customers, too; they used them for water storage.
- *Exploring latent dissatisfactions or inadequacies that customers have accepted as normal*. Dyson vacuum cleaners did away with bags, which were both inefficient and expensive, even though consumers have used them for decades.
- *Paying careful attention to abnormalities*. An unusual pattern of sales of washing machines in India revealed that they were being used for making a local yoghurt-based drink.
- *Learning from other industries*. A neonatal unit at a medical hospital has been working with a professional racing team to bring the Formula One pit-stop know-how to help in the resuscitation of new-born babies.

When observing customers, the objective is to glean customer insights into every stage of the consumption chain,[6] as summarized in Table 3.2.

This consumption chain reflects the entire customer experience from awareness to purchase, use, service, and replacement. That means that each part of the company has interactions with the customer from which you can learn something that may be useful. It is a multifunctional problem. Product owners, marketing teams, and field sales may have the most frequent contact with customers, but the richest insights may be in call centers or

Table 3.2 Understanding the consumption chain.

	Customer Experience	What works well	Even better if. . .
1	How do customers become aware of the need for your product or service?		
2	How do customers find your offering?		
3	How do customers make their final selection?		
4	How do customers order and purchase your product or service?		
5	How is your product or service delivered?		
6	What happens when your product or service is delivered?		
7	How is your product installed?		
8	How is your product or service paid for?		
9	How is your product stored?		
10	What is the customer really using your product for?		
11	What do customers need help with when using your product?		
12	How is your product repaired or serviced?		
13	What happens when your product is disposed of or no longer used?		

other high-touch, but low-power, parts of the company. Insights that challenge deeply held beliefs often come from the fringes of the organization that are less vested in reinforcing "the way we do things around here." That makes challenging the company's fundamental beliefs best done as an all-company, cross-functional activity.

LEARN FASTER

Great companies fail not because they do not see change coming, but because they do not believe it and fail to act. Corporate Explorers that see the opportunity to create new businesses and business models often find themselves at the sharp end of this problem. They see a genuine business opportunity that, if we do not act, can quickly become a threat. However, the company's toxic assumptions about their business, customers, and market constrain thinking.

Corporate Explorers can make colleagues and potential sponsors more receptive to breakthrough insights, if they start from the premise that they need to reveal and challenge these assumptions. The presented tools are a way of doing this work that creates the opportunity for genuine organizational learning. It is a process that can lead to insights that inform incremental improvements in the core business, just as much as it enables a business to see the potential for radical innovation to create new revenue streams.

Corporate Explorers are more than just advocates for how to solve a customer problem, they are contributing to the vitality of the company, helping it to learn the value of outside-in challenges to its strategies. As a noted scholar once said, "The ability to learn faster than your rivals is the only sustainable competitive advantage of the future."

APPLICATION CASE STUDY: THE CIGNA STORY

(Based on an interview with Arjan Toor by Narendra Laljani, Fall 2022)

Cigna is a global health service company headquartered in the United States and serving more than 190 million customers around the world.

At Cigna Europe, chief executive Arjan Toor and his colleagues have been undertaking a significant business transformation, from being a traditional medical insurance company to being a "whole health" partner to its customers. This process has required challenging much of the conventional wisdom of the insurance industry, overcoming significant internal skepticism, and leveraging distinctive customer insights gained in unusual ways.

"Innovating within a large organization is hard work," says Toor. "You have to help people understand that what got us here, won't get us there. It is tempting to remain focused on the legacy business model as that's what delivers your current revenue.

For us, the most important shift was to redefine the business we are in. We realized that insurance is and will remain important, but it's a narrow part of a much broader value proposition, which is to help people improve their health, well-being, and peace of mind. If we want to be that real health partner we know our customers are looking for, it's really important for us to understand what drives the individual perceptions of their health and well-being. That means not just paying their bills when they are sick, but helping people improve their overall health, to make sure that they don't have to access healthcare in the first place. So, we're trying to take a holistic approach to healthcare, and help customers address all aspects of their health."

As a result, Cigna has moved away from the belief that their competitors are other insurance companies.

"In this new world, there are thousands of other companies that claim to help people stay healthy, often without any clinical evidence. The role we see for ourselves is not necessarily to be a competitor to these companies, but more an aggregator who can provide a range of health services in a seamless manner to our customers. That means we're doing our own quality assessment of which services will make a meaningful impact. We acknowledge that we can't manufacture every relevant health service, nor should we. We want to partner with the best of the best and be the ones that create the most impactful and personalized customer experience.

Along the way, the notion of who the customer is has also been challenged. As we expand our range of healthcare services, we're discovering that this appeals not just to clients buying our health insurance products, but also to clients who are interested purely in health services. Even some of our traditional competitors can now become our clients because they're interested in adding our health service capability to their own proposition for their customers. By offering stand-alone health services, we've significantly expanded our strike zone."

Toor acknowledges the internal assumptions and beliefs that also needed to be challenged. "You have people who want to focus on insurance products only and are challenging whether customers are actually looking for these types of solutions. Others say that it may be valuable to offer these services, but wonder if it is going to help us make money. So, we've had to change the nature of the conversation and make a very clear business case to support the required investments. It's not about insurance or offering a 'nice to have' employee benefit; that's a toxic belief. It's about helping our clients to improve productivity, engagement, and talent retention, all key drivers for business success. In addition, for those clients for whom we do have insurance solutions in place, keeping their population healthy also has a direct impact on reduced claims costs."

This paradigm shift within Cigna is underpinned by distinctive customer insights, including spotting unusual patterns. Toor explains: "Earlier today, I met with a large corporate client, and I asked them if they knew that there is a significant increase in musculoskeletal-related claims within a segment of their workforce. As a consequence of this insight, we were able to talk about everything from onsite physiotherapy to the provision of more ergonomic office equipment. We were able to use data to show them that they had a problem – which they didn't know they had – and begin to offer them relevant solutions.

"Finding ways to listen to the voice of the customer is critical," says Toor, who regularly joins customer service agents talking to customers. "This is powerful because it gives you direct insights into why people are calling, and what they're worried about. Bringing customer service agents together in groups gives you valuable insights into what's going on. We're now testing software in our call centers that uses artificial intelligence tools to analyze every call, and capture customer sentiment. It literally captures the tone of voice.

We know that people are usually anxious when they call us, because they are contacting us with questions about their health or the health of a loved one. So, if you want to improve your service, it's important to ask challenging questions. For example: "If the Ritz-Carlton got into health insurance, how would they do it?" You then quickly appreciate the value of a high degree of employee empowerment, combined with a desire to consistently exceed customers' expectations. So based on the Ritz Carlton model, we've introduced a program called Wow Moments. We've basically told our frontline staff: 'If you pick up something in a customer conversation that you think is worth following up, you are empowered to send something nice and personalized to that customer. If you've just had a conversation about a sick child, send a box of crayons with a nice handwritten card that says we hope your child quickly recovers.' We had a patient who was diagnosed with cancer and was passionate about running, and our agent decided to send her some nice running gear, with a personal letter saying, 'We hope you can continue to run while recovering from this terrible disease.' The customer feedback we receive is incredible, and it's usually very personal and

(Continued)

very emotional. What's even more powerful is how it makes our colleagues feel. When we launched this program, not everyone was convinced. People worried that this would quickly spin out of control, and that it would become really expensive. But in reality, we spent very little, and the program had a huge positive impact internally and externally.

We've tried to build a culture where the customer is at the heart of everything we do. I believe the things we're doing are working. We continue to attract new clients and are also able to retain our existing clients. I'm incredibly proud that we've had client relationships spanning decades. But it's something we never take for granted, and we're constantly trying to innovate and improve further."

CHAPTER 4

Jobs-to-be-Done: Defining a Market by Customer Outcome

Tony Ulwick

MARKET DEFINITION

Many aspiring Corporate Explorers doom themselves to failure by making a fatal mistake even before getting out of the gates, because they don't properly define the market they are targeting to serve.

Why does this happen? Because while a clear and precise market definition is a prerequisite for success of any new venture, an effective process for defining a market is often missing from the innovator's toolkit. For example, Lean Startup, one of the most popular methodologies available to entrepreneurs, takes for granted that entrepreneurs know the best way to define the market they are pursuing.

This turns out to be a questionable assumption: in a survey, we found that 70% of product teams do not agree on the best way to define a market.

Managers use various, seemingly random classification schemes to define the markets they serve. Some innovators choose to define markets around a product, for example, the vacuum cleaner market or the espresso maker market. Others choose to define markets around verticals, such as the financial services market or the healthcare market. We've seen markets defined around demographics (the people-over-45 market), technologies (the brain sensor market), customer activities (the fitness market), and product portfolios (the heavy equipment market), to name just a few.

The larger point is that the market definition process is obscure, random, and often left to chance. Managers routinely enter a recursive process, in which they are iterating on the market definition, customer needs, and the value proposition simultaneously, with no logical way to exit. As a result, they often define markets in ways that cause them to frequently pivot, churn cash too fast, and eventually fail.

The truth is that innovators don't create markets; they create products to serve markets. Just as you wouldn't iterate your destination as you are trying to plot a course, entrepreneurs should avoid iterating the market they are targeting while trying to establish product/market fit. The market must be defined and validated in the innovation process *before* moving to the need discovery and product definition.

A market-definition process is, therefore, urgently needed that would reduce uncertainty and iteration in the effort to establish a product/market fit and would align the team around the business objectives.

That is why we have created the Jobs-to-be-Done Market Definition Canvas.

HOW SHOULD A MARKET BE DEFINED?

First, what constitutes a "perfect" market definition? We believe a market should be defined in such a way that . . .

- It becomes a constant in the product/market fit equation, not a variable. It should not change as the study of that market unfolds.
- It is stable over time. It does not disappear when different solutions or technologies come along, thus making it a valid long-term focal point for value creation.
- It is unambiguously defined, making it distinguishable from any other markets.
- It does not assume a product or a solution. Rather, it is defined as a problem.
- It points to targets for value creation, making it clear which group of people to focus on.
- It makes the discovery of customer needs quicker, more effective, and less costly.
- It reveals all sources of competition, making disruption and other unpleasant surprises less likely.
- It is relevant to and aligns with the entire organization, including sales, marketing, product development, and so forth.

Second, we should understand why people buy products and services in the first place. Jobs-to-be-Done (JTBD) theory states that people buy products and services to get a "job" done. A job is a task people are trying to accomplish, a goal or objective they are trying to achieve, a problem they are trying to resolve, or something they are trying to avoid.

JTBD opens the door to a new way of thinking about how a market can be defined. Since people buy a product or service to get a job done, a market is best defined as *a group of people and the job they are trying to get done.* For example, parents (a group of people) trying to pass on life lessons to children (JTBD) constitute a market. As do surgeons (a group of people) trying to repair a torn rotator cuff (JTBD), or clinicians (a group of people) trying to diagnose the cause of a patient's sleep disorder (JTBD).

This approach enables us to see that thousands of unique, distinguishable markets exist. They are stable over time; focus on problems people are facing rather than solutions to this problem; offer a fixed, stable focal point for analysis; and form a solid and valuable foundation for understanding customer needs.

Most importantly, a market defined in this manner will not change as the study of this market unfolds, which dramatically reduces the number of iterations and pivots when using the Lean Startup and other methodologies. This happens because the market is optimally defined before engaging in customer-needs discovery. Consequently, the innovator can jump directly into understanding the customer's "problem" by thinking about customer needs through a JTBD lens.

JOBS-TO-BE-DONE MARKET DEFINITION CANVAS

To help you define your market correctly at the start of your innovation process, we have created the Jobs-to-be-Done Market Definition Canvas (Figure 4.1). In conjunction with Steve Blank, the pioneer of the Lean Startup methodology, we want to make this canvas available to all innovators who want to avoid unnecessary pivoting and churn.

If you have a product in mind for your venture, you have already assumed a market but may not have formally defined it. The JTBD Market Definition Canvas is designed to help you define the market you are in or have chosen to serve through a JTBD lens. The canvas lets you start by defining your market in solution space and guides you to redefine it in problem space as (a group of people) + (the job they are trying to get done).

The Market Definition Canvas is designed to accommodate both business-to-consumer (B2C) and business-to-business (B2B) applications. While it is optimized to define one-sided markets, it can be used twice to define both sides of a two-sided market. For component manufacturers who sell to original equipment manufacturers (OEMs) or who are at the top of a long distribution chain, a canvas can be completed for each constituent in the distribution chain, including the end-user, because each constituent has its own unique job to get done.

Let's explore, step by step, how the canvas can be used to define the market you have chosen to serve.

Step 1. Traditional Market Definition

The market definition journey starts with something you're familiar with, namely, a product. We ask: "What is the product, service, or idea you're looking to innovate around?" We use this as the grounding point, and the subsequent steps will help transition you from a product view to a JTBD view of your market.

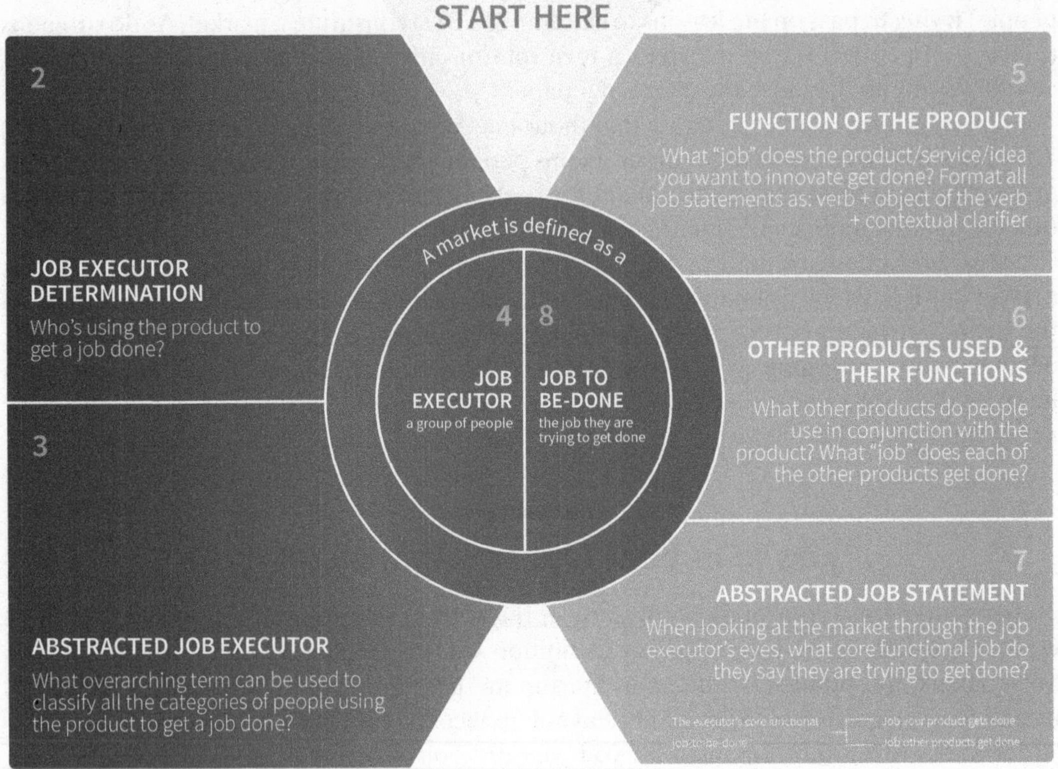

Figure 4.1 JTBD Market Definition Canvas.

Step 2. Job Executor Determination

The transformation begins with this step. Ask yourself or people on your sales and marketing teams: "Who's using your product (or who would use your product once released) to get a job done?" The goal of this step is to reveal the diverse set of potential product users. List all the categories of people who use or would use the product. Keep in mind that we are focused here on stating the job executors. Do not list influencers, economic buyers, people who support the product throughout its lifecycle, or other customer types, just job executors.

For example, Bosch used this approach when trying to enter the North American circular saw market (yes, they began with a product-based market definition in mind). They concluded that finish carpenters, framers, roofers, general contractors, electricians, and plumbers use circular saws. Notice they did not use the formal job titles of the job executors; instead, they listed the categories of people who use circular saws.

Step 3. Abstracted Job Executor

With a list of all the distinct categories of people using or potentially using your product, next you want to define *the one overarching term that can be used to classify all the categories of people using the product to get a job done*. Remember, we are defining a market as a group of people + the job-to-be-done. When defining the group of people, try not to use an actual job title. Instead, look for an all-inclusive term that encapsulates all job executors, usually a higher-level, generic term.

The Bosch team, for example, abstracted roofers, framers, plumbers, finish carpenters, and so forth into a higher-level category using the term *tradespeople*. In other words, the "group of people" using circular saws was conveniently referred to as *tradespeople*.

For those of you who produce consumer product goods, the job executors are often referred to simply as "consumers."

Step 4. Job Executor

You may have come up with more than one way to describe the "group of people." Here you will make and document your final choice. Choose a label that fittingly represents all types of people using the product, service, or idea you have in mind. For example, you may choose the term *surgeons* over *cardiac surgeons,* or *tradespeople* over *tradesmen* to be more inclusive. Other examples include educators over teachers, accountants over tax preparers, or consumers over adults.

It is important to define the "group of people" before defining the job-to-be-done, as you will be interviewing representatives of the group to determine the way *they* define the job they are trying to get done.

Step 5. Function of the Product

Products don't have JTBD; people do. But to uncover the targeted group's JTBD, it is often helpful to understand what function/job the product in question performs. To make this determination, you can work with your product team, or, preferably, you can go directly to the "group" of people (defined in Step 4) and ask the question, "What does/will the product or service in question help you accomplish from a functional perspective?"

Collect and arrange the responses into a single statement according to this formula: the product will help the group of people [verb] + [object of the verb] + [contextual clarifier] (optional). For example, a kettle may be used to "heat + water + to the desired temperature," or a dental drill may be used to "contour + the shape + of a tooth."

Keep in mind that this isn't the customer's JTBD. It's the job that the *product* gets done, which is often only part of the job the customer is trying to get done. For example, while people may use a kettle to "heat water to the desired temperature," the overall job they are trying to get done may be to "prepare a hot beverage for consumption." (Always remember: the goal of the market definition canvas is to help innovators uncover the JTBD as perceived by the customer, not the product developer.)

Step 6. Other Products and Their Functions

To get a feel for the entire job your customer is trying to get done, ask them *what other products they use immediately before, while, and immediately after using your product/ service*. For example, when tradespeople use a circular saw to "cut wood," what other products are they using in conjunction with a circular saw? Perhaps they are also using a T-square, a measuring tape, sandpaper, and a pencil.

List the products they use in conjunction with the one you have in mind. Next, document the jobs/functions that each of these other products gets done for the group of people. Use the same format used previously: [verb] + [object of the verb] + [contextual clarifier] (optional).

The Bosch team, for example, determined through customer interviews that while the function of the circular saw was to "cut wood" (a job statement), tradespeople were using a T-square to ensure they "make a cut in a straight line" (a job statement), and that they were using a pencil to "mark the cut path" (a job statement).

Step 7. Abstracted Job Statement

Putting all the pieces together helps reveal the customer's ultimate JTBD at the right level of abstraction. Assume that your product is getting part of a job done. Also assume that people are using other products to complete the entire JTBD.

Now, you want to define your customer's JTBD in a way that includes your product's function (job) and rationalize why customers are using all other products as they cobble together a complete solution. The Bosch team, for example, determined that tradespeople are using a circular saw along with other products so they can "cut wood in a straight line" (the abstracted job statement).

The reason for defining the market at this level of abstraction is that you can evolve your product over time to help customers get more, and eventually all, of their job done – preferably before competitors do. Therefore, defining a market in this manner offers the innovator a built-in path and vision for growth tied directly to what customers are trying to accomplish.

Complete Steps 5–7 employing customer interviews and make sure you encapsulated the job of the product you have in mind in the abstracted job statement. If the job of the product is not represented, you have abstracted the job statement at a too high a level. This will ultimately prevent you from capturing customer-need statements that will help inform the improvement of the product.

Step 8. Customer's Job-to-be-Done

Now that you have your customer's job abstracted appropriately, you can document that job in Box 8. If you have multiple versions of the job statement, work with job executors to gain consensus on the best version.

With this, the Market Definition Canvas is completed, and your market is defined for you through a JTBD lens.

APPLICATION CASE STUDY: WEARABLE SLEEP-STAGE DETECTION

Ted Thayer

Before we began the customer development process, we attempted to define the market we were targeting with the product we had in mind. We debated if we should define it as the "productivity" market, the "sleep technology" market, or the "sleep-disorder treatment" market. We weren't sure if we should define the market narrowly, broadly, around the technology it employed, or around event and treatment detection.

Right off the bat, we abandoned the idea of defining it as the "productivity" market because this ambiguous definition made the market feel unapproachable. The "sleep-disorder treatment" market, we concluded, was too narrow a market focus, because the product we had in mind had additional possibilities. So, we defined our market as the "sleep technology" market, because this aligned best with our thinking.

As we conducted our customer interviews, we eventually discovered that different groups of people – for example, sleep apnea patients, business travelers, and those who were sleep deprived or had insomnia – all had different problems and needs, each requiring a different solution and value proposition. This finding introduced uncertainty into the whole process. We were unsure where to focus and concluded that we must have defined the market too broadly. We tried to redefine the market around demographics but found the same divergent responses. So, after several additional weeks of research, we pivoted again, this time choosing a disease-based definition of the market. This, too, proved to be equally ill-defined.

In retrospect, we failed to define the market optimally before we began needs discovery. Consequently, we spent months doing customer-discovery research, and the startup had nothing to show for it. It's a regrettable outcome, the one every Corporate Explorer wants to avoid.

But here is a success story. Back in late 2001, the data-recovery company Kroll Ontrack was attempting to enter a new market that offered a significant opportunity for its software development business.

"The term 'paperless office' was just coming into vogue," notes Andrea Johnson, Kroll Ontrack's vice president of marketing and communications. "Lawyers were finding that many

(Continued)

documents relevant to a legal proceeding were available only in electronic form. Competitors who had historically served the market were able to meet the paper discovery needs of lawyers but were ill-equipped to manage the discovery of these electronic records."

Kroll's company had an exciting technology that would allow them to digitize legal document discovery for the first time, but they failed on their first two attempts to bring it to market.

When Kroll applied a JTBD approach to the challenge – to understand what was going wrong – they discovered they had incorrectly defined their market. Kroll had always created and marketed products for IT teams, so they targeted this product at IT teams as well, positioning it as a solution that would allow them to efficiently retrieve data off a hard drive.

However, in this instance, it's the legal team that needed document discovery tools, and the legal team was not trying to retrieve data from a hard drive. Instead, they were trying to find information to support or refute a case.

Kroll redefined their market as legal teams (group of people) retrieving data from a hard drive (job they were trying to get done) and subsequently made some critical adjustments:

- They added search capabilities to their data retrieval technology, and
- They marketed this new product to legal teams rather than IT departments.

Thanks to the corrected market definition, Kroll's third launch attempt was a huge success. The company's electronic document discovery product went from $0 to $200 million in sales in approximately 3 years – and they have remained the market leaders in the space for nearly 12 years.

CHAPTER 5

From Explorer's Insight to Opportunity Story

George Glackin

STARTING POINT

Corporate Explorers face the daunting task of sorting through dozens of ideas on how to create the next blockbuster business. Ideas are easy to come by, but which are the most promising and which truly align both with the Corporate Explorer's passion and with the ambitions of the corporation? No matter how good the idea, you can only make progress when you can persuade others that you have identified an opportunity worth pursuing and motivate them to commit resources to enable you to get started. Although corporations get a bad rap for failing to back good ideas, this challenge is the same for entrepreneurs. Ideas can fail not because they are not worth backing, but because an entrepreneur or Corporate Explorer lacks the ability to persuade others to follow them. This chapter is about how the explorer makes the decision of where to explore and then builds a bridge between that and the stakeholders whose support they need to make progress. I will illustrate with examples from the original Corporate Explorer book, UNIQA Cherrisk and Deloitte Pixel.

EXPLORER'S INSIGHT

Aspiring Corporate Explorers operate within an existing business. Typically, that business is doing well, generating solid top- and bottom-line numbers, and its leaders have forecasted many more promising years ahead. There may even be a portfolio of upgrades and improvements that can be expanded to the market as needed.

What excites Corporate Explorers is an insight that something is changing. They spot early warning signs that the happy *status quo* may be at risk. This is a sign of opportunity and that now is the time to start to prepare for the future.

The early warning signs could come from a *new entry to the market* that at first appears small and nonthreatening, but which has attracted a small number of passionate followers. The insurtech startup Lemonade was a warning sign to traditional insurance companies because it showed that a digital business model for insurance was possible. Another warning sign could be a *shift in end-user tastes or habits* or *the way people buy or consume a product is changing*, thereby affecting how they spend money.

In either of these cases, the original product could start to lose sales, or its market share could shrink. For example, bricks-and-mortar retailers have been watching e-commerce changing buying habits for more than a decade, though only a few understood the scale of the opportunity. In business-to-business markets, the Corporate Explorer Balaji Bondili at Deloitte Pixel capitalized on a shift in the professional services industry toward consuming technology consulting via crowd-sourced platforms. In many cases, the customer's "job-to-be-done" remains the same, but the way they do it changes. These insights are the starting point for the Corporate Explorer journey.

Some companies adopt systematic ways to pressure test the current business model and pinpoint potential strengths and weaknesses that may create disruption risks and opportunities. Most rely on enterprising Corporate Explorers to act as the challenger. The skilled Corporate Explorer has an effective mindset and toolbox to address these challenges. This includes being curious and probing, understanding that business success is always at risk, and questioning what in the business model is working and what is vulnerable. They take an insight – see the tools described in Chapters 3, 4, 6, 7, and 9 that help generate it – and rally others around an idea to act on it. There are two tools that can help in this work: the *opportunity screener* and the *opportunity story*. The opportunity screener helps an explorer make the decision of where to explore. The opportunity story is a format for building a compelling narrative that can elicit the support of key stakeholders. Together, these tools enable an assessment of both the emotional and logical power of each idea.

OPPORTUNITY SCREENER

Most Corporate Explorers start with a personal experience or insight that drives them to solve a problem. Krisztian Kurtisz at UNIQA in Hungary converted his frustration with the insurance industry into a new, digital disruptor, which is now available across Europe (see Case Study). This journey from a personal frustration to business concept is typical for the successful Corporate Explorer. However, personal enthusiasm for an idea is rarely an accurate predictor of its commercial viability. Corporate Explorers need a way to quickly assess whether what they see as a possibility has the potential to be worth additional work.

There are three killer questions to screen an opportunity:

1. Is there *sufficient opportunity* to make it worth pursuing?
2. Is the end user experiencing *"hair on fire" pain*, sufficient to motivate them?
3. Do you have an ownable *claim* to being the provider of a delightful solution?

I will describe each of these questions and how to use them to objectively assess an idea. A blank opportunity screener is shown in Figure 5.1.

- **Sufficient opportunity.** A potential market needs to be large enough to justify the effort to develop it. However, sizing a market that does not exist can be challenging, because there are no historic benchmarks on which to rely. One approach (advocated by Tony Ulwick in Chapter 4) is to size a market by the number of people who want to complete the "job" performed by the innovation. Another is to look for proxies in other related markets to understand the potential market size and rate of adoption. Yet another factor to consider is whether there are competing solutions for the idea, such as branded competitors or workarounds that the end user can reasonably do. It is easy to forget that "nonconsumption" (that is, not using a solution or doing it yourself) is often the innovator's largest competitor.

  We can create an opportunity score for this factor by multiplying the size of the market by the number and strength of competing solutions, where a high opportunity score can be achieved based on a large market and few competing solutions.

- **"Hair on fire" user pain.** A problem needs to matter sufficiently to an end user that they are interested in finding a solution. It helps if the task customers are performing is frequent, perhaps part of their daily life or routine. The value of the opportunity increases even more if the task takes a long time to perform or requires a lot of resources to complete. If there is a high-level of frustration with a task you need to perform every day and that takes a long time, then you are likely to pass the "hair on fire" test.

  We can create an opportunity score for this factor by multiplying the frequency of doing the task by the time and frustration of doing the task, where a high opportunity score can be achieved based on a high frequency of doing the task and a high time or frustration in doing the task.

- **Likely ownership.** Entrepreneurs often work in a "virgin" territory with few legacy resources to develop an innovation. However, Corporate Explorers operate within an organization that has resources. This is what gives them an edge but only if they can figure out how to use it. That makes it important to know whether there is a viable solution that the company can produce. This could come from product or technology assets, customer access, or perhaps a position in the value chain. Ideally, these assets will add up to some sort of protection from competitors who could try to copy the solution.

			OPPORTUNITY?	EVIDENCE
SUFFICIENT OPPORTUNITY?	Size of Market	Number & Strength of Competing Solutions	Total = Size X Improvement	
	3 = Large 2 = Medium 1 = Small	3 = Few 2 = Some 1 = Many	9 = High 4 = Medium 1 = Low	Evidence
END USER "HAIR ON FIRE" PAIN?	Frequency of Task	Time & Frustration to Do Task	Total = Frequency X Frustration	
	3 = High 2 = Medium 1 = Low	3 = Few 2 = Some 1 = Many	9 = High 4 = Medium 1 = Low	Evidence
SOLUTION OWNABILITY & DELIGHT?	Available & Ownable Solution	Solution Improvement vs. Current Solutions	Total = Ownable X Improvement	
	3 = Large 2 = Medium 1 = Small	3 = Few 2 = Some 1 = Many	9 = High 4 = Medium 1 = Low	Evidence

Figure 5.1 Blank opportunity screener.

The other aspect of likely ownership is whether you have a reason to believe that end users may see the solution as being *delightful* when compared to current solutions. We need to believe they will rapidly adopt the habit of using the new solution and be enthusiastic advocates of the solution to others.

We can create an opportunity score for this factor by multiplying the availability and ownability of the solution by the degree of solution improvement against current solutions.

The opportunity screener allows a Corporate Explorer to take a step back and assess an idea against these three key criteria – sufficient opportunity, "hair on fire" pain, and likely ownership. However, there is a risk of "confirmation bias" when all the data leads to a eureka moment that confirms your own brilliance! Expect to find shortcomings in an idea, so that it needs to be modified and made a stronger opportunity. It may help to start with several ideas and do comparative ranking, to make sure it is an objective assessment of which is the strongest idea to pursue.

OPPORTUNITY STORY

The opportunity story brings alive the specifics of the *promise you are making to the end user*. Humans have used storytelling to cover their thoughts and engage others for millennia. Developing and pitching a new business idea is no different. The following are the key questions to answer to start to construct the story:

What is the enemy? Every story needs an antagonist – the Darth Vader role. In business, this often shows up as a frustration. What is the frustration that the end user is experiencing? The end user may or may not talk about getting poor performance from a product or service – the frustration can be conscious or unconscious – and they may learn to work around the deficiencies of a product to get the necessary job done. Airbnb is an example where prior to experiencing the simplicity of Airbnb, the end user was not aware of the challenges of choosing and booking a hotel room. But once made aware, end users readily adopted the new and better solution. In other cases, the frustration may be both obvious and annoying, such as when Uber solved the problem of not being able to find a taxi. At Deloitte, Balaji Bondili's enemy was the consulting industry itself and the lifestyle that made it difficult for them to hire the best digital technical talent.

Who is frustrated? Personalize the frustration, give it a subjective identity that people can relate to and understand as a potential viable audience for the solution. This does not need to be a mass market; it is best to find specific, clearly identifiable groups, making the case more vivid. At Deloitte, Balaji Bondili attached his crowd-sourced consulting talent value proposition to specific industries, such as banks and financial institutions, which struggled to hire digital natives.

What is our hero? Every story needs its Luke Skywalker who will resolve the frustration customers feel. In the opportunity story, this is the solution with a value proposition to address or resolve the customer's pain or frustration. There are many ways of describing a value proposition that emphasize its logical value; however, the opportunity story aims to motivate stakeholders to support the Corporate

Explorer, and so it must engage the emotions as well as logic. The solution is a promise to the customer that they will receive value. Here are three elements to creating an emotionally compelling "hero" value proposition:

1. Our hero solution should be *delightful and memorable*. Describe what would compel its end users to brag to friends about the amazing new product or service they have found. These descriptors should relate to an experience, a benefit, an attribute, and a feature.
2. Our hero should be *trusted by the customer*. Be able to claim how much better, cheaper, faster, the solution is, and do so in a way that the customer finds believable. This could mean quoting an authority the user trusts.
3. Our hero should be *easy to use or adopt*. Communicate to the end user how simple it will be to get the new product or service, and to ensure that the company has thought through how simple it must make this step to remove barriers to trial and purchase.

At Amazon, managers who want to propose new business ideas must complete a PR/FAQ. The PR is a one-page press release addressing the emotional elements, with the quotes from fictional customers talking about their reactions to the product or solution. The FAQ covers the rational element, providing answers to Frequently Asked Questions about the idea.

What is the ambition of the Corporate Explorer? Corporate Explorers often underappreciate the fact that the quality of their commitment to the venture is a critical factor that stakeholders use when deciding whether to fund an idea. Venture capital firms often invest in a leadership team, not in a specific idea, and whether we recognize it or not, it is no different inside corporations. The management wants to see commitment to sustain the venture for the long haul, with evidence that the Corporate Explorer will commit time and reputation to making it a success.

The opportunity story should describe an explorer's personal passion for vanquishing the enemy. Explain the excitement about working in a new or emerging market sector, or developing a wholly new technology, product, or service. Connect with personal experience of the challenge that the venture will solve? What personal experience in the life of the Corporate Explorer or that of a family member or friend drives the commitment? At Deloitte, Balaji Bondili explains how creating Deloitte Pixel was partly a response to solving his own career crisis caused by the endless travel associated with the consultant's lifestyle. A few years earlier, he had been part of a crowd-sourced effort to provide humanitarian relief to the Asian

Tsunami victims. Now, he wondered whether the same approach could help solve the problem of recruiting high-quality technical talent to solve problems for corporations. These experiences helped connect his sponsors to his idea and experience his passion for the project in human terms.

What is the ambition of the company? In Chapters 1 and 2, my colleagues talked about the value of a clear ambition that gives Corporate Explorers the "license to explore." The opportunity story needs to link back to this ambition to provide the strategic rationale for investment: Why will backing this idea help realize the company's objectives?

What is the threat? Anyone familiar with superhero stories knows that just as all problems seem to be resolved and we are headed to a happy ending, a threat re-emerges and places the future in jeopardy. This "Oh no, he's not dead after all" moment adds a sense of reality and makes the final resolution of the story easier to believe. A good opportunity story can do the same by highlighting the consequences of inaction. This is the point to highlight the early warning signs of disruption that should provide the imperative for action. For example, "If we do not act, these are the players that are already starting to make moves in the same space, and could prove disruptive to our core business in the future." The challenge is to persuade stakeholders that the market changes are important or threatening enough to justify diverting funds from its current business to exploring a fundamentally new one.

The logical case of the opportunity screener is added to the story to answer the questions of size, market need, and potential competitors. Taken together, they complete the case.

It helps if the story brings these two components together in a memorable way. Here are three ways to do this:

1. Personal anecdote – There is nothing as powerful as the authenticity of the first-hand anecdote. When Corporate Explorer Yoky Matsuoka at Panasonic talks about her innovation, an AI-enabled concierge service for working parents, she talks about her own life as a mother of four that she pursued in tandem with a career at Nest, Apple, Google, and Panasonic.
2. Analogy – Connecting an innovation with something that people already know is a great way of grounding a concept into reality. Robin Chase, the co-founder of Zipcar, pitched his idea of a car-sharing service, which at that point did not exist, by drawing a parallel to how people feel about getting cash out of an automated teller machine. He said Zipcar was "like an ATM, but its wheels when you want them."[1]
3. Image – See the Cherrisk story of how Krisztian Kurtisz presented a single PowerPoint chart with an image of a company weighed down by the traditional insurance model to explain why it was so important for UNIQA to act.

Taken together, the *story of the idea* and the *opportunity screener* provide powerful tools for the Corporate Explorer to think through the logic and appeal of an idea, to objectively screen and sort multiple ideas, and to pitch the opportunity represented by the idea to key organizational stakeholders.

APPLICATION CASE STUDY: CHERRISK

In 2018, the Hungarian business unit of UNIQA Insurance, a firm with 20 million customers across Europe, launched a new digital service called Cherrisk.[2] It broke five rules of the insurance industry. First, it was a digitally native insurance service, with the entire transaction managed online. There was no involvement from agents, brokers, or even customer service staff. Second, the service was available on a monthly subscription basis, not the usual annual contract, with extremely simple product features. Third, it required a fraction of the usual administrative staff to manage Cherrisk. It could service millions of customers in Hungary and across Europe at a fraction of the normal cost. Fourth, customers could choose to reinvest some of the profits (that the model made possible) to charitable causes of their choice.

Finally, and most radical of all, it made a promise to pay customers' claims for loss within three days, as opposed to the standard of many weeks. It did this by reversing the usual logic that the insurer should first assess whether the claim was valid. Cherrisk assumed that customers were honest and followed up with potentially fraudulent claims only when an AI algorithm detected anomalies.

Today, Cherrisk has a rapidly expanding customer base in nine countries and is teaching UNIQA how to build and market low-cost digital products.

It would have been easy for UNIQA's leaders to dismiss Cherrisk. UNIQA is a highly performing company, with growing revenues and a stable customer base. Its primary market of Austria has one of the lowest rates of market penetration for digital financial products in Europe (still less than 10%, compared with over 50% in the UK). Yet, it decided to invest in an unproven concept that was deliberately breaking five separate rules of the insurance industry.

There are key reasons for this decision. The first was the quality of the critical thinking and analysis done by its originator and Corporate Explorer Krisztian Kurtisz; an overview of his analysis is captured in Figure 5.2. This analysis was followed up by Krisztian's compelling Cherrisk Opportunity Story. Here is my reconstruction of that logic.

Cherrisk Opportunity Story

What is the enemy? Cherrisk's enemy was the industry itself. Insurance had started in the seventeenth century as a way for communities to pool resources so that money would be available to people when they faced misfortune. This community-centered purpose had been replaced by an industry-centered objective to sell policies, administer them, and prevent losses, not on helping communities. Products and the paperwork required were complicated, and the insurer may not pay a claim. Customers had become a cost to manage, not a community to serve.

			OPPORTUNITY?	EVIDENCE
SUFFICIENT OPPORTUNITY?	Size of Market	Number & Strength of Competing Solutions	Total = Size X Improvement	
	3 = Large 2 = Medium 1 = Small	3 = Few 2 = Some 1 = Many	9 = High 4 = Medium 1 = Low	
• Insurance is a known & desired product • No or few competitors are offering digital solutions aimed at simplifying insurance & building community	3	3	9	• Market research of competitor offerings
END USER "HAIR ON FIRE" PAIN?	Frequency of Task	Time & Frustration to Do Task	Total = Frequency X Frustration	
	3 = Large 2 = Medium 1 = Small	3 = Few 2 = Some 1 = Many	9 = High 4 = Medium 1 = Low	
• Insurance must be renewed at least annually • It either takes lots of time to properly consider options, or high frustration in having to buy insurance without sufficient option analysis	2	3	6	• Observations & interview with current customers • Clear understanding of insurance purchase process with clear time sinks & gaps identified
SOLUTION OWNABILITY & DELIGHT?	Available & Ownable Solution	Solution Improvement vs Current Solutions	Total = Ownable X Improvement	
	3 = Large 2 = Medium 1 = Small	3 = Few 2 = Some 1 = Many	9 = High 4 = Medium 1 = Low	
• Insurance is a known & desired product • No or few competitors are offering digital solutions aimed at simplifying insurance & building community	3	3	9	• Existing expert in-house • Strong & favorable customer feedback on solution mock-ups

Figure 5.2 Cherrisk opportunity screener example.

(Continued)

Who is frustrated? UNIQA found that younger customers living in urban areas were less likely to buy insurance, particularly in Eastern Europe, where the very habit of buying insurance had not yet been developed. This is a sizable group of tech-savvy customers who would be expected to embrace digital insurance products.

What is our Hero? Cherrisk is a user-friendly, low-cost line of insurance products that is available, like Spotify, through a monthly subscription. Its focus on giving profits back to the community made it a friend of the people. Also, by committing to pay claims, no questions asked, Cherrisk was saying that it trusted its customers. The simplicity of the digital experience made it easy to use.

What is the ambition of the Corporate Explorer? Kurtisz used his own story of frustration with an industry that he had served for 15 years as an actuary. He was a credible insider describing precisely why the old model of the insurance industry needed to die. He described how his idea already had interest from venture capital firms, which demonstrated to his stakeholders that he was "all in" on the idea and ready to pursue it outside the firm if necessary. Kurtisz also benefited from being a trusted manager, who had just completed a successful turnaround of his business unit.

What is the ambition of the company? Kurtisz knew that there was no immediate threat to UNIQA in its core markets. However, he also understood that it had to compete with larger European rivals, such as Allianz, Generali, and AXA. These firms had deeper pockets, particularly when it came to spending on information technology. If Cherrisk could teach UNIQA how to become a digital business, then, he argued, this could help them leapfrog larger, slower firms to the next generation of the industry.

What is the threat? Kurtisz used a visual image to describe the threat of inaction by UNIQA. On one side, he showed a large office building, segmented by the percentage of cost represented by the different administrative departments of the company. The other side was the cost to serve Cherrisk customers – in the initial plan, just two people. The CEO of UNIQA immediately understood the implication: "If we do not act and our competitors do, then this will put a bomb under our business."

SECTION II

INNOVATION DISCIPLINES

CHAPTER 6

Ideation from Within: How to Generate Breakthrough Ideas from Within Large Corporations

Kaihan Krippendorff

IDEATION

For a Corporate Explorer, the ideation phase can seem like an easy step – you're likely a creative, self-motivated problem solver who has already had a few transformative ideas. However, the most powerful internal innovators have developed a way of thinking that allows them to come up with dozens, if not hundreds, of game-changing ideas every year. They don't put all their chips on one idea, and they throw in the towel if they fail. Instead, they create a portfolio of ideas that have the potential to change their organizations for the better. The process doesn't stop after coming up with the idea. Imagine, dissect, expand, analyze, and sell – IDEAS is an easy-to-remember acronym representing a framework that will increase your chances of generating truly innovative strategic options. This chapter explains how to apply that framework, from the ideation phase to getting others in your organization on board with your ideas.

IDEAS

As a Corporate Explorer, you know that your best chances for success come from generating a lot of strategic ideas . . . and I mean *a lot*. I'm not talking about two or three big ideas that seem perfectly primed and ready for excellence. That's the mistake many corporate innovators and teams make. They apply the routines and frameworks they're used to, then come up with three great options. In the meantime, they kill off the most exciting, "out there," strategic possibilities, the ones they think won't work because they're too different from the norm. This leads corporate innovators into recycling the same few ideas and applying the old rules year after year. Then suddenly – *bam!* – the game changes. A new technology arrives, a new entrant emerges, a new customer preference sets in – and they feel blindsided and stuck in the past.

It doesn't have to be this way.

It's no surprise that companies feel disrupted when the game changes; you can't win a new game with an old playbook. Leaders in strategy have long recognized this. Niccolò Machiavelli was one of the first to point out innovation's fundamental challenge when he wrote, some 500 years ago:

> There is nothing more difficult to take in hand, more perilous to conduct, than to take a lead in the introduction of a new order of things, because the innovation has for enemies all those who have done well under the old conditions and lukewarm defenders in those who may do well under the new.[1]

The IDEAS framework, described in this chapter, is a program I developed in an attempt to solve that challenge: to convert innovation's enemies, and energize its lukewarm supporters. The ideas that have come out of the application of this process have so far generated over $2.5B in new annual revenue. Businesses that apply it, on average, accelerate their growth rates by 50%. I can claim very little credit for that growth. The credit should go to the people, like you, who have applied the process, come up with the ideas, and then did the hard work to execute them.

The IDEAS framework[2] is composed of the following steps (Figure 6.1):

- Imagine: Step back from the future and choose an "impossible" goal.
- Dissect: Choose strategic leverage points.
- Expand: Generate more potential ideas.
- Analyze: Choose disruptive ideas.
- Sell: Build support and alignment within your organization.

I don't pretend that the process is magic. However, because I have seen it applied so many times, with so much success, I can say without hesitation that it works. I know that internal innovators who apply it see new options for solving real challenges. By applying the framework, you will come up with a defined game plan composed of a few priorities you can immediately begin executing or validating. And finally, you will begin developing new strategic thinking habits that allow you to apply the framework again and again.

The process does not deliver prepackaged solutions, already boxed up and tied with a bow. What it does do is enable you to rapidly generate unorthodox strategic ideas and begin creating a new context that encourages more innovative strategic thinking. When that becomes your standard way of thinking, there is no limit to what you can achieve.[3]

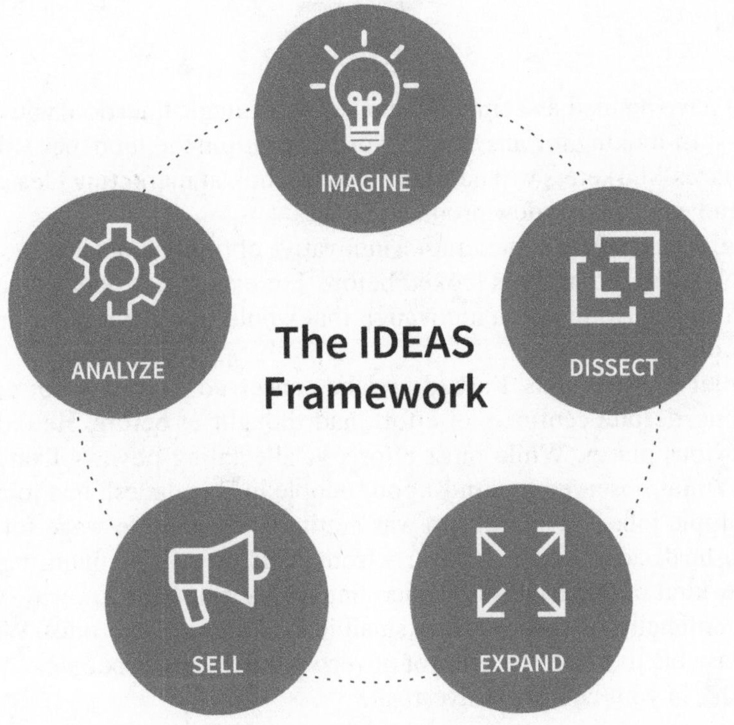

Figure 6.1 The IDEAS framework.

IMAGINE

To think differently about a problem or opportunity, it helps to start out by defining an "impossible" goal. By "impossible," I mean a goal that is unattainable by the solutions already in hand. In contrast, setting "possible" goals encourages a conversation about execution because you already have a solution that almost gets you there, so the easiest path seems to be tweaking that existing solution to be a little bit better.

To get your team to set an "impossible" goal, work backward from the future. You can do this in the following five steps:

1. **The mess:** Step out 10 years into the future and imagine the "mess," the undesirable but realistic future that would occur if you continued along your current path.
2. **Long-term trends:** Still standing out 10 years from now, think about the trends that will affect the future in which you will be operating.
3. **Long-term ideal:** Envision your ideal outcome 10 years from now.
4. **Near-term ideal:** Then ask, "In 18 to 36 months, what must be true for us to know, without a doubt, that we are on the path to realizing our long-term ideal?"
5. **Strategic question:** Finally, convert your near-term ideal into a strategic question.

DISSECT

Now that you have defined a seemingly impossible strategic question, you and your team will naturally start looking for answers. A word of caution: the tendency will be to look in the obvious places. Marketers will naturally want to look at marketing ideas, salespeople at sales tactics, and engineers at new product features.

To increase your chances of generating innovative options no one has thought of before, it helps to look where no one has looked before. For example, Nobel Peace Prize winner, Muhammad Yunus, introduced an innovation that would transform the lives of millions of the world's poor: microfinance.

When I interviewed Yunus, I asked how he conceived a strategy for combating poverty that no one, despite centuries of effort, had thought of before. He did it by looking in the less obvious places. While most efforts at alleviating poverty fixated on creating employment, Yunus observed that most poor people in Bangladesh had jobs. Indeed, they often had multiple jobs. Their problem was getting a sustainable wage for the jobs they performed. So, he decided to attack poverty from a different angle: financing. Yunus's solution was a new kind of financial tool – microfinance, as it became known – which enabled would-be entrepreneurs to take out very small loans at reasonable rates. With one simple idea, Yunus was able to break the cycle of poverty for millions of people.

To apply this in your company, investigate:

- Where are things working?
- Where are things not working?
- Where are people primarily focusing?
- What areas of the problem are people ignoring?
- Given all of these, where do we want to focus?

EXPAND

You are now primed to brainstorm solutions. The more ideas you generate, the greater your chances of finding a truly innovative idea. Follow a few basic rules:

- **Start small:** Rather than attempting to dream up a large-scale innovation, identify a seemingly small pain point experienced by customers or users.
- **Turn an internal capability into a business:** Andy Jassy convinced Amazon to turn its internal capability at managing technology into a service that manages technology for other retailers and, eventually, for any kind of company. The resulting Amazon Web Services offering grew into a $17 billion business. What internal capability can you turn into a business?

- **Do good:** Working to solve social problems is the source of inspiration for many internal innovations.
- **Find an unorthodox path:** We often get so used to delivering value in one way that we overlook opportunities to deliver it through different pathways. The Louvre, for example, delivers its experience through the landmark museum in Paris, but this limits its market to tourists willing and able to travel to France. The Louvre is now essentially franchising its model through a partnership with the Abu Dhabi government, which allowed Louvre to open a museum in the Middle East.
- **Apply an abandoned innovation:** Your organization has a junkyard filled with failed innovations. You can pick innovations out of the trash and apply them in new ways. What has been abandoned that you could repurpose?
- **Coordinate the uncoordinated:** The growth of platform models like Airbnb points to the notion that we can now coordinate things (empty rooms, personal automobiles) that before we needed to control.
- **Serve "superusers":** We often focus on customer segments that represent the largest portion of our market. But on the periphery, you can find "superusers" who are trying to use your product or service in new ways, pushing the limits of your offering. Look at what those users are asking for.

ANALYZE

Finally, you will want to prioritize your ideas. As you do so, you may find you want to ignore the ones that are the most innovative. There is a logical reason for this: the most innovative ideas are departures from the past. They will be inconsistent with prevailing dogma and practices, so they are easy to discount. But you can avoid this through the following simple three-step process.

1. Sort Your Ideas on a Two-by-Two Matrix – Easy or Difficult, High or Low Impact

For each idea, assess whether it is easy or difficult to implement. Then, for each idea, ask what its potential impact would be if you successfully implemented it. Would it have a high or low impact?

This gives you four groupings of ideas (Figure 6.2):

1. **Wastes of time:** Difficult, low-impact ideas. Get rid of them.
2. **Tactics:** Easy, low-impact ideas. Put them on a to-do list; implement them when you have the time.
3. **Winning moves:** Easy, high-impact ideas. These are the ideas you think you should focus on. But we have found that the truly breakthrough ideas tend to fall into the fourth category . . .

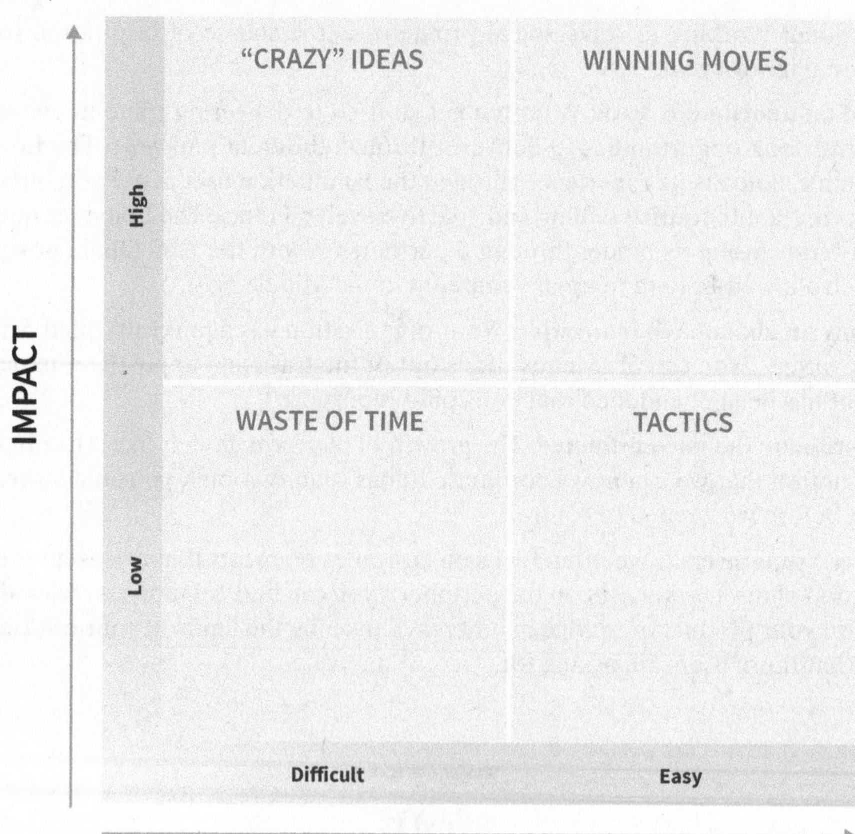

Figure 6.2 The "difficulty-impact" matrix.

4. **Crazy ideas:** Difficult, high-impact ideas. They appear to be impossible, but if you could figure out how to implement them, they would have a major impact. Your breakthrough ideas are likely to reside here.

2. Break Down Some "Crazy" Ideas

Force yourself and your team to sit with a seemingly impossible idea for 10 minutes. List three big barriers that make the idea look crazy; for each barrier, brainstorm three ways to remove it. If you think it will cost too much, for example, you might write, "Partner with someone who has the money. Find a customer to fund it. Outsource to reduce the up-front cost."

Then sit back and ask, "Does this idea still look crazy?" You will often find that what at first appeared to be a "crazy" idea is worth exploring further.

3. Document Your Idea Portfolio

Select about five innovative ideas you are committed to testing. Circle, highlight, or write them down in a notebook. Maintain a list of ideas you are working on, a list of those you have implemented, and a list of those you have ruled out. When you implement or rule one out, pull another innovation idea from your backlog and start working on it.

The key difference between successful serial innovators and frustrated ones is that the successful ones view the political challenge as part of the problem-solving process. The final stage, as you are working with your team, is to lay out an influencing strategy: identify the stakeholders (investors, partners, colleagues, gatekeepers) you need, and think through how to get them on board.

Consider:

- How can you sell the strategy to win the interest and support of key stakeholders needed to bring the idea to fruition?
- How can you build support and alignment for the execution of the strategy?

OVERCOMING BARRIERS

The innovation ideas most likely to disrupt the competition will do so because they preempt resistance in, as Machiavelli put it, "those who have done well under the old conditions." For an idea to really break through, it helps having the competition ignore and ridicule it. The competition will do this because the novel idea is inconsistent with prevailing logic and belief. This makes the idea seem impossible.

And therein lies the true dilemma of innovation: because you and your team have grown up in your industry and, therefore, likely hold similar beliefs as your competition, disruptive ideas are likely to initially seem impossible to you and your team as well.

The IDEAS framework helps overcome this dilemma by addressing five common barriers that might otherwise lead your discussions away from truly breakthrough ideas:

1. **Imagine** addresses the barrier we call "practical." Often, we don't have time to think about the long-term future because we should deal first with near-term challenges. You can flatten this barrier by zooming out 10 years before defining your near-term goals.
2. **Dissect** addresses the barrier we call "obvious," the tendency of focusing on the area of the problem we have the greatest expertise in.
3. **Expand** addresses the barrier we call "expert," the common habit of those who have considerable experience to limit ideation by saying things like "we tried that before."

4. **Analyze** addresses the barrier we call "what works," the tendency of saying, "We have all of these big, out-there ideas, but for this year let's just focus on what we know works."
5. **Sell** addresses the barrier we call "the cog," a concern expressed by many would-be Corporate Explorers that "we are just a cog in the wheel, they will never listen to us."

You can break down any problem-solving conversation into one of these five. At any given moment, you are either imagining, dissecting, expanding, analyzing, or planning how to sell internally. Using the steps proposed in this chapter will help you become aware of which conversation you are having and overcome, systematically, the barriers that might otherwise stop great ideas from making it into your organization, market, and the world.

APPLICATION CASE STUDY: A GLOBAL MEDIA AND ENTERTAINMENT COMPANY

The head of strategy of one of the three leading global media and entertainment conglomerates requested help to think more expansively about their strategy. Industry dynamics was changing shifts in streaming, technologies for digital rights management, M&A, regulations, and changes in consumer behavior.

We scheduled a day-and-a-half strategy meeting for about 50 members of the leadership team to review the IDEAS process.

There were two major reasons the company wanted a new approach to their strategy. First, the company faced a period of historic flux and needed more "big ideas" to manage its way out of the situation. While it had a tradition of creative thinking in their programming, it was not as inventive when designing elements of their business model. Second, the leadership team wanted a more inclusive experience, so that it could feel a shared ownership of the strategy, not a top-down process whereby a central team sets strategy to be "cascaded" down to each function.

Before the planned meeting in an offsite location, we met with leadership to lay the foundation for *Imagine*. We polled participants for their feedback, then collected the results into an initial "Imagine" statement. Doing this in advance would ensure the meeting was as productive as possible.

We also conducted a survey on the current state of the company's business model using an "8P" framework: position, product, promotion, pricing, placement, physical experience, processes, and people. We asked whether they thought each P was currently an advantage, a weakness, or neutral.

Finally, we divided the attendees into groups that would focus on a different P of the business model. We renamed the Ps to apply to the company. Product became production. Promotion became ad sales. Placement became distribution, and so forth.

On the first day of the meeting, we started with an overview of the IDEAS process and jumped into imagine. We shared the survey feedback and facilitated an imagine discussion – what is the mess, what are the trends, what is our shared long-term ideal, what is our near-term ideal, and what strategic questions does this imply? We captured the conversation in a word document, projected in front of the room.

Ultimately, we landed on a clear near-term vision – a statement of about 70 words including a set of quantifiable goals that the leadership wanted to achieve in the next 18 months.

Having aligned the team on the overarching goal, we gave each group 30 minutes to translate that goal to their area of the business model. For example, if the overarching goal was to increase revenue from streaming, the ad sales team might set a goal of strengthening the capability and relationships to sell streaming.

We then ran an ideation discussion. We introduced five core strategic patterns that, according to our research, the most successful companies are using more frequently than their peers:

- **Move early to the next battleground.** Play for tomorrow rather than today.
- **Coordinate the uncoordinated.** Imitate platform business models, distributed blockchain models, and social models.
- **Force a two-front battle.** Define yourself not by your industry but by a capability or purpose that allows you to behave differently.
- **Be good.** Pursue strategies in which your business benefits multiple stakeholders like communities, society, the country, and the environment.
- **Create something out of nothing.** Focus on new customers, categories, occasions, and needs.[4]

Each group considered the resulting patterns and wrote down ideas on sticky notes, generating at least 50 strategic options totaling over 500 ideas – far more than one would expect from traditional strategic ideation processes.

Groups plotted their sticky-note ideas on flipcharts using a two-by-two matrix, assessing the ease or difficulty of execution and the potential impact of the idea. Each group followed these steps:

- Sort all ideas on the matrix.
- Agree that the difficult, low-impact ideas are wastes of time and should be removed.
- Review the easy, low-impact ideas and agree that these are tactics. These ideas may be acted on in the future, but they are not priorities.
- Work on a crazy idea: pick one idea from the high-impact, difficult quadrant and break it down. Each group had 10 minutes to outline three barriers to implementing the idea (like figuring out the technology or raising the required investment).
- Brainstorm three ways to remove the barriers. (In each case, the group found that an originally labeled "crazy" idea shifted to something they might explore further.)

(*Continued*)

- Finally, list the top-10 ideas on a flipchart. It's important to have the ideas properly numbered (as you will see in the next step), so group "A" will number their ideas A1, A2, . . . A10, group B number their ideas B1, B2, . . . B10, and so on.

We combined all ideas into a master list. Naturally, there were duplicates. To adjust for that, each group presented their top-10 ideas while other groups noted ideas that could be the same. For example, if group D thought that their seventh idea was the same as group B's second idea, they would cross out their idea and write "same as B2."

We then asked each participant to pick their top eight ideas, with at least three of them being "crazy" ideas. This is important because often, when you reach the Analyze phase, and the leadership is starting to commit to ideas to pursue, it's the moment when the "rubber hits the road." We are no longer dreaming about what might be possible, but, instead, deciding where we are going to invest time and resources. There is a tendency to pull back and choose ideas that are more reasonable. To correct for this, you must force people to pick some "crazy" ideas.

We collected flipcharts with top-10 lists.

After the session, with applause and celebration behind us, we entered all the ideas and votes into an Excel spreadsheet. We grouped them into themes like: "creating a culture of analytical innovation," which included building data-analytics capabilities to allow the launching of new products, or "positioning for the short-form content," which included cutting up existing and new content to be delivered into new platforms and occasions.

Seven strategic themes have emerged as a result. These themes, when executed, would lead to one overarching mission.

Summarizing the result of the session, it has set the foundation for what became a meaningful transformation of the whole business.

The strategy development goes through three phases. First, the assessment and realization that things need to change. Second, the loosening of priorities leads to the willingness to try new things. And finally, the identification and commitment to new options must take place. The new collection of ideas would fit primarily within the second phase. The company seeded several new themes that would later blossom into new ideas, the ideas that would transform the company from a traditional content business into the one that is fit for the new era of media.

CHAPTER 7

Ideation from Outside: A Step-by-Step Guide to Challenge-Driven Innovation

Bea Schofield and Simon Hill

OPPORTUNITY FOR EXPLORERS

The benefits of accessing the wealth of ideas, insights, skills, and experiences within and outside organizations offer tremendous opportunities for Corporate Explorers to find breakthrough ideas to customer problems. Platforms enabling organizations to connect to brainpower inside and outside their walls are becoming commonplace; tools and approaches for harnessing a global network of capabilities are getting more sophisticated yet more accessible.

NETWORKED PROBLEM SOLVING

In 2009, a well-known carbonated drinks company posted an open call for ideas on how to manipulate the size of bubbles in soft beverages. Posting anonymously on a platform called InnoCentive, the company shared its belief that changing the size, shape, and texture of bubbles would distinguish its products from competitors and make the company a market leader.

Eight thousand miles away, in Mumbai, India, Manish M. Pande was working on a PhD in metallurgical engineering. Having spent three and a half years in the steel industry, Manish had developed a knowledge of metallic foams and the physics of foaming in metals. The challenge piqued his interest, and Manish went about proposing a method to manipulate the characteristics of bubbles based on his knowledge. His idea turned out to be the winning solution, and Manish was awarded a $15,000 award.[1]

Imagine that for every problem that a company has failed to solve by itself it can find someone like Manish.

Although it's well-known that ideas feed off one another, and innovation thrives when multiple hunches combine, organizations often do the opposite to letting this happen. Instead of allowing ideas to enrich one another, they make their innovation departments lockboxes for ideas and exclude participation of people within and outside their organization who might have a solution to important problems.[2]

This chapter provides Corporate Explorers and innovation practitioners with an approach to leveraging the collective experiences, insights, and problem-solving capabilities of networks of people by taking an outside-in approach to ideation. It provides a set of principles for how to connect with the Manish Pandes of the world and accelerate problem solving through tapping into diverse audiences in a sustainable way.

OPEN IDEATION'S UNIQUE POTENTIAL

Diversification of the problem-solving process is the strongest argument in favor of open innovation as opposed to its "closed" alternatives.[3] A metallurgical engineer based in India coming up with ideas for how to solve a problem in the carbonated drinks industry is just one example of such diversity. Corporate Explorers want to benefit from allowing ideas to come from multiple and diverse sources, then mingle, and breed.

Another benefit of the open innovation approach, not immediately evident to many, is the motivation of the people taking part in an open-call ideation contest. No one was forcing Manish Pande to take on the bubble-size problem. He *self-selected* to work on it because he felt he had appropriate knowledge and experience to solve the problem. Compare that to situations in which people are *assigned* to work on innovation problems, whether they are interested in them or not.

What Corporate Explorers need to realize the unique potential of open ideation is a robust idea generation system that would create a space in which ideas can circulate and take shape.[4] Corporate Explorers then should channel the energies of talented audiences, inside and outside their organizations, into important problems that need to be addressed. This creates an environment in which exchanges of ideas around problems are constantly happening, thereby increasing the probability of finding the right idea at the right time. We call such an idea generation system challenge-driven innovation (CDI) (Figure 7.1).

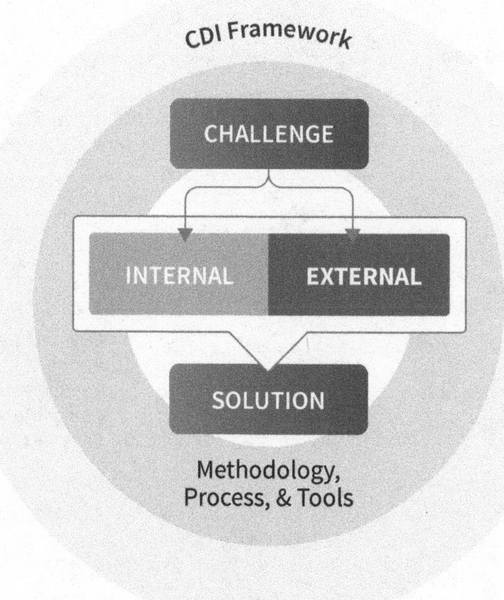

Figure 7.1 Challenge-driven innovation framework.

CHALLENGE-DRIVEN INNOVATION

In the core of the CDI framework lies the process of dissecting a large problem into smaller elements, or challenges, which are then distributed among a network of problem solvers. Solutions that arise from the network are integrated back into one large solution to the original problem.[5]

CDI differs from other problem-solving techniques in that it is focused on breaking larger projects into portable blocks of work, so that these blocks could be easily outsourced, distributed among various channels, and then reintegrated back into the organization. CDI also uses platforms to bring together independent people and groups of people, allowing them to collectively create what any of them alone is incapable of creating.[6]

The CDI process has five major steps (Figure 7.2). For a Corporate Explorer seeking to generate disruptive ideas, the most vital are the first three: problem identification and prioritization, challenge definition, and selecting an appropriate channel. The downstream processes of idea incubation and scaling will be described in later chapters of this book. But before we proceed to describe these first three steps, let's first discuss what represents a "good" challenge.

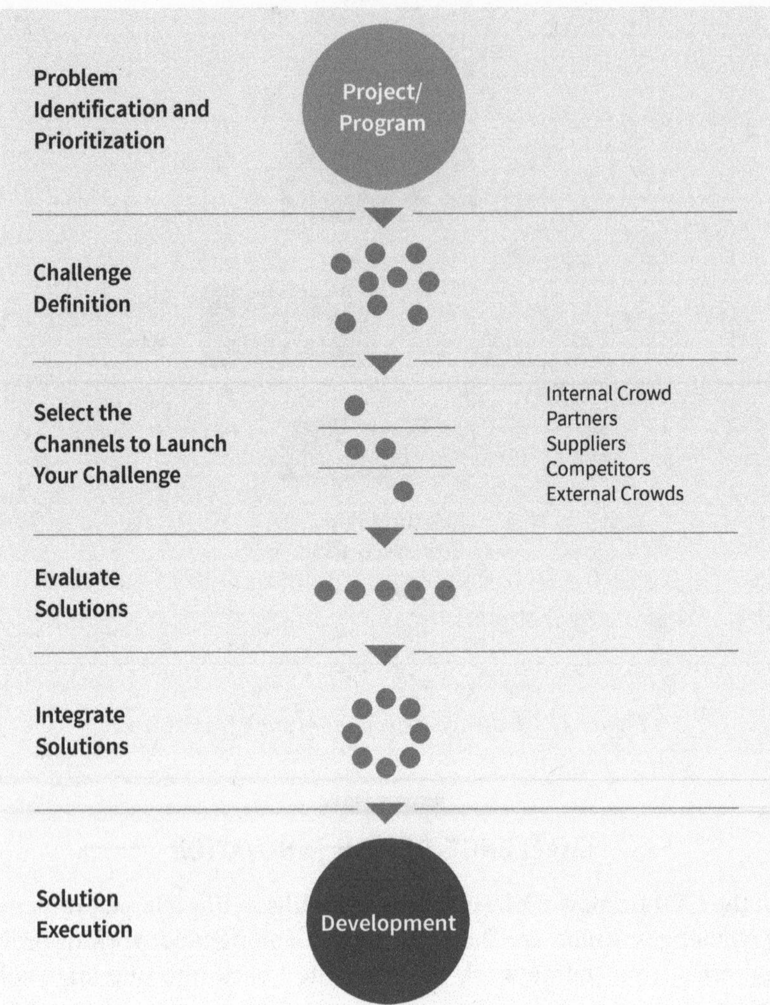

Figure 7.2 The CDI method: A step-by-step guide.

FIVE TRAITS OF A "GOOD" CHALLENGE

Not every problem can be successfully solved by using the CDI framework. To improve your chances of using the framework successfully, the challenge should display five important features: be limited in scope, be actionable, be specific, be supported, and be owned. We call this approach the LASSO approach.

Limited in scope. A typical challenge is supposed to be solved in a fixed timeframe (usually a month) by one person or a small team. As mentioned earlier, to achieve that, a larger job should be broken into smaller parts. (We'll discuss this process in more detail later in the chapter.) Depending on the type of challenge, access to necessary equipment should also be considered. If a solution requires testing in the field, the timeframe should be appropriately extended to reflect this, too.

Actionable. Make sure that your challenge requests solutions that are not so complex or out of scope that it would be impossible to develop or implement them within your organization. Solutions should be something you can act upon. As an example, a challenge that seeks new packaging may be of no use if you are not producing the packaging. Challenges should be viewed in the same way as internal innovation projects, ensuring that the value of the future solutions is worthwhile.

Specific. Problem solvers need to know precisely what is expected of them. If the challenge is vague, then the solutions will be most likely vague as well. Or, worse, they will be largely irrelevant because the problem solvers will simply tell you what you already know. So, for instance, instead of asking "Does anyone know how to do complex math using Excel?" ask, "How can we fit nonlinear sigmoidal curves using an Excel-based macro or add-on?" Specificity will generally increase as you move from asking for just ideas to more complex solutions. But in any case, the problem solvers, as well as you as the problem owner, should immediately know when a solution to the challenge has been found.

Supported. Challenges should be aimed at solving problems that are of high value to the explore strategy. An idea that helps solve a problem that is aligned with ambition and hunting zones is much more likely to get funding.

Owned. Challenges must be owned by someone who has a vested interest in their solution and can, therefore, be the driving force of the solution implementation. This gives the solutions the greatest chance of being acted upon. The deep insight into the challenge topic area brought by the owner helps ensure that the challenge is well formulated (that is, limited in scope), and the solutions are actionable and valuable. For cross-disciplinary challenges, problem owners would collaborate to ensure all technical requirements are covered in the writing process, and all future solutions can be properly assessed.

BASICS OF THE CDI PROCESS

As mentioned earlier, the first three steps of CDI – problem identification and prioritization, challenge definition, and selecting an appropriate channel – are the most relevant to Corporate Explorers at the ideation step of the innovation process.

Problem Identification and Prioritization

Step one in the CDI process is to identify problems and opportunities that need to be addressed. We recommend taking a broad approach and not putting any limitations on the number of problem areas you identify at this point. The first task is to build a list of problems, roadblocks, or opportunities you have encountered at work. For example, you may want to start with the following sentences:

"Technologically it has been difficult for us to . . ."

"An important project is delayed because . . ."

"What is a suitable, superior, and more cost-effective way to . . .?"

When conducting initial brainstorming, refrain from judging or censoring problems as you write them down; the goal here is to go for volume. Also, do not try to solve the problem; just capture it along with a description of what the problem is.

Once you have completed the brainstorming, the identified problems, roadblocks, or opportunities need to be filtered. If projects do not fit with corporate objectives, then they can be culled at this point. To repeat it once again: a successful challenge must be aligned to the strategic goals of the company for the solutions to this challenge to stand a chance of being implemented.

We would recommend prioritizing identified topics using the grid presented in Figure 7.3. The *x*-axis reflects how important the problem is to customers. The *y*-axis assesses its alignment to the company's explore ambition and strategy: Is this something you are likely to invest in solving? You can assess this strategic alignment by asking the following questions:

- How important is this problem to customers?
  - Is there evidence of customers looking for new solutions?
  - Are competing solutions coming to market?
  - Is venture capital money flowing to startups engaged in solving this problem?

- How aligned is the problem with your company's explore ambition and strategy?
  - Does it connect with your ambition statement?
  - Is there evidence suggesting there is a market for solving this problem?
  - Do you have assets relevant to solving the problem (for example, customer access)?

You can also filter problem areas using the opportunity screener described in Chapter 5.

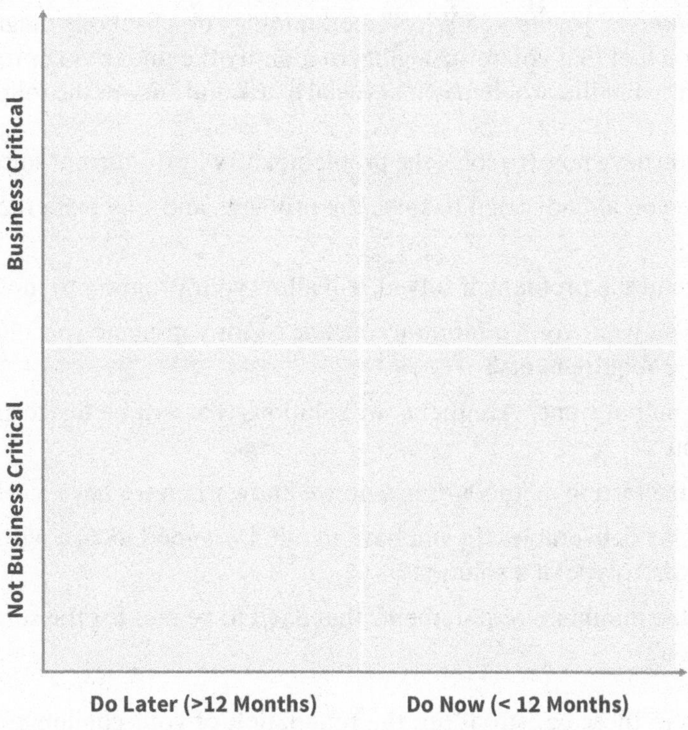

Figure 7.3 Prioritization grid.

Challenge Definition

Topics and problem areas that fall into the top-right quadrant of the grid in Figure 7.3 should move to the topic refinement. Others can remain in a backlog until there is evidence that they are valuable to customers and aligned to the explore strategy.

It's at this point that the problems are broken down into discrete modules that can be worked on separately (see the LASSO approach earlier). One way to think about a portable unit of work would be to take the example of a self-driving car. Asking a crowd to design the entire vehicle would be too big, but the process of designing a car could be broken down into smaller parts which can then be outsourced. For example, autonomous vehicles depend on the ability to sense and analyze the surrounding environment. A problem statement could, therefore, ask, "How might we allow for faster edge detection in video streams?" This is a scope that is limited enough to ensure that you have better chances of succeeding, because a solution to this problem will be portable enough, too, so it can be reintegrated back into the research and development (R&D) process.

Once you have determined which problem to take forward, it's time to start refining it. The first thing you do is asking yourself: "What is the actual problem?" Please, note that you aren't asking, "What might be a solution to this problem?" The focus at this stage is on *problems*, not *solutions*. Toyota's "5 Whys" methodology or a fishbone diagram can be used at this point if you feel that you're struggling to identify the underlying problem.

After defining what the problem is, it's crucial to ask and answer the following questions:

- What do you have now (to solve the problem) and why do current solutions not work?
- What have you already tried to solve the problem, and why were these attempts not successful?
- What piece of the problem, if solved, will allow your program to move forward?
- What do you want your solution to include? Can you name specific *must-have* and *nice-to-have* requirements?
- What do you not want? Are there any solutions that will be unacceptable, for whatever reason?
- What are the testing methods? How do we know when we have a solution?
- What specific deliverables do you have in mind – a good idea, a written proposal, or a working prototype of a solution?
- What are the minimum requirements that need to be met for the solution to provide value to you?

The answers to these questions are the foundation of your challenge. They are also a great indicator of how much you really know about the problem you are trying to solve. At this point, it could be useful to engage subject matter experts (SMEs) who may have a deeper knowledge of the problem and any previous attempts to solve it. It's likely that you may take your problem through several iterations of the listed questions to ensure that you have adequately broken a problem into portable units of work.

The challenge definition process culminates in writing a challenge statement summarizing the goal, objective, and scope of your challenge. There are some solid, time-proven good practices to follow when writing an effective challenge statement:

- Your challenge has an objective that is clearly defined and focused.
- Your challenge doesn't ask people to do the work you have already done.
- Your challenge includes a clear set of solution requirements that, at the same time, would not prescribe a solution.
- Your challenge contains all the information that problem solvers would need to develop a potential solution.
- Your challenge is engaging and appealing to as broad a pool of solvers as possible.
- Your challenge uses the minimum amount of jargon, domain-specific lingo, and uncommon acronyms.
- Your challenge provides an appropriate incentive structure.

There are also a few things you should avoid:

- Avoid ill-defined boundaries to your challenge. Uncertainty increases the perceived risk for the solvers and invites solutions containing partly or even wholly irrelevant content.
- Avoid making the cost for participating in the challenge too high in terms of time or resources.
- Avoid posting problems that are so tightly tied to a specific technical domain that only experts in this domain could understand the problem.

Select the Channels to Launch Your Challenge

The channel you should consider first for launching your challenge is an internal crowd. It is composed of employees of your organization; it can also include its close partners, such as contractors and suppliers. The specifics of internal ideation were discussed in detail in the previous chapter. Here we want to highlight two important aspects of dealing with internal crowds.

First, it's always a good idea to run a challenge first with an internal crowd. This ensures that a solution to the problem doesn't already exist within the organization, hidden in some "remote" department or function. Besides, running a challenge internally allows more stakeholders to read the challenge statement, and this may prevent possible mistakes committed at the stage of problem definition from being broadcast to external crowds.

Second, when asking for ideas from an internal crowd, always address the "what's in it for me?" question (especially if you are not offering a substantial financial reward). Different employees may have different motivation to participate in a challenge, depending on their role, tenure, and seniority. So, the incentives might be different for junior employees trying to develop their problem-solving skills as opposed to a senior person who's more interested in gaining visibility through solving an important problem.

If you ran a challenge internally but haven't come up with a satisfactory solution, it's time to employ external crowds. This external pool of talent might be composed of individuals or organizations with which you share some common DNA: your suppliers, partners, academic institutions, or even competitors. In addition, this pool may also be composed of the people you don't know and who might not be familiar with your organization or share your expertise. It's this part of external crowd that often comes up with the most original, unorthodox solutions to a problem (the "long-tail" phenomenon), as argued by Bingham and Spradlin.[7]

For external challenges, the most common incentive is a financial reward that should be properly aligned with the amount of work required from the problem solver. Failing to choose an optimal award amount may result in losing potential solvers.

You should remember, however, that for many solvers, the importance of solving a problem, especially with a potential social impact, is equally, if not more valuable than the financial award. Your ability to inspire your audience by communicating the importance of solving the problem is, therefore, crucial.

The most convenient way to run an external challenge, especially for an organization that is new to this process, is by using a commercially available crowdsourcing platform. Choosing a crowdsourcing platform and working with it should follow a set of rules discussing which, however, lies outside the scope of this chapter.

IDEAS MATTER

Make no mistake: ideas matter. No innovation, whether disruptive or incremental, can start without a great idea at the beginning of the process. But ideas, by themselves, are not enough. Ideas must be properly incubated, and then the best of them scaled for innovation to happen. This chapter described one of the most efficient ways of generating breakthrough innovative ideas. How these ideas can be converted into new products and services will be described in the following chapters.

APPLICATION CASE STUDY: UK MINISTRY OF DEFENCE CHALLENGE-DRIVEN INNOVATION

By Stuart Laws, Assistant Head in the Defence Innovation Directorate at the UK Ministry of Defence

The UK Ministry of Defence (MOD) uses Challenge-Driven Innovation (CDI) in several ways, primarily for acquiring solutions from outside the MOD. Different MOD agencies and industry partners are engaged. Some of them are focused on working with military branches to review existing challenges and transform them into problem statements that will be posted to the pools of external solvers. Other agencies are charged with the review of submitted proposals to decide, along with the problem holders, whether any of the received contributions are feasible and could be integrated into ongoing research projects.

The MOD also uses CDI as part of a new approach to the defense-related innovation that it calls cross-sector innovation. In this case, the MOD is looking for nondefense partners willing to share a challenge with the MOD. The purpose of these challenges, targeted at the solvers in academia and industry, is to develop solutions that would result in a new commercial product. MOD considers these collaborations as an effort to help create products that could make UK exports more attractive.

The funding for the cross-sector innovation approach reflects its collaborative character. The MOD works with Innovate UK, the country's leading innovation agency, to create a cofunded allocation that is distributed as grants to syndicates. The partnership with Innovate UK is especially cost-effective because the latter has a wide network of companies it can approach to participate in a challenge.

One of the recent challenges the MOD was involved in was the High-Altitude Intelligence challenge focused on humanitarian aid and disaster relief efforts following natural disasters. One part of the challenge focused on new methods of obtaining earth observational imagery of affected regions without waiting for satellite images (which could take up to a week).

Another part dealt with organizing rapid first response. Solutions were sought to design effective ways of directing first responders to places where they were needed the most (for example, to the locations where images identified large numbers of survivors). Yet another aspect of the challenge was to tackle the problem of communication: the communication of first responders with one another, as well as the restoration of phone and internet connections to the civilian population in the affected area.

The second scenario the Challenge focused on was maritime safety and security.

There are a lot of objects floating in the water that represent a danger to shipping. How can we identify these objects and warn the ships that they are there?

Currently, this problem is being solved by coastal services sending a boat that would sail next to the object and broadcast its position. This is an expensive and not sustainable solution. The challenge looked for an automated solution that would allow identifying hazardous objects remotely and sending information about them to the ships in the area until the objects have been removed or left the monitored zone.

Another part of this scenario was devoted to the issues of finding survivors of a maritime accident, which normally can take several hours. The challenge asked for technologies that could identify a survivor in the water and then direct first responders to that location as fast as possible.

As mentioned earlier, the MOD often partners with nondefense entities to run joint challenges. One example of such a challenge is the one run by the Royal Navy in cooperation with an offshore oil and gas company. The purpose of the challenge was to explore options for next-generation underwater uncrewed vehicles. This challenge hasn't yet resulted in a marketed product, but a few positive options emerged: one was focused on high-quality underwater imagery; and another provided swarming maintenance capability for offshore windfarms, intended to significantly reduce the frequency of specialist divers being sent into often hazardous waters.

Using the CDI approach, the MOD doesn't define what the final product should look like; instead, it creates a problem statement outlining different possible scenarios, and then requests a solution fitting each scenario. Of course, the MOD could potentially develop these solutions by itself; however, there is no guarantee that these solutions are going to be the best. Engaging external pools of talent would ensure the MOD always knows what is already available in the marketplace, and what parts of various solutions could be combined to create yet even more powerful ones.

This is what happened with the high-altitude challenge: one of the solutions was a proposal to create a new capability through combining known component parts. Given that such "follow-up" projects are not starting from scratch, the final product usually reaches the market faster.

Besides clear commercial advantages of using the CDI approach, we see three more, equally important, benefits. First, challenges not only bring together people investing time and money; they also invite *conversations* about important issues. Second, CDI forces people and companies to be more open and collaborative. Finally, CDI creates new partnerships and networks. To this end, the Royal Navy believes that it generated more value through meeting companies they didn't know existed than from the challenge itself, for which it calculated a 12:1 return on investment

CHAPTER 8

Business Model Maturity: Using Customer Evidence to Validate New Ventures

Michael Nichols and Uwe Kirschner

CUSTOMER FIRST

"Customer first" is a phrase every corporate executive utters, but what does it really mean? Much like the phrase "digital transformation," it depends on the context. The context of the core business is fundamentally different from a new venture. Corporate management is well schooled in how to efficiently extract more cash out of the core business, but the tried-and-true principles of managing the core are, at best, counterproductive and, at worst, value-destroying when applied to the exploratory business ventures. As a result, many new business ventures are asked to scale to revenue before they are fully mature. There is a technology or product solution, but no clarity on how to create a repeatable business model from solving a customer problem.

This "maturity gap" can be closed by adopting customer first practices of customer discovery, customer validation, and maturity assessment. In this chapter, we describe these practices and their application. We then provide an example of how Bosch, the German technology company, has developed a repeatable methodology for customer validation through its Bosch Accelerator Program.

MATURITY GAP

The inside-out model of innovation is dominant in many technology- and engineering-focused businesses. As described in Figure 8.1, it starts with a technology or product-driven insight into what the market needs.

Unfortunately, well-developed product offerings often reach the market with immature business models, which causes potentially good ideas to fail. This happens because the inside-out approach focuses only on the product, ignoring the other aspects of the innovation, such as go-to-market. Consequently, innovative products reach the sales team with an immature business model that struggles to succeed.

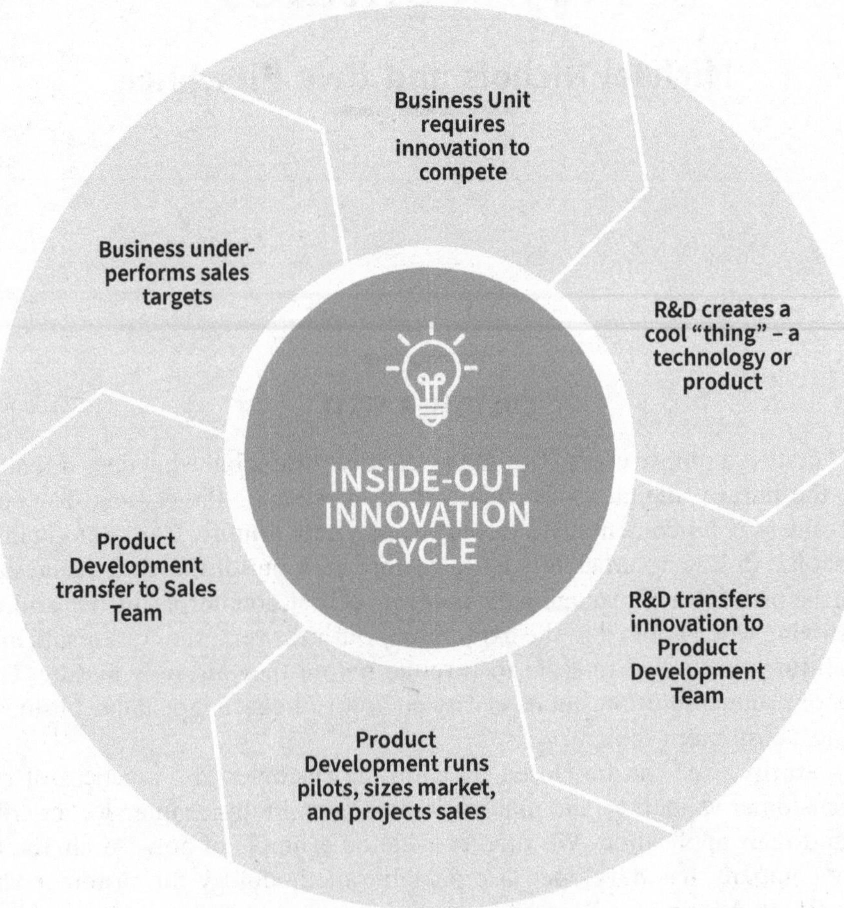

Figure 8.1 Inside-out innovation cycle.

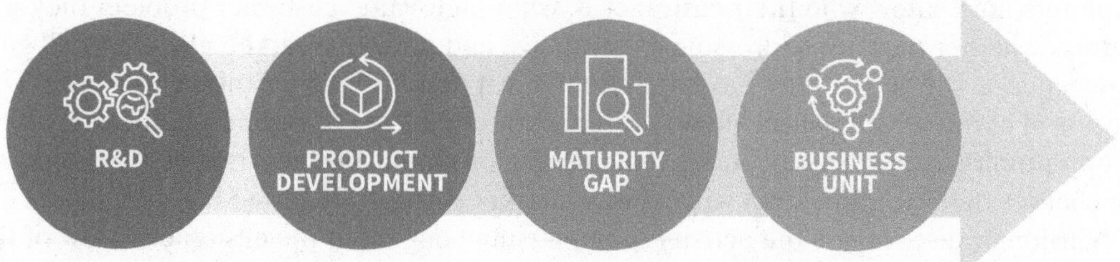

Figure 8.2 The maturity gap between predevelopment and business units.

The business model maturity gap leaves the prospect of converting a tremendous technological innovation into a scalable, profitable business to chance. It could work, but mostly it does not, and as a result, large firms miss markets that they could have dominated.

This is how the business model maturity gap works (Figure 8.2). Imagine that you have a new technology you need to validate. You have listed numerous use cases and ascertained that the technology works for those use cases. Maybe you have even done a few pilots.

Next, you look at high-level market research data, typically based on verticals and the listed use cases, to estimate market potential. Then you consolidate your learnings and attempt to hand the technology over to a relevant business unit, believing that the market research is sufficient.

Despite your excitement, the business unit is underwhelmed. Why? Are they simply shortsighted? In fact, they are not shortsighted; they are probably correct to reject the technology at *this* stage. A technology is not a product, and it is certainly not a business model or business – and that is the origin of the maturity gap. Business units are core business machines. They know how to sell existing products and how to exploit the current business model. If there is a deviation from that model, then business units are reluctant to undertake the new technology, especially if it requires more investment either in product development or at the go-to-market stage.

This maturity gaps means that most of the innovation budget is tied up solving the problem of how to get more customers to buy a product they do not want, instead of investing in the area where the maturity gap exists – namely, customer validation and go-to-market. This is expensive, time consuming, and results from not being customer first.

CLOSING THE MATURITY GAP WITH EVIDENCE

The alternative is to adopt the practices of customer discovery and validation, followed by a rigorous assessment of the business model to ensure it has matured. These practices focus prospective Corporate Explorers on potential customers early in their journey, forcing them to learn "outside-in" what the market values.

We want Corporate Explorers to be able to produce evidence for all elements of a business model before a business unit tries to scale it in the market. This means Corporate

Explorers must know who their customer is, what high-value customer problem they will address, whether they are addressing an attractive and growing market, how they will generate value, and whether they have the required capabilities and partners to succeed. This process of customer validation allows the Corporate Explorer to decide whether they have an opportunity to create a repeatable, scalable, and profitable business model. This improves the chances that the innovation will come to market with a fully tested business model.

Customer discovery is the activity of immersing yourself in the customer's view of the world so that you can develop an outside-in appreciation for the problem they are trying to solve. The greatest learning comes from repeated interviews – we recommend more than 100 – so that you are forced to challenge your initial hypothesis and genuinely see the world from the perspective of the customer. During the interviews, a Corporate Explorer learns to evolve, adapt, reinvent, or refute their understanding of the customer's biggest pain points. If done well, the Corporate Explorers either end up with a full understanding of whether to proceed with the project or, if the evidence suggests, they do not have a severe enough customer problem to solve.

During the customer validation process, Corporate Explorers build a minimum viable product (MVP) to test all elements of their intended business model and determine whether it could be repeatable, scalable, and profitable. An MVP is not a technical prototype; it is the first version of a product that can be used to test and iterate all elements of your business model.

The goal of customer validation is to find out whether you have accurately identified a high-value customer problem that you can solve in a repeatable way. This means you need to test the MVP with real customers and get their reaction. Does it solve a severe problem? Does it offer a convincing value proposition that they are willing to pay for? Who are the highest priority customer segments; who are the most likely to adopt the solution first?

These practices are embedded in the Bosch Accelerator Program (see later). At Bosch, we have found that roughly 70% of teams make their own no-go decision at the end of customer discovery because they were not able to find a repeatable and severe problem to justify moving forward. At the end of the customer validation phase, again, approximately 70% of the teams make a no-go decision and kill their respective business model idea. The application of these practices at Bosch speeds up the rate of innovation and reduces the amount of time and resources spent on ideas that will never succeed in the market.

INDICATORS OF BUSINESS MODEL MATURITY

There are eight key success factors showing that you have a mature business model.

Repeatable and Severe High-Value Customer Problem

The top threat to any business idea is the unwillingness of customers to change their behavior, because existing solutions are good enough. This is your biggest competition. We want Corporate Explorers to identify problems that are so severe and high value that customers are willing to change behavior and adopt them. Even more, we want them to be willing and able to pay for the intended solution. These problems also need to occur frequently enough that there is a market to serve. It is not enough to focus on niche problems; one needs to focus on the problems that, if solved, will lead to a strategically relevant market opportunity with enough customers. This focus on repeatability is critical if you are going to scale a new business, because it implies the strength of your long-term market demand.

How Customers Solve the Problem Today

This criterion follows directly from the previous point. To understand how severe a problem is, it is necessary to understand how well it is currently diagnosed and addressed, if at all. This is the starting point for your competitive analysis. You should look at substitutes, competing technologies, and even doing nothing. Doing nothing is a special case where we hear lots of interesting remarks. One refrain is "the customer is unaware of the problem," the point being that if we just launch, the customer will be blown away and money will rain down. However, there are two reasons for the customer's ignorance. Either the problem doesn't exist (bad news), or the problem is real, but they are unaware of it (potentially bad news). Why is the latter bad news, too? If customers are unaware of the problem, your company had better be good at marketing to create awareness, which is expensive. We are not saying: "Do not proceed." However, you will have to consider marketing as a fundamental part of your business model and MVP testing. A second common refrain is "there is no solution for this problem." Be careful when this happens; there may be a good reason nobody is solving it. Again, the point here is that thorough validation must happen instead of just launching on faith and pure enthusiasm.

Prioritized Customer Segmentation

The most important aspect of this criterion is a thorough understanding of exactly who the customer is. Interviews, persona templates, and customer archetype templates are indispensable for helping articulate the key characteristics of the customer. These tools serve as a reminder that customers are people. We have a nasty habit in business of listing entire verticals or organizations as customers. While that might work in core business where the business has already been validated, it is dangerous in exploratory ventures. Again, customers are people, and knowing their job titles, roles, behaviors, and beliefs matters the most at this stage.

Customer Ecosystem and Value Chain

Note that having proper segmentation is only the beginning of the work. You must next begin to understand the entire customer ecosystem. Map out how customer decisions are made, and what role each stakeholder plays. Knowing the identity of the user, the economic buyer, the decision maker, the saboteur, the influencer, and the recommender will be vital for creating a workable business model. We cannot count the cases when teams got excited about finding a user who loves a solution but is not a relevant decision maker or has no budget. Customer decision diagrams, influence maps, stakeholder maps, and other templates are very helpful for sorting out these often-complex ecosystems. But your work is still not done. You must map out the value chain from your suppliers to you, to channels, to the end customer, and, on top of that, analyze each ecosystem along the way. The mentality here should be that if anyone says no, and your business model fails, you must talk to them and understand their problems. Again, if you have no channel to the user or buyer, there is no business.

Convincing Value Proposition and Willingness to Pay

If you have thoroughly validated the customer problem, the value of resolving it should be intuitive. However, one mistake we see at this point is that teams list product features as value propositions. The key word here is *value*. Teams should articulate the emotional, social, or functional value of solving the problem. Tools such as the Value Proposition Canvas (see Chapter 10) or methods such as jobs-to-be-done (see Chapter 4) can be very helpful in thinking about what the real value is. In the end, products deliver this value to customers, and features are a key component of that. The ability to deliver value is a key criterion for MVP testing in customer validation, and we must also be able to measure this value (see Sticky Solution, below). Ultimately, we measure whether there is sufficient value for the customers via their willingness to pay.

It is crucial at this stage that you do not end up in proof-of-concept hell. What we specifically mean is asking customers to pay for MVPs during customer validation. We must begin measuring the commitment of the customer early on – and free MVPs don't do that. It is not difficult to find customers who are willing to push all the cost and risk on to you, but you do not learn much about your business model. You do not want to make endless free MVPs part of your sales process. That is a recipe for enormous customer-acquisition costs. Finding the customers with the true must-have is much more difficult, and this is exactly the task of this phase.

Sticky Solution

The key word here is *sticky,* meaning that the customers start and keep using the solution. We are not so concerned if there is no solution at the beginning of customer validation, but we should have a solution that delivers and measures the value proposition by the end of the phase. In our program, we do not allow MVPs to be built until the customer interviews are finished, and there is enough justification for starting building anything at all. We know from experience that technologies teams developed in customer validation are often wrong if built in advance rather than in tandem with their customers. The most important thing at this juncture is to make sure that your MVP delivers and captures value and that you have metrics for measuring this value.

Solving a Sufficiently Large Problem

Let's say you have somehow managed to accomplish everything up to this point. You are now standing in front of an executive and explain excitedly how much your customers love your product. You even have paying customers! The executive seems underwhelmed and asks: "How many customers do you have?" The ambition in large corporates is to solve problems that will lead to a $100M revenue – and nothing less. This target may seem arbitrary, but it is important for large corporates that must constantly replace vanishing businesses. Anything smaller makes for a good startup or a small company, but it is not worth the time of large corporates. At least, that is the attitude. Fortunately, if you have followed the aforementioned criteria, you have already found something repeatable and severe, which can be the basis of such a large business, and if it is not, you will know why.

Repeatable, Scalable, and Profitable Business Model

Provided we have done everything already discussed, we now have reached the final checkpoint of customer validation. As we do our MVP tests, we want to ensure that we do testing with the right, paying customers; our solution does not need significant adaptation from one customer to the next; and our sales funnel is beginning to take shape. If we have evidence of these final items, we now have the foundation for what comes next in the venture building process.

ASSESSING THE MATURITY GAP

Every company has some version of an investment-readiness framework. It is vital for validating and evaluating exploratory ventures. Corporate Explorers can take it to the next level – not just knowing the investment criteria, but also governing their portfolio of ventures and enabling these ventures to fill the gaps in their business models. At Bosch, we have developed a systematic set of criteria and deliverables for both investors and teams to use, something we call the business model maturity assessment.

When we began validating ventures in practice at Bosch, we often ran into the situation that, despite knowing the investment criteria, we were unsure of what exactly to do next with our venture teams and what precisely would constitute evidence that we had met any given criterion. What we found is that criteria alone are insufficient for corporate venture teams. What is necessary is a set of clear deliverables and best practices for each stage of maturity to answer the question, what should we prioritize and work on today?

These deliverables help teams produce the right evidence at the right time and to demonstrate they have met the investment criteria. Without such deliverables and criteria, decisions will be made on gut feel. We do not believe that you can completely remove gut feel, but the ambition should be to remove it as much as possible. Such deliverables force both investors and teams to play by a common set of rules which are transparent to everyone.

Every venture must meet the same standards and produce the same evidence to move forward and receive more funding. So, goal number one was transparency, fairness, and governance. Goal number two was to enable the teams to fill any gaps they may have in their business models.

Telling teams they do not meet the criteria is not good enough; we must be in a position as Corporate Explorers to show them how they can meet the criteria, to coach them, to enable them to overcome the maturity gap mentioned above. Governance and enabling are the cornerstones of the business model maturity assessment and removing the maturity gap to make the ventures ready for scale.

The assessment is organized according to maturity stages. At Bosch, we have created the following phases: strategic framing, problem definition, concept ideation, concept validation, and incubation. These phases describe the typical maturity stages corporate ventures must traverse to validate and scale their business models; they roughly correspond to other commonly used investment stages (pre-seed, seed, Series A–D). These describe the typical criteria and deliverables one should expect from a venture at any given time.

This point is crucial, because you should not be judging a mature business and a seed-stage venture by the same criteria. Asking for a five-year revenue forecast from a venture that is not even sure of the problem it is solving or the value of solving it is counterproductive at best. We have witnessed several ventures damaged from being given mature-business criteria too early. Some day in the future, such questions will be appropriate, but not today. The maturity gap is still too big.

There are four roles in the assessment: venture team member, assessor, enabler, and investor.

The venture team members produce evidence that will be assessed. They are the ones running experiments in the market, talking to real customers, and building MVPs.

The assessor's job is to seek the truth together with the team. The assessment is not an audit. The goal is for the team, the assessor, and the investor to all get on the same page and understand where the venture is today and what can be done to push it forward. No advantage exists for sugar-coating the evidence, since it is clear to everyone whether the evidence is sufficient or not based on the transparent deliverables. You either have it or you do not. In fact, our favorite answer is, "We don't know," because it is honest and leads to the best question: "How do we find out?"

The assessor also has the role of enabler. They must both determine the maturity level and gaps in the business model and provide advice to enable the team to fill the maturity gaps. The assessor must avoid being adversarial. The most important job is to let the team tell the current story of the venture and to ask probing questions to calibrate the maturity level according to the evidence.

The investor does not normally take part in the assessment itself but receives it afterwards. The role of the investor is to use the assessment in future investment decisions: whether to deploy more resources given the gaps or stop the project.

At Bosch and beyond, we have performed this assessment on over 75 ventures. In our experience, ventures are grateful for the honest look at their progress, the advice given, and the clear prioritization of what to do next. Investors are likewise grateful because they now know exactly where the gaps in the maturity are and how to fill them. We know that not every venture will ultimately be able to overcome the maturity gap. That is just the nature of exploration, but the only way to start is by knowing what and where the gap is. The maturity assessment does not just provide the *what* but also the *how*. It has and will remain an indispensable tool in our exploration efforts at Bosch and beyond.

APPLICATION CASE STUDY: BOSCH ACCELERATOR PROGRAM

At Bosch, we have turned the customer discovery process into a repeatable process for closing the business model maturity gap. Launched in 2017, the Bosch Accelerator Program enables rapid, systematic, and cost-effective (in)validation of a very large number of business model ideas. Each program has 20–25 cross-functional teams of four to five members from across Bosch Group. The team is 100% dedicated to the program, a requirement that demonstrates the sponsoring business unit has skin in the game. If the unit cannot commit sufficient capacity, the project is rejected. Although this precondition for program entry sounds harsh, it sets an expectation that exploratory projects should be treated just as seriously as core business, where all hands are on deck, and the starting point must be full commitment even if the most likely result is a failure.

The program has two phases: customer discovery, with a duration of two months, and customer validation, with a duration of six months. At the end of each phase, the teams decide whether to pursue the innovation project further, pivot, or stop. A foundational pillar of the program is that the teams know whether to proceed based on the available evidence, and whether they meet the criteria of the program. Therefore, it's the teams that should be the drivers of the respective go/no-go decision, not pitch juries or senior executives, who are often disconnected from the evidence on the ground. This approach requires a lot of trust and empowerment, and we have observed very few cases where the team's decision to proceed or stop was unjustified.

Here is an example of this process in action.

"How can we provide recreational vehicle users with maximum mobility and freedom without sacrificing comfort or safety?" This was the question that the "48-Volt Camper team" set out to answer when it began the Bosch Accelerator Program. The team entered Phase I (customer discovery) of the program and managed to execute more than 100 customer interviews within the span of merely eight weeks. Based on the extensive customer interviews, the team figured out how to cluster RV users into different segments according to their respective needs, expectations, and traveling behaviors.

One problem stood out for many RV users: in remote places with no external power source, they frequently run out of electricity, and, therefore, cannot use air conditioning or the fridge for perishable goods.

(Continued)

As mentioned earlier, having users is not sufficient when your company has no natural channels to these users. Therefore, the team made sure that the idea was potentially high value for RV manufacturers as well. With the RV manufacturers on board, the team decided it had enough evidence to fulfill all the deliverables of Phase 1.

After a clear go decision, the team then moved to Phase 2 of the program (that is, customer validation) to focus on MVP development and iteration. In addition, the team worked on all the aforementioned deliverables of Phase 2. After several MVP iterations, the team managed to generate energy with an electrified axle and store it in scalable 48V lithium-ion batteries to power various systems in the RV.

The project successfully exited the Bosch Accelerator Program to further incubate the innovative business idea. During the incubation phase, however, the team decided to suspend the idea because of the limited availability of key system components during the worldwide supply chain crisis. In addition, due to the COVID-19 pandemic, RV manufacturers invested heavily in production capacity expansions and less in explorative solutions to address the strongly growing vehicle demand.

This example demonstrates that even successful initial validation of an innovative idea with users is no guarantee for success when incubating a venture. Timing, dependence on manufacturers, behavioral trends, and many other factors matter, too, when validating a new business model.

CHAPTER 9

Get Out of the Building: How to Gather Customer Discovery Data with Interviews

Vanessa Ceia and Sara Carvalho

OUTSIDE-IN LOGIC

Interviews help Corporate Explorers generate deep qualitative insights about their customers and de-risk ideas for new ventures across the innovation funnel – from ideation and incubation to scaling. However, the research goals and interview techniques you employ to achieve them will differ at each stage of the process and depend on the maturity of the idea. This chapter outlines the *why*, *when,* and *how* of interviewing customers. It describes the insights interview data can provide that quantitative methods cannot; it also outlines a step-by-step process of designing interviews and selecting participants that will help you achieve your research and business goals.

One of the biggest obstacles to becoming a successful Corporate Explorer is the "inside-out" mindset of corporations. This is the self-referring logic of being a part of a large, successful organization that views customers and competitors through the lens of your existing business. This mindset is highly destructive to any new venture, because it leaves Corporate Explorers with unchallenged biases and assumptions about customers: what they need, what they value, what solutions they prefer, and their willingness to pay for them. Customer discovery interviews are a way of overcoming the biases of "inside-out" by getting you outside of the building and talking directly to potential customers.

TALKING TO CUSTOMERS

Customer research comes in many forms – case studies, surveys, data mining, focus groups, and usability studies being among the most popular – and research methods are broadly categorized as either quantitative or qualitative. Whereas quantitative research collects data that is measured numerically, qualitative methods generate non-numerical insights about customers' attitudes, feelings, and experiences. The former is great for gathering large amounts of data that help create general insights – the *what* – about a sizable sample of customers, but the latter can result in a deeper and more nuanced understanding of customers and of the *why* driving their behaviors.

Interviews and focus groups are two of the most common qualitative research methods employed to generate deep insights about customers. Focus groups can be a time-saving way to measure customer reactions to your product or idea, but it can be difficult to avoid a "groupthink" and get honest answers from each participant. Meanwhile, although conducting several one-on-one interviews can be more time-consuming than running one or two focus groups, interviews also tend to yield richer and more honest insights about individual decision-making processes, experiences, attitudes, feelings, and behaviors.

In this chapter, we outline the *when* and *how* of interviewing customers. Our step-by-step guide will help you design interviews and select participants that can help you achieve your research and business goals. Just as your research and innovation goals change depending on the level of your idea's maturity, so will the interviewing techniques you will employ at each stage of your discovery process.

CUSTOMER INTERVIEWS FOR IDEATING, INCUBATING, AND SCALING

Depending on which stage of the innovation process you are in – ideating, incubating, or scaling – your research goals will differ, as will the focus of your research questions. Similarly, the purpose of your research will determine whether your interviews will be more open or targeted.

The more open an interview question is, the less it restrains the interviewee. Open questions are designed to help you identify potential customers, and begin to understand their attitudes, feelings, perspectives, and experiences. Open questions also help develop a hypothesis about a problem that the customers have and want to be solved. In the early ideation or exploration phase, you are still identifying your customer segments, creating hypotheses, and identifying the problem you aim to solve. The less you know, the more open and exploratory your questions should be.

Likewise, the more you already know about your customers, and the more mature your product or idea is, the more targeted your questions should become. Targeted questions validate an existing product or hypothesis and are, therefore, more practical, operational, and detail oriented. They are also more focused on a defined target customer.

How you approach the interviewing process and design your interviews depends on the level of your innovation maturity and research goals. There are three major stages of the innovation process: ideation, incubation, and scaling. Each stage will have a different **purpose** (primary research goals), **interviewees** (target research participants or customers), **focus** (topics that interview questions should center on), and **target outcomes** (ideal outcomes of your interviews). This is how we suggest applying these stages in practice.

Interviewing at the Ideation Stage

During the ideation stage, you may or may not have a hypothesis to test. As noted earlier, the less you know, the more open your questions should be. This will ensure that you don't overly restrain your customers during the early ideation (and, therefore, the most exploratory) stage. If you have already developed a hypothesis about a problem that needs to be solved, your questions will be more targeted as you aim to generate data that validate or invalidate your hypothesis and ensure that you are ideating a solution to a problem that your customers do face and want to be solved (Table 9.1).

Table 9.1 Interviewing at the ideation stage.

Purpose	• Define a customer problem or unmet need using the information that you gathered from observation or deduced from collected data. • Formulate and test an initial hypothesis. • Get acquainted with the targeted customer audience. • Immerse yourself in the point of view of the customer. • Discard "problems" that don't really exist.
Interviewees	• Decision-makers. • Users. • Field experts.
Focus	• Is the problem that you have identified real? • What are the consequences of not solving this customer problem now? • Have your customers attempted to adopt alternative solutions? • Are they satisfied with existing alternatives or still seeking out additional solutions? Why or why not? • Are there other, bigger problems that customers need to solve first?
Target Outcomes	• Customer problem that needs to be solved is identified. • You understand your potential customers' wants and needs. • You are ready to kick-off an ideation session focused on the question, "How might we solve this problem?" • You understand your target customer's profile before ideating the value proposition.

Interviewing at the Incubation Stage

At incubation, you need to validate the problem- and solution-market fit; improve customer segmentation; deepen and sharpen customer profiles; ensure that your early prototype (minimum viable product or solution, MVP) meets user requirements; and repeatedly collect customer feedback that you will use to iterate and improve your offering. To do so, you should interview target users to understand their needs; influencers and recommenders to understand what they love (or would improve) about your offering; testers for product usability tests and feedback; decision makers; buyers to identify barriers to purchasing your offering (and learn what they would be willing to pay for it); and saboteurs to understand why they oppose your offering (Table 9.2).

Table 9.2 Interviewing at the incubation stage.

Purpose	• Validate problem- and solution-market fit. • Improve customer segmentation. • Deepen your understanding of customer profiles. • Ensure that your early prototype (MVP) meets user requirements. • Collect feedback to improve MVP.
Interviewees	• Target users. • Influencers and recommenders. • Testers. • Decision makers. • Buyers. • Saboteurs.

Focus	• Problem-market fit:
	  • Who is who in your customer decision tree?
	  • Is the problem you are solving relevant to the most important stakeholders in the customer decision tree?
	  • Are you trying to solve a "must-solve" or a "nice-to-solve" problem?
	  • Will people pay for a solution to this problem?
	  • What are the characteristics of the customers facing this problem?
	  • How many potential customers have a similar problem?
	  • What is the value proposition that customers are looking for? Does it have emotional value?
	• Solution-market fit:
	  • Does your solution solve the problem?
	  • Does your solution deliver the value you expected?
	  • How is your solution better or worse than previous or alternative solutions?
	  • Is there a market for your solution?
	  • Does it delight customers from end-to-end of the customer journey?
	  • Will the customer be willing to pay for your solution?
	  • Does it make business sense to pursue this solution? Can it win in the market?
	  • Will your ecosystem partners follow through on commitments to the project?

Target Outcomes	• You have refined customer segmentation and personas. • You have refined the customer journey. • You have validated the feasibility, viability, and desirability of the MVP.

Interviewing at the Scaling Stage

Preparing to scale is a critical point in the innovation process not only because you are going to market, but because it is a time when new and unexpected blockers to success are likely to arise. These blockers may include the lack of operational capacity, resistance of other business units, and absence of partners to sustain the scale of your new venture. At the same time, you will need to continue validating customer traction. That means that the list of interviewees should include not only all stakeholders from the customer decision tree (target users, influencers, recommenders, decision-makers, buyers, and saboteurs), but also people representing your own organization: your partners, your sales team, and heads of relevant departments (logistics, purchasing, marketing, and others) (Table 9.3).

Table 9.3 Interviewing at the scaling stage.

Purpose	• Validate organizational support for scaling. • Ensure that your product or service has customer traction.
Interviewees	• All stakeholders from customer decision tree (target users, influencers, recommenders, decision-makers, buyers, and saboteurs). • Key stakeholders within your organization, including department heads and operational colleagues. • External partners.
Focus	• Can and should we pursue this project? Is the organization willing and capable of pursuing this project without negatively influencing the customer experience? • Is the business model as scalable as expected? • Do we understand all the processes required across the customer journey? Can we support them? • What are the obstacles to delivering our value proposition? Are there any internal saboteurs of the process integration between our core and explore businesses? If so, what is driving them? • Are our key internal stakeholders supporting the implementation of our new offering? If not, what do they need to do to change their attitude? • Can our operating services implement the new processes? What will it take to create a positive user experience for them? • Does our sales team understand our solution and have the means to sell it? Do they have the right incentives to sell? Can they track sales and keep learning from customers? • How will we get continuous customer feedback to improve processes? • Is our product or solution sticking with customers? If not, why? • Are we creating obstacles that prevent customers from buying again?

(Continued)

Target Outcomes	• Evidence of scalability: customer base is growing as expected. • Proof that internal processes are working. • No internal saboteur can block business implementation. • A customer feedback loop process is established, so we can continue to improve our offering.

DOS AND DON'TS OF CUSTOMER INTERVIEWS

The interview process itself has three key phases: preparation for interviews, conducting interviews, and summarizing and analyzing collected data. Each stage has specific *dos* and *don'ts*.

Preparing Interviews

If you are new to interviewing, you might be wondering, how do I overcome nervousness when I get started? Where do I find people to interview? How can I prepare for my first interview? These questions are to be expected. Preparation is key to conducting a quality interview. Here are some points to consider when designing your research plan and interview guide (Table 9.4).

Table 9.4 Preparing interviews.

Do	Don't

• Plan to interview several people from your target customer segment. Be aware that you may mistakenly validate a business model if all target users show great interest in your solution, but decision makers and buyers do not. Have a purpose and a plan:
  • Know who you are meeting and why.
  • Prepare a list of questions to validate your business model hypotheses.
  • Plan an interview guideline for each persona.
• Be creative about where to find your target customers to interview. Do they go to a specific location, for example, a mall? Go there! Use social media, ask your contacts if they know someone, and never forget to ask your interview partner if they have someone in mind for you to interview.
• If you have financial resources, hire an agency to find the right people for you to interview. But you and your team should be the ones to hear the answers firsthand.
• Practice with people you know before you start interviewing and ask feedback on your performance. If possible, film it so you can observe and correct mistakes.
• Establish roles in advance, such as moderator and note taker.
	• Outsource the interviews to interns or external companies.
	• Rely on a small list of potential customer interviews.

Conducting Interviews

Once you have prepared your interview guide or list of interview questions and have a list of interviewees, you need to answer a question: How many interviews are enough? Carnegie Mellon's Professor M. Granger Morgan and his co-authors conducted a study on this topic and found that no new concepts emerged after 20 in-depth interviews.[1] Moreover, they found that most new data emerged in the first five or six interviews, and 80–90% of concepts were identified in the first 10. Similarly, Greg Guest and his colleagues found after conducting 60 in-depth interviews that 70% of the themes identified in their research emerged in the first six interviews and 97% emerged in the first 12.[2]

If your time is limited, five or six interviews will help you identify most of the key themes within your target segment. As a rule of thumb, we recommend conducting 5–12 interviews per customer segment, with 8 being, in our experience, what you might call a "saturation sweet spot," a moment when new data begins to repeat the data previously collected (Table 9.5).

Table 9.5 Conducting interviews.

Do	Don't

• Conduct at least five interviews per customer segment.
• Follow an interview guide, or list of questions.
• Iterate and improve your interview guide after the first one to three interviews.
• Have at least one colleague review your interview guide to ensure that your questions are designed to achieve intended outcomes and do not introduce unintended bias.
• Come prepared to listen and learn:
  • Set a relaxed tone.
  • Be open to surprises and insights.
• Have one moderator and one note-taker at each interview, so that the moderator can focus on the interviewee.
• Record and generate an interview transcript if circumstances allow that.
	• Come unprepared, without an interview guide and list of questions.
	• Continue interviewing when you have reached saturation; this is a waste of time and resources.
	• Stop conducting interviews until you validate or invalidate your hypothesis.
	• Give up if the interviewee is only giving you 10 minutes of their time. However, if your participant is not showing interest in the discussion, this is evidence that you are likely not addressing the right problem.
	• Assume you understand your customer problems and jump to questions about the solution; be sure you define and understand the problem first.
	• Ask only closed, yes-or-no questions.

Summarizing and Analyzing Interview Data

Once you have reached a saturation spot, it is time to synthesize and analyze your data. While there are many ways and tools you can use to do this – spreadsheets, whiteboards, stickies, digital collaboration tools – the key is to conceptualize and cluster your data into themes, then analyze the clustered data, and write the results of your research as actionable insights. Generating actionable insights should be the primary goal of your analysis as this will enable you and your team to make informed decisions about next steps, including how to improve processes, refine your offering, and make data-driven decisions. If possible, at least two to three people should analyze the data to avoid a researcher bias in your analysis (Table 9.6).

Table 9.6 Summarizing and analyzing interview data.

Do	Don't
• Summarize and note key observations and insights as soon as the interview concludes. • Create thematic clusters based on the interview data to cross-check patterns suggested by your hypotheses. • Have participants, note takers, or other members of your team validate the data to ensure that your summary is not biased. • Revisit your business model hypotheses and make the necessary adjustments to your interview guide for future interviews. • Determine if there are other people you should interview, and add them to your research plan, if needed. • Include the entire project team (including the project leader and decision makers) in the interview and data analysis process to ensure that as many interpretations as possible are considered. • Write down key insights and separate "must-resolve-now," "nice-to-have," and "unimportant" problems. • Generate a summary of actionable insights and, if possible, specific next steps to take based on the interview data and insights.	• Delay analyzing and writing down the immediate observations and insights from your interview. • Conduct and analyze data alone unless you have no other option. • Forget to check your interpretations for bias (including confirmation bias).

APPLICATION CASE STUDY: PAY-AS-YOU-OWN WATER HEATERS IN KENYA

While backpacking in Peru, I (Sara) stayed at a family house in Lake Titicaca. It was a cold day; I was tired, sweating, and asked my hosts if I could take a hot shower. They became embarrassed as they did not have hot water. I was equally embarrassed as I had simply assumed that they would have it. This was an unplanned instance of customer immersion that revealed an actual customer problem. My hypothesis was that hot water is a worldwide need for health and comfort but many people living in developing countries do not have the financial means to afford the significant one-time expense of a water heater. A pay-as-you-own model could, therefore, be their best option.

To test my hypothesis, I conducted the following interviews before investing in the ideation of solutions (Table 9.7).

Table 9.7 Interviewing potential customers in Kenya.

Interviewee	Sample questions
My Bosch colleagues living in developing countries like Kenya, Colombia, and India	• How would you describe hot water needs and access in your country? • What are the current options for heating water in your country? Who uses what? • Who does not have access to water heaters? Why?
A co-founder of M-KOPA, a pay-as-you-own solar energy device company in Kenya	• Who are your customers and why do they buy solar energy using a pay-as-you-own revenue model? • What other products or solutions are you selling using this model? Why? • Do you think this model could work for water heater sales? Why?
Kenyan farmers	• Do you use hot water? How often? • How do you heat water? Why? • What prevents you from owning a water heater?

After finding initial evidence that the idea of selling water heaters through micropayments could make sense, I decided to dig deeper. First, I needed to validate the problem-market fit. To do that, my team and I interviewed three different personas representing different customer segments. In total, we conducted 101 customer interviews, as we tested various segments.

(*Continued*)

Some of the key questions we asked included:

- How do you currently heat water?
- How satisfied are you with your current heating system and process? Why?
- What prevents you from switching to another solution?

Table 9.8 provides a sample of my key insights.

Table 9.8 Customer interviews key insights.

Persona	Maji	John	Baraka
	Twenty-eight years old, single, rents apartment in urban area	Forty years old, married, two kids, owns apartment or house in urban area	Fifty-five years old, married, four kids, owns house in a rural area
Main Water Heating Method	Electric shower head	Electric storage tank	Firewood
Satisfaction Level	Low	Somewhat low	Extremely low
Pain Points	A fear of an electrical shock; high energy bill.	Huge energy bill; hot water not available during electric blackouts.	Health problems due to smoke; time consumed in preparing the firewood; high costs of charcoal and wood.
Why not switch to a different water heating solution?	Landlord doesn't allow any changes, and he can keep the rent deposit if this rule is violated. Maji is not the decision maker.	They would prefer a solar water heating solution, but it is cost prohibitive. Would prefer to pay monthly if possible.	They would prefer a solar water heating solution since many are not connected to the electrical grid, but the upfront investment is too high for their irregular income.

After understanding and validating the problem, we decided to focus on the Baraka segment and put the John segment on hold, as we had not identified a "must-have need."

The solution to be tested was a solar water heater with an integrated valve connected to a payment controller. Customers would use their mobile phones to pay the number of credits or days they could pay, and at the end of a certain number of credits or days, they would own the complete device.

With every customer interview, we began to better understand our customer profile: major pains in life, their decision-making processes, and their buying patterns (Figure 9.1).

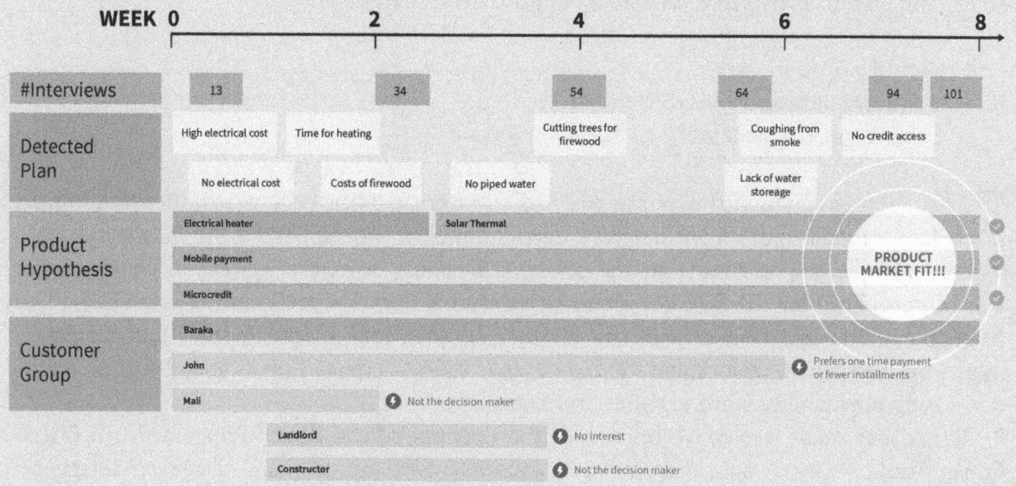

Figure 9.1 Customer discovery timeline.

During the problem identification research, we observed patterns in our customers and concluded that only the "Barakas" that owned more than two cows were willing to go for a pay-as-you-own model. In contrast, the "Barakas" who owned fewer than two cows used all available money to feed their families.

We then moved on to validating the solution-market fit. To do so, we created 12 MVPs to understand if the solution would deliver the value customers expected and be feasible at the same time. After installing the systems, we regularly interviewed the test users to collect more insights.

We asked the following types of questions:

- What is your satisfaction level with the solution? Why?
- How often did you use the system and why less (or more) than before?
- Is your payment pattern faster, on time, or slower than it should be? Why?
- Would you recommend this solution to your friends and family? Why or why not?

These helped assess if the real value proposition aligned with the value proposition we identified in the problem-market fit phase. To address the viability pillar of the business model, we also included some tests and interviews around the payment method, preferred communication channel, partner concept, go-to-market strategy, and customer journey.

(Continued)

The combination of these interviews and real customer sales testing did validate that we had a solution-market fit.

Finally, we moved on to the scaling phase with the goal of answering the question of scalability and also to prove that we had an organization-market fit:

- Should we do it?
- Is the organization able to do this?
- Can we get the necessary customer traction?

To collect evidence in this phase, we had to interview not only customers but, importantly, internal colleagues from different departments as well as partners and salespeople.

For example, we learned that the available business software system in Bosch Kenya was not prepared for the B2C (business-to-consumer) type of business. As a result, we had to redefine our relationship with our partner so that they would receive the micropayments on our behalf. Unfortunately, this complication decreased profitability. Other issues decreasing profitability were logistics and taxes.

To address these issues, we borrowed the concept of the Bosch Rangers (from Bosch Power Tools, a Bosch subsidiary), the salespeople who move from village to village on motorbikes. We also had people on the ground helping us understand what went well and poorly in their sales activities and what might improve our solution. This had created a feedback loop between our target customers and our team. In the process, we revealed additional issues such as, "customers on my route aren't working" and "customers on my route are too healthy, so this customer segment is not there." We also asked phone representatives at our partner call center to regularly interview customers until we felt that their satisfaction hit high levels.

Questions asked at this stage included:

- Are you satisfied with this process? Does it help you to perform your job? Why?
- What was the most successful sales route you had this week? Do you have any ideas on how to improve it?
- How easy is it for you to pitch the sale? What points are customers struggling to understand?

In the end, internal interviews revealed that our idea did not find an organization-market fit. However, by continually getting out of the building, listening to customers, and learning throughout all stages of the innovation process, we saved ourselves and Bosch valuable time and resources that could instead be allocated to exploring other promising innovative ideas and projects.

CHAPTER 10

Value Propositions: Using Value Flows and Design Criteria Maps to Create Customer Delight

George Glackin

INSIGHT TO DELIGHT

Corporate Explorers face multiple challenges when bringing a business opportunity to market. They must identify a market insight and craft an opportunity story about how this insight will dramatically transform or expand the company's business. They must persuade colleagues and management to follow them in developing and launching this opportunity. And they must truly delight the customers they intend to serve. In this chapter, we will explore how to use value flows and design-criteria maps as best practices to develop a delightful value proposition. We'll also learn from the Swiffer Wet Jet case study.

An aspiring Corporate Explorer often starts with an insight that can dramatically transform or expand a company's business. Bringing this insight to life, enlisting the support of colleagues and company leaders, becomes their personal ambition. They embark on in-depth customer discovery work to validate their insight and prepare to start the hard work of incubation. The critical first step of this work is developing a value proposition with the potential to truly delight the customer. They need to know what will make the customer see the solution as a "hero" that transforms their daily routines.

The Corporate Explorers should start work on the value proposition with skepticism about their own experience. It is good and useful to have personal experience of a market, to know the problem you are solving from the user's point of view. What's dangerous is to believe that what you think is true. You are just one data point. It may be rich in experience, but it is also heavily biased by your own self-interest. That is why customer discovery is so vital. Only by diving deep into the lives of *many* target customers can you disentangle your own beliefs from the needs of your potential users.

What do you do with that work when it is complete? How do you convert masses of customer insight into a value proposition? This chapter introduces two analytical frameworks for developing a value proposition. In this chapter, we will cover the steps needed to create a value flow and design-criteria map that shows how our innovation will deliver a delightful value proposition, something that is at the heart of every strong new business model.

CREATING VALUE FLOW AND DESIGN CRITERIA MAP

The term *value proposition* is often misunderstood. For our purposes, let's define the value proposition as "the value a company promises to deliver to customers should they choose to buy their product." We've upped the ante a bit more by declaring that the Corporate Explorer is going to provide a "delightful" value proposition, as that's the only way to deliver the big business impact that we're seeking.

In Chapter 5 on Opportunity Story, the Corporate Explorer had crafted a narrative about a specific "who," someone who is frustrated by a problem, and "enemy," something that needs to be resolved. A "hero" solution has been identified that is believed to be the solution to this problem. We now need to bring this opportunity to life.

As a first step, we need to convert our insights from customer discovery interviews to define the customer's journey for solving their problem. This lays out, to our best understanding, the steps an individual is currently taking to accomplish the solution and achieve a specific outcome. We do this with a tool called a value flow. As a basic example, let's assume that a six-year-old girl is barefoot and wishes to be wearing shoes and socks. Her parents want her to wear shoes as well and want to see their daughter master this important developmental skill.

The girl would likely follow the steps in Figure 10.1. She has the manual dexterity to put on socks and shoes. But tying laces is a challenge for a six-year-old, so this may take many attempts to tie them even loosely.

Now imagine that an innovator, after observing many six-year-olds' attempts to tie their shoes, had the insight that Velcro might be much easier and faster for a six-year-old to fasten, with a more secure result. By employing the value flow approach, the innovator can lay out current steps needed to put on a laced shoe, and then the envisioned steps needed for a Velcro shoe. As we can see in the Velcro value flow in Figure 10.1, at least one step has been

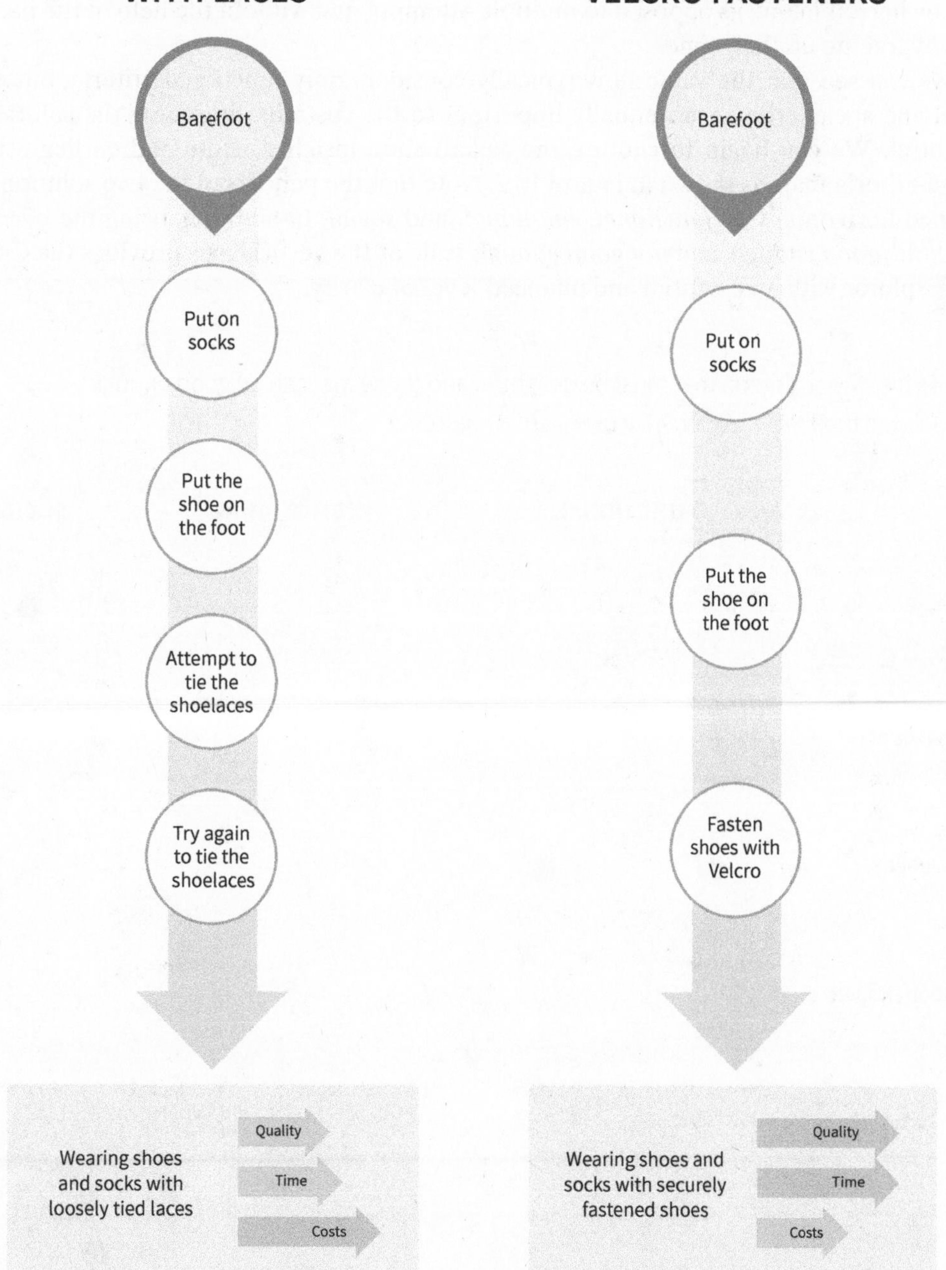

Figure 10.1 Value flow for putting on a shoe, with and without Velcro fasteners.

eliminated, and as an output of the process, the shoes are fastened more securely and in less time. The solution is delightful for both the parents and the child, as the child can fasten the shoe by herself in one as opposed to multiple attempts, and without the help of the parents, thereby freeing up their time.

We can see that the value flow typically considers only functional criteria, but emotional and social criteria are equally important to the customer in seeing the solution as delightful. We can begin to capture the Velcro shoe insights mentioned earlier using a design-criteria map, as shown in Figure 10.2. Note that the benefits of the two solutions are grouped horizontally as *functional*, *emotional,* and *social*. In addition, using the *overshot*, *delightful*, *good enough*, and *not good enough* scale as the vertical axis provides the Corporate Explorer with an essential and nuanced level of clarity.

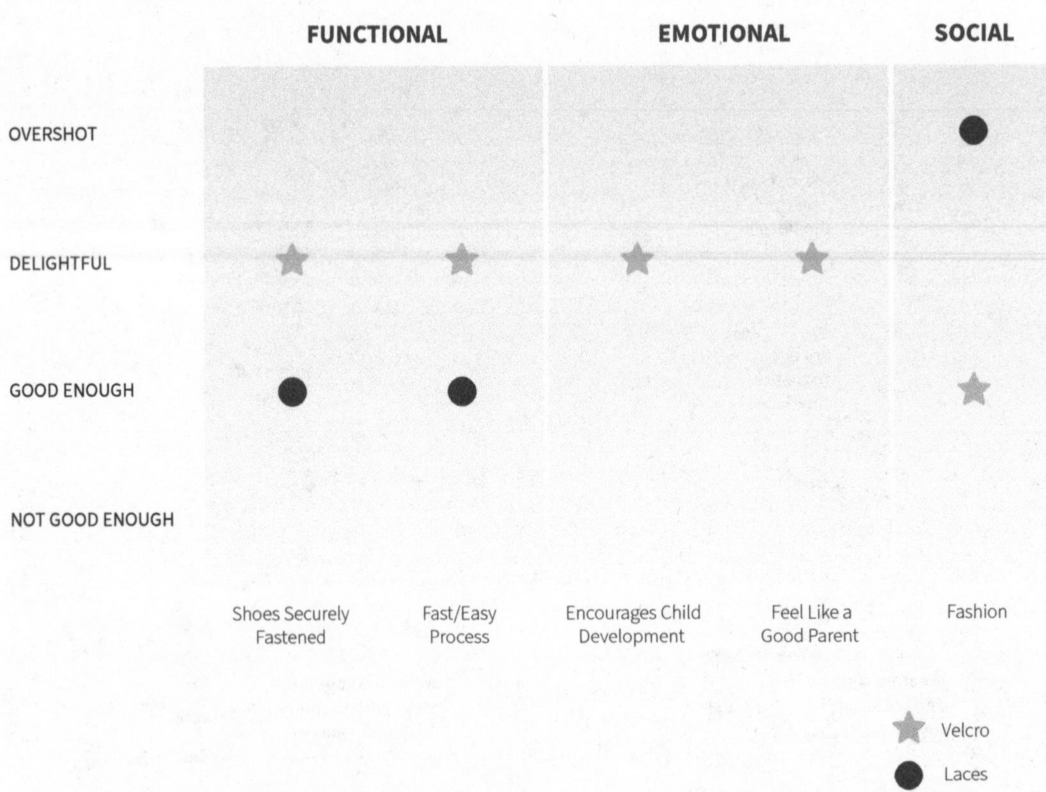

Figure 10.2 Design-criteria map for putting on a shoe, with and without Velcro fasteners.

Let's bring the design-criteria map to life using our Velcro shoe example. A Velcro shoe delivers "delightful" functional benefits for more secure fastening and a fast and easy process. The Velcro design also delivers "delightful" emotional benefits for the child, because she has the satisfaction of being a "big girl" by independently putting on her own shoes. The parent also receives the "delightful" emotional benefit of being a "good parent" by enabling the child to develop and grow. The social benefit of being "fashionable" is only "good enough," because when first launched, Velcro fasteners were considered unexpected or odd looking as compared to laces.

These points help bring to life the vertical scale of *overshot*, *delightful*, *good enough,* and *not good enough*. To deliver a delightful solution, the shoes must be more secure, and faster and easier to put on. The offering solidifies the *delightful* status when it gives both the child and the parents emotional satisfaction and fulfillment. These benefits are so powerful that they overshadow any social impact, such as the shoe looking less fashionable and only *good enough*.

Note that, in the case of *child development* and *feel like a good parent* benefits, the laced shoe offering is *not good enough* when compared to the *delightful* performance of Velcro. This poorly laced shoe performance was heavily exploited by the makers of Velcro shoes and provided a key reason for customers to choose Velcro over laces.

Finally, note that laced shoemakers are delivering *overshot* performance for the fashion benefit, meaning that they have pushed their designs to the illogical extreme by adding colors or licensed characters that no longer have incremental appeal or differentiate them from competition. They have fallen prey to the mindset that "if a little was good, a lot will be even better," and have missed the innovator's insight that there may be new benefit vectors to consider that could add delightful value.

In summary, a delightful new product or service should be *delightful* where it must be and *good enough* where it can be. If all design criteria were boosted to *delightful*, the cost of the offering would increase, or the time to market would expand, undercutting sales and profitability.

Taken together, the value flow and the design-criteria map provide powerful tools for the Corporate Explorer to think through the logic and appeal of an idea. They also provide a structured way to capture insights gleaned from observation of the customer performing the task. This enables the Corporate Explorer to design a solution that will truly delight customers and develop a strong and winning value proposition.

APPLICATION CASE STUDY: P&G'S SWIFFER

Let's look at how these tools were used by Procter & Gamble (P&G) during the development and launch of the Swiffer Wet Jet.[1] In 1994, P&G was seeking organic business growth through innovation and new product lines. With these corporate goals in mind, Corporate Explorer Craig Wynett studied the steps that it took to clean his kitchen floor. He noticed that just to sweep and mop the floor required many complex steps. Intrigued, Wynett had assembled a diverse cross-functional team to study the problem and to invent a better way to clean the floor.

Using a value flow mindset, the team studied the heart of the process, which was mopping the floor and wringing the mop. The team also looked at the process in its full context, and found that at the front end, users had to sweep the floor, because the mop was not very good at getting up loose particles. They also looked at the end of the process and found that very often, streaks were left on the floor (and needed to be dried with a towel). The mop itself needed to be cleaned, a dirty and time-consuming process. And then, as the mop inevitably soiled whatever the user was wearing, the user needed to change clothes! As we can see in Figure 10.3, a seemingly simple task of mopping a floor had a surprisingly large number of steps. Moreover, the process delivered a mediocre result and was often avoided due to the hassle.

The development team had the benefit of including a very diverse set of designers and thinkers, with a broad range of technology and market sector experiences. (P&G operated in both the home cleaning and personal care markets, with specific experience in hard-surface cleaning and baby care.) The "ah-ha" innovation moment came when the team decided to combine a disposable nonwoven pad (such as used for diapers and diaper wipes) together with a cleaning chemical. As we can see in the lower half of Figure 10.3, the number of steps was cut in half, and the quality of floor care improved.

While the functional improvements offered by Swiffer were immense, the emotional and social benefits proved even more powerful. With Swiffer, floor cleaning was no longer a hassle. Users described the process as quick and fun, both for adults and children. And users were able to always have their homes guest-ready, without the rush of a last-minute cleaning. These benefits are captured in the Swiffer design-criteria map in Figure 10.4.

As noted in the Velcro shoe example, a delightful new product or service should be *delightful* where it must, and *good enough* where it can. While Swiffer was able to clean floors a bit better than *good enough*, earlier versions did not seek to be *delightful* for this attribute. The team could have considered additional benefits, such as being fully streak free, delivering a bright shine, or providing a protective coating. However, additional benefits are best considered down the road, and should not be considered initially, due to the inevitable cost increase, reduced profitability, and launch delays they will incur.

Swiffer was launched in 1999 and later became one of P&G's "billion-dollar brands" and one of its most successful new business launches.

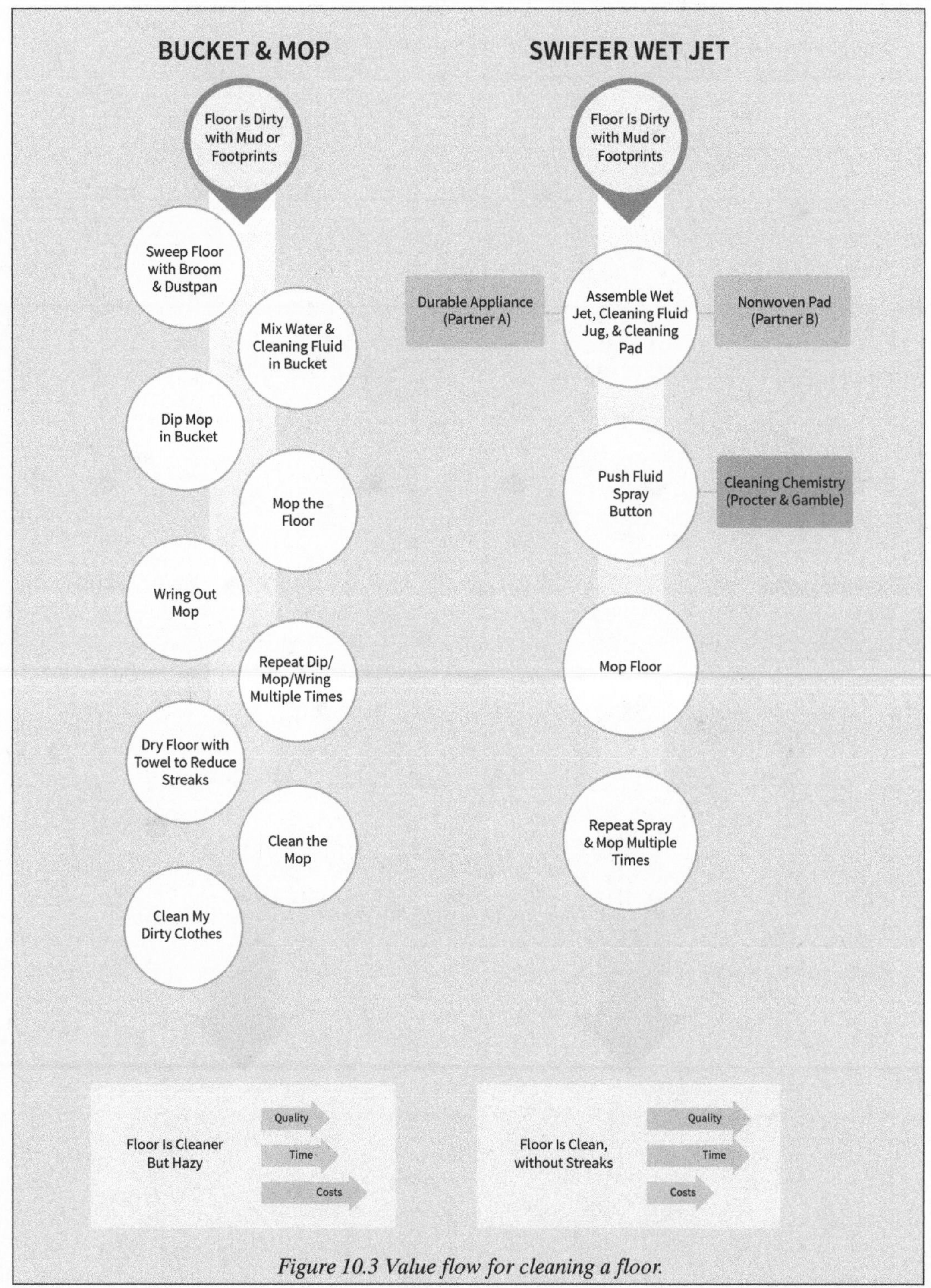

Figure 10.3 Value flow for cleaning a floor.

(Continued)

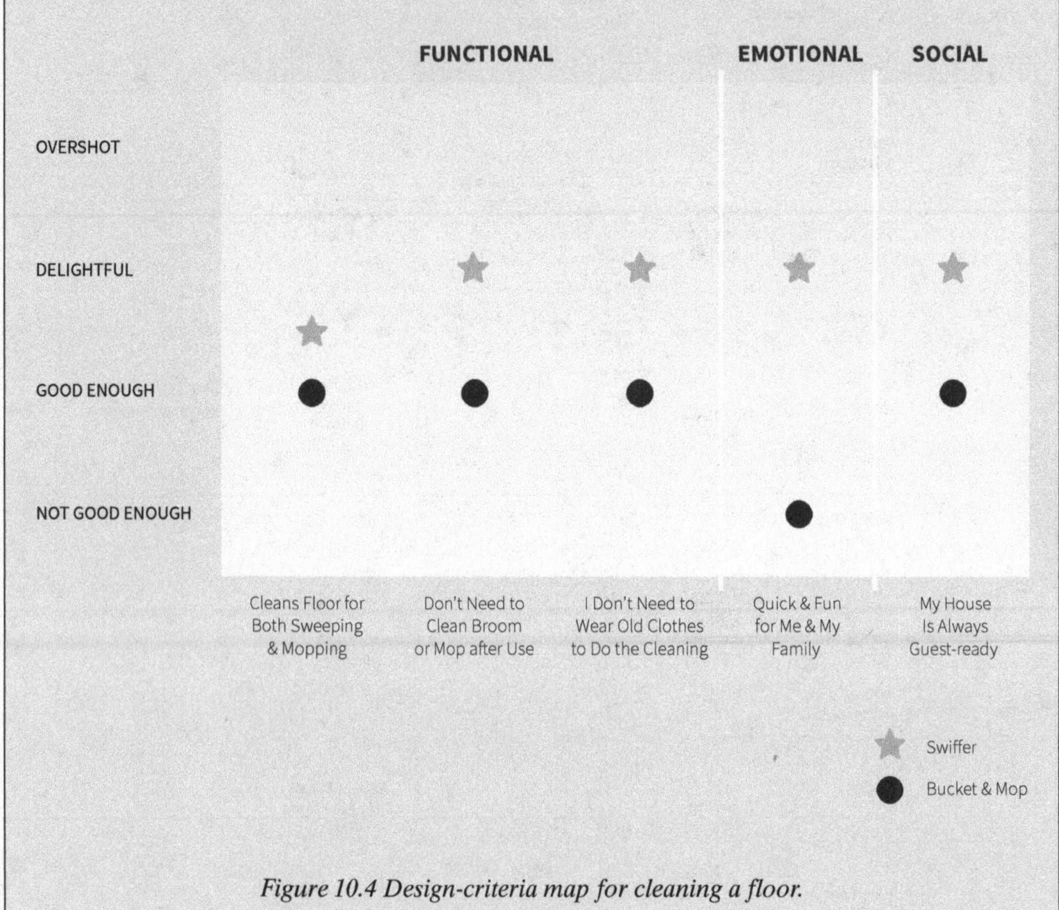

Figure 10.4 Design-criteria map for cleaning a floor.

CHAPTER 11

Business Experiments: De-risking Execution Spend Through Experiments

Sarah Spoto and Vincent Ducret

INSTINCT OR DATA

There are many examples of how even the most successful entrepreneurs and business managers can fail when they put personal conviction and opinion ahead of data. Andy Grove, Intel's legendary CEO, committed the business to videoconferencing equipment in the late 1990s.[1] Jeff Immelt, another storied CEO, bet GE's future on the "industrial internet of things." The browser company, Mozilla, reportedly spent $400 million on a new phone operating system. These are decisions made on instinct that failed.

How does a Corporate Explorer replace, or at least supplement, instincts and opinions (assumptions) with data and evidence to demonstrate whether an idea is worth pursuing, or if it requires a pivot or a shutdown? How does a Corporate Explorer answer questions that have a major potential to jeopardize the project's progress and ultimately its future success if not addressed upfront? This chapter describes how incubation tests unproven assumptions of an idea for a new business by de-risking each element before committing scarce resources to the project.

DE-RISKING INNOVATION

The high level of uncertainty involved in exploring a new business opportunity makes it very different from the operation of a core business. A new venture has none of the performance information and reference points that come from operating an existing business. The new venture is entering an immature market, with emerging or new customer needs, and no historical performance data.

The first impulse for many corporates is to trust their employees' experience, knowledge, and skills to address these uncertainties. They have earned this trust by delivering high-performance results from the existing businesses for many years. However, the reality is that an idea rarely survives its first contact with a customer. The uncertainties of an emerging business make your first ideas highly susceptible to bias, meaning that there is a strong correlation between the "trust" approach and failure of corporate innovation. Paraphrasing Ash Maurya, the creator of Lean Canvas and author of *Running Lean*,[2] the true job of a Corporate Explorer is to systematically de-risk new business designs through gathering, analyzing, and interpreting real market evidence, before making data-driven decisions. This may mean Corporate Explorers have to confront deeply ingrained corporate habits and behaviors. Many organizations are used to decisions being made by the most senior person or the one with the best argument. This likely contributes to the reality that 80% of new products fail to get market attraction, with the lack of clearly identifiable customer needs being reported as the main cause. Corporate Explorers need to teach their colleagues to use evidence to de-risk their investments in new ventures.[3]

In the absence of data or evidence to back up decision-making, the risk of building the wrong solution increases over time. Adopting a systematic way of continuously de-risking new business designs allows earlier decisions (that is, persevere, pivot, or pull-the plug) before the sunk cost of the investment makes it hard to admit that your initial assumptions were wrong.

This chapter outlines the steps to perform iterative experimentation (from assumption identification through experiment design and execution to data-driven decision-making). This approach will be illustrated by its application at General Motors China Premium Import (GMPI) for the development of The Durant Guild platform, GM's first scaled direct-to-consumer business model.[4]

STRUCTURED LEARNING CYCLES

Business experiments operate on a continuous learning cycle (Figure 11.1). It starts with a long list of *assumptions*, which are narrowed to the ones that are *highest priority* to the business. The latter list then becomes part of an *experiment* or test, from which *learning* is extracted and used to *iterate* the business design.

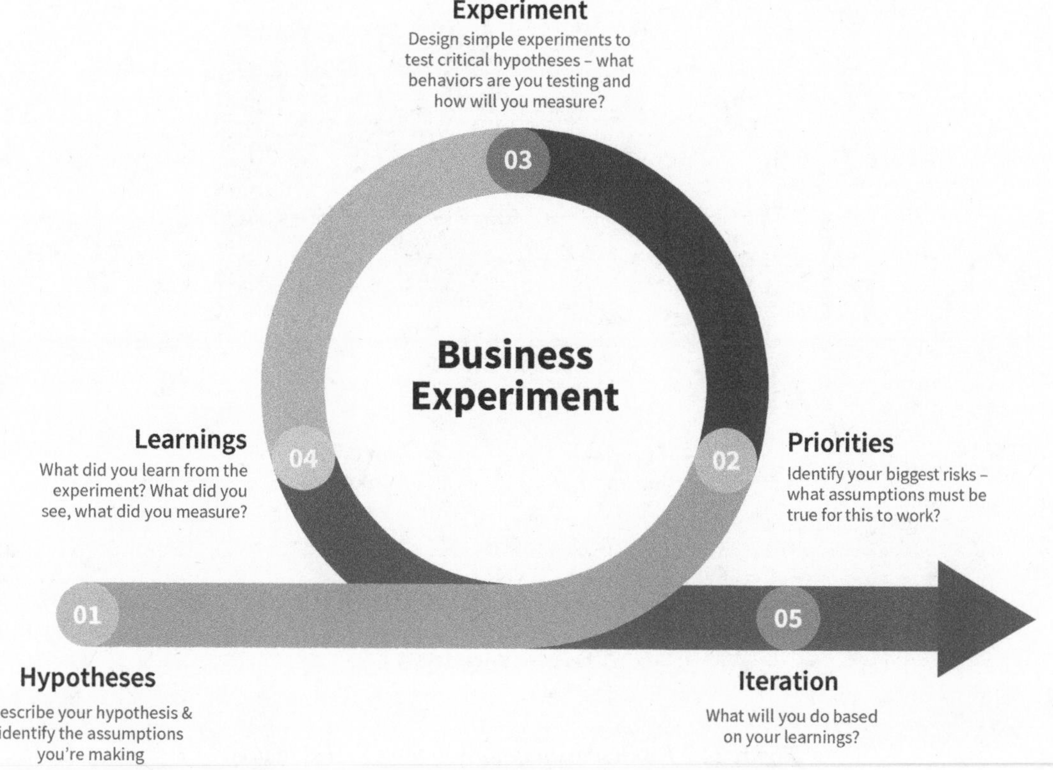

Figure 11.1 Business experiment learning cycle.

Assumptions

Assumptions are underlying guesses or beliefs that are presumed to be true, even though there is no evidence that they are. Every business idea has assumptions embedded in it about what customers want, how much they will pay, how they want to buy a solution, and so on. You make your assumptions explicit by taking any risk, question, unknown, or uncertainty and then stating, "We believe that . . ."

For example, you are enthusiastic about the solution you want to offer customers and believe there is a market, but you are unsure how large this market is and how many people will spend money. You can convert this into an assumption by saying, "We believe that 20% of consumers will be willing to pay for our solution." Your assumption just became testable. New business ventures are de-risked by testing these sorts of assumptions in a series of experiments. Each experiment seeks to turn the assumption into knowledge that validates or invalidates the assumptions of your business design.

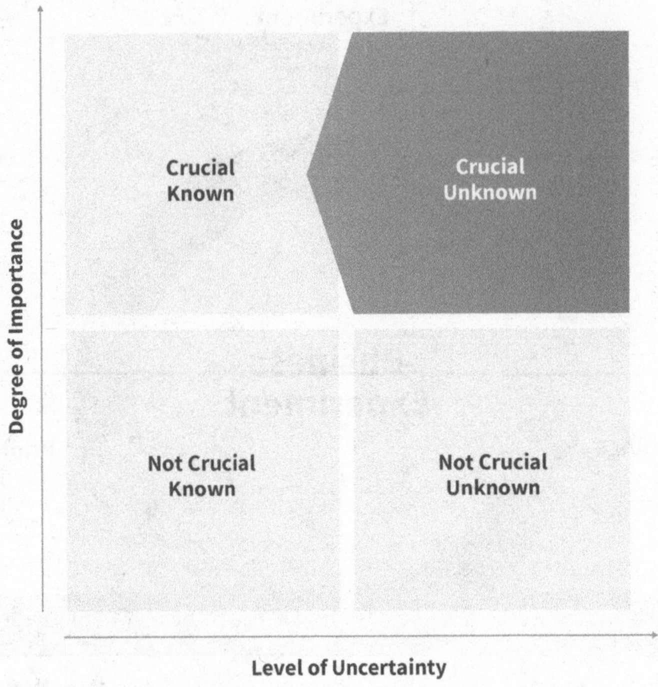

Figure 11.2 Riskiest assumptions to test (RATs) matrix.

Priorities

Not all assumptions are equally important to the success of business, so decide first which assumptions are the most critical. Corporate Explorers can use a two-by-two matrix presented in Figure 11.2 to sort out assumptions and identify the riskiest assumptions to test (RATs).

The matrix classifies assumptions according to the degree of importance and the current level of uncertainty ("Do we already have market data or evidence for the assumption?"). The assumptions in the Crucial Unknown segment are the RATs. As the name suggests, these are the first to be tested in a business experiment.

Experiments

Experiments expose RATs to live customers in conditions as close as possible to market reality. The goal is to produce evidence of an observable or measurable customer action or behavior – do they do what we expect them to do? Some examples of the experimental methods used for this purpose are listed in Table 11.1.

Table 11.1 Experiment method examples.

Experiment method	Examples
Smoke test: gauges market's consideration for a hypothetical problem or opportunity to be solved, or for a product idea by triggering market willingness to exchange "currency."	• Landing Page/video trailer asking visitors to sign up to obtain more information, for example, about a hypothetical product. • Events confirming customers' interest for a hypothetical problem or a product idea through investment of personal time or money (for example, with paid event). • Presales accepting customers' payment in exchange for a promise to deliver the product at a later stage (for example, crowdfunding platforms like Kickstarter).
Survey: asks a fixed set of questions via various communication channels (email, social media, or instant messaging).	• Open-ended or qualitative-focused survey whose answers to questions are not constrained by a predefined set of choices, which allows participants to respond with their own words and level of details. This survey type usually targets small participant sample and helps turn high-level assumptions into future testable hypotheses. • Closed-ended or quantitative-focused surveys constrain participants' answers to a predefined set of choices, thus contributing to the creation of structured quantitative data. This survey type usually targets big participant sample helping test hypotheses.
Concierge: customizes and manually delivers products or services to select stakeholders (like a hotel concierge).	• Rent the Runway, an online dress rental business, wanted to test their solution before going online. They used an in-person service with college students supporting customers in trying on the dress before renting it. This approach provided understanding of the main deficiencies of the service, which allowed the company to develop further testable hypotheses. • Swap Devices, a consumer goods company selling electronic devices, wanted to test customers' desirability to swap out-of-battery devices with fully loaded ones. Before automating this process through dispensers, they deployed a few manual device swap points like booths in a mall to test customers' interest in swapping devices. • Food on the Table wanted to develop a family meal planning service based on dietary preference and shopping deals. Rather than build the technology first, the founder manually gathered information and had the chef design the plans. Performing the service as a concierge helped them validate the solution before building it.

(Continued)

Table 11.1 (Continued)

Experiment method	Examples
Wizard of Oz (WoZ): simulates fully functioning product features without the use of technology. All inputs, outputs, and algorithms are performed manually by humans, but without the knowledge of the customer, unlike Concierge.	• Zappos.com wanted to validate consumers' desire for buying shoes online, knowing that consumers couldn't try shoes before purchase. Before building a full e-commerce automated site, the founder collected consumers' orders through a simplified website and mail exchanges, and manually purchased the ordered shoes in physical stores; he then packaged the shoes and sent them to the customers. Testing the service through a WoZ approach helped Zappos.com to (in)validate riskiest assumptions before moving forward with building the e-commerce solution. • Aardvark, a former social question asking and answering service (later acquired by Google), used a WoZ approach to learn about how their service concept would work without building all the technology. Aardvark employees would get the questions from beta-test users and route them to users who were online to answer these questions. This was done to test out the concept before the company spent the time and money to build a technology to eventually replace humans. • Cardmunch application was created to help alleviate the pain of having to keep a handful of business cards at a networking event. For that purpose, the application would allow people to take photos of the business cards, and then would digitalize the information captured from the card. Before developing any complex technology, the application owners used a WoZ approach to test their overall approach with beta testers by having people from Amazon's Mechanical Turk service manually analyze the photo and transcribe its content into the Cardmunch database.
Dry Wallet: simulates a "check-out" experience to confirm the extent of customers' interest in purchasing a product.	• An automotive company wanted to validate customers' willingness to pay for unique driving experiences. To this end, the company organized an online auction where selected customers could bid on the events while being asked to fill in a payment form for their credit card should they win the auction. The winners of the auctions were informed that no money would be charged to their credit card as events were not yet scheduled but they will get free access to those events in the future.

Experiments take many shapes (smoke tests, surveys, concierge, Wizard of Oz, dry-wallet, and so on) depending on the type of data to be gathered (qualitative as opposed to quantitative) and the dimension of the business idea being tested (market or product) (Table 11.1). For instance, critical assumptions with a customer desirability dimension are usually tested through minimum viable product (MVP). That is the most basic version of your business idea that you can test with customers, allowing you to learn about their needs and preferences as fast as possible and at the lowest cost. Zappos.com, an online shopping site, is a great example of MVP where assumed interactions between customers and a business solution were first executed by unseen humans at a very low cost.

In addition, Corporate Explorers should keep in mind a few principles in identifying the most adequate experimental method to test a given assumption:

- Proceed fast and at low cost in the early stages ("test often, learn quickly").
- Increase the strength and solution fidelity over time (smoke tests, prototype before MVP).
- Be prepared to run multiple experiments to validate a high-risk assumption (for example, by increasing the sample size over time).
- Choose the experiment that will produce the strongest evidence given your constraints (time, money, or people). Note that while evidence requires value exchange with the targeted customers, the quality of the data depends on what customers do (medium-strong evidence) as opposed to what customers say (weak evidence).
- Remember that not every assumption requires experimental testing. The evidence might be available from other sources, both internal and external (Critical/Known in Figure 11.2).

Should Corporate Explorers end up with too many experiments to conduct, they may leverage prioritization techniques (see earlier) to figure out which experiments to conduct first. Figure 11.3 shows an experiment card template that we recommend using when testing assumptions. This helps ensure a disciplined, not random, process to learning.

Learning

Extract data from testing critical assumptions, translate these experimental results and observations into important insights, and make sense of them. What did you see, hear, and measure? Pay close attention to unexpected customer behaviors, too. What did you learn from your customers and collected data? What did you *not* expect? Why did the customer behave this way? What did you conclude from all those observations and data?

As best practice, learnings from experiments should be documented and shared across the corporation in a structured and systematic way – for example, through a corporate knowledge repository. The experiment card includes a learning section to keep experiment and learnings from it together.

ASSUMPTION	[What we want to discover (qualitative data) or test through the experiment (quantitative data)]		
LEARNING OBJECTIVES	[What we expect to learn through the experiment]		
HYPOTHESIS (If testable assumption)	[Which hypothesis we derive from the assumption, i.e., if we do __, then __% of people will do __]	SAMPLE SIZE (If testable assumption)	[The number of people we plan to test through the experiment]
EXPERIMENT METHOD	[Which method we will use to collect data or/and measure people behavior]		
EXPERIMENT LENGTH	[How long it will take to do the experiment]		
EXPERIMENT PLAN	[The steps we will conduct to do the experiment]		
LEARNINGS & DECISIONS (once experiment completed)	[What we learned through the experiment and agreed to do next]		

Figure 11.3 The experiment card: Structuring testing of an assumption.

The completion of experiments also provides the opportunity for Corporate Explorers to measure the impacts and the learning curve of the innovation team in exploring new ventures. For that purpose, metrics like experiment velocity (the number of experiments completed per week), learning velocity (the number of learnings per week), experiment efficacy (the ratio of experiments with learnings), and average cost of learnings should be regularly captured and processed.[5]

Iteration

Use the learnings to decide what to do next. Should the collected evidence not be strong enough for pointing to a clear decision, design new tests and experiments for those critical assumptions to find out if you are getting closer to the answer. Or you might use the evidence to decide whether to persevere, pivot, or kill the idea. Pivoting or killing a business idea might bring Corporate Explorers to revisit the business concept of an idea or to ideate for a different solution to the problem.[6]

Once a decision has been made, document it, update your business design and artifacts, and, if applicable, iterate by looking back at your next critical assumptions.

APPLICATION CASE STUDY: BUILDING THE DURANT GUILD PLATFORM AT GENERAL MOTORS

Founded in 1908, General Motors Company (GM) is an American multinational automotive manufacturing company headquartered in Detroit, Michigan. It is the largest automaker in the United States that is committed to delivering safer, better, and more sustainable ways for people to get around. In China, GM and its joint ventures[7] sell passenger cars and commercial vehicles under the Cadillac, Buick, Chevrolet, Wuling, and Baojun brands. In 2021, GM delivered more than 2.9 million vehicles in China.

Early in 2022, GM publicly unveiled their plan to create an independently owned premium import platform in China. The new GM Premium Import (GMPI) business, tailored for the country, will present a curated collection of iconic GM vehicles through an innovative platform-based business model known as The Durant Guild. The portfolio will range from full-size SUVs and pickup trucks to performance cars. It will address evolving demand in the niche market, complementing GM's model and brand lineup produced locally. Critically, it sells these cars direct to consumers, rather than via a dealership network.

GMPI started by segmenting customers into several personas, the definition of multiple high-value customer problems and opportunities, and the development of related potential solutions (from services and experiences for consumers to online communities and the vehicles themselves). An early alignment and clarity on the target personas ensured that solutions that added real customer value (for the right customers) were prioritized.

The team started its experimentation work by asking "what needs to be true" for these solutions to be adopted by our targeted customers. It also explored which of these beliefs were most critical and should be tested first.[8] Assumption tree and 2x2 sorting matrix (Figure 11.4) technics were used to define smaller and testable assumptions, organize those assumptions between them, and finally identify the most critical ones to test.

Once assumptions to test were prioritized, time came for the value-proposition team to design the experiments to either (in)validate them or turn them into more testable assumptions. While the use of the experiment card template referred to in the illustrations section brought structure to the team in designing their experiments, a particular attention was focused at this stage on setting up learning objectives per experiment and, when applicable, on decision metrics. Defining up-front decision criteria for testable assumptions is crucial to support data-driven decisions vs. opinion-based ones, once data was captured

(Continued)

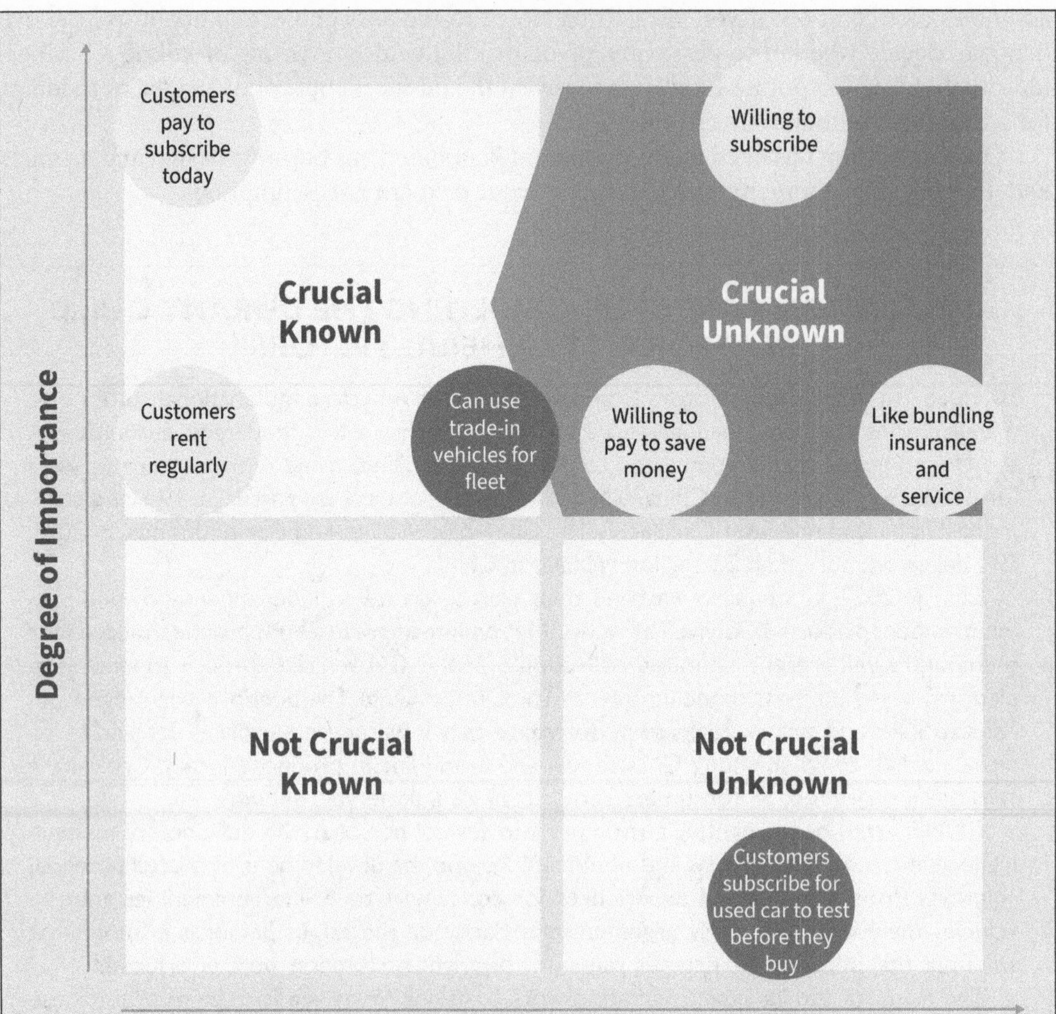

Figure 11.4 Vehicle subscription service: Identifying assumptions to test first.

(see introduction section). Figure 11.5 outlines an experiment designed to test if target customers would place more value on a multibrand vehicle subscription offering (as foreseen by GMPI) than on a single brand (as proposed by competition).

Once the team completed the experiments, they documented learning and decisions on the experiment card and shared with other teams via a corporate knowledge database.

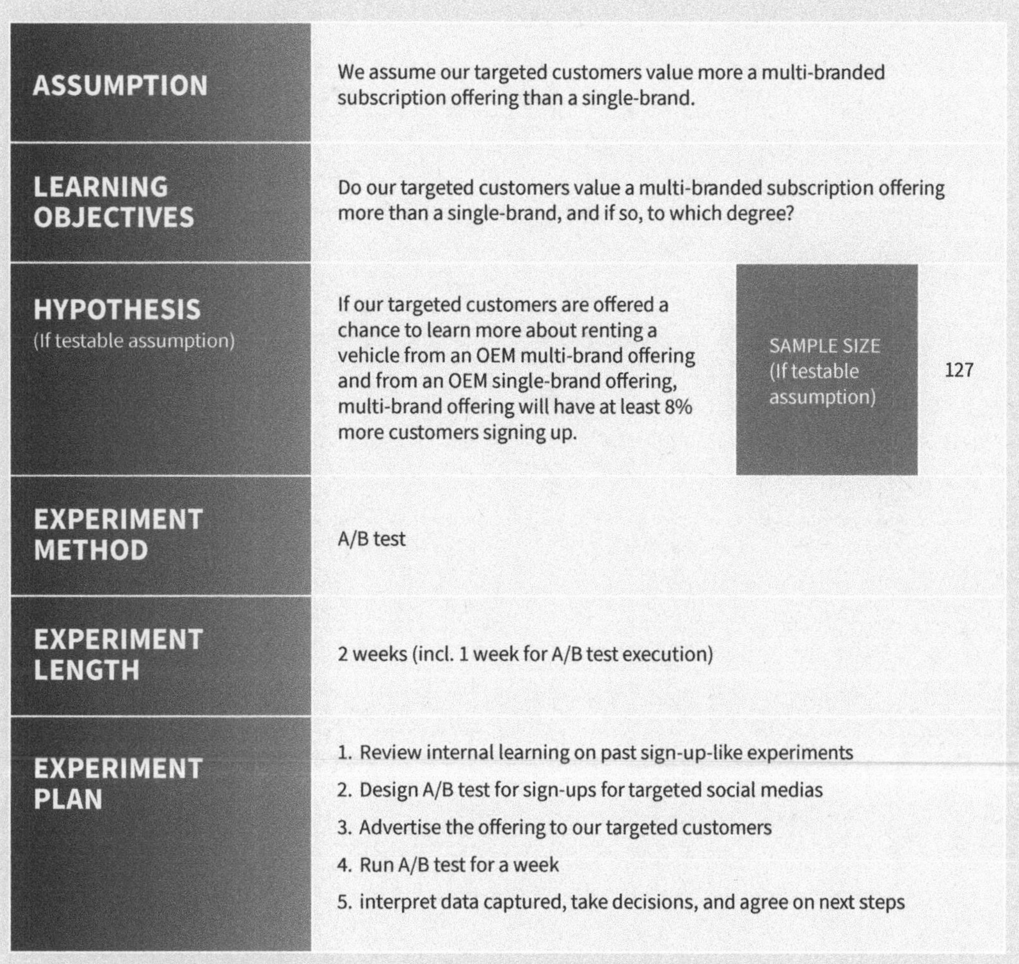

ASSUMPTION	We assume our targeted customers value more a multi-branded subscription offering than a single-brand.		
LEARNING OBJECTIVES	Do our targeted customers value a multi-branded subscription offering more than a single-brand, and if so, to which degree?		
HYPOTHESIS (If testable assumption)	If our targeted customers are offered a chance to learn more about renting a vehicle from an OEM multi-brand offering and from an OEM single-brand offering, multi-brand offering will have at least 8% more customers signing up.	SAMPLE SIZE (If testable assumption)	127
EXPERIMENT METHOD	A/B test		
EXPERIMENT LENGTH	2 weeks (incl. 1 week for A/B test execution)		
EXPERIMENT PLAN	1. Review internal learning on past sign-up-like experiments 2. Design A/B test for sign-ups for targeted social medias 3. Advertise the offering to our targeted customers 4. Run A/B test for a week 5. interpret data captured, take decisions, and agree on next steps		

Figure 11.5 Vehicle subscription service: Testing customers' interest for multi-brand subscription offering.

Depending on the decisions made by the team, another experiment was started or not. During the first half of 2022, the GMPI team ran more than 20 experiments to test the team's ideas for value propositions. The team used various methods including A/B testing and live communities to run those experiments.

The iterative experiment has contributed to GMPI making decisions backed-up with real customer data rather than opinions or conviction. This has helped the team to speed-up decision making (including killing or pivoting potential solutions despite initial convictions[9]), to look beyond usual interviews and survey approaches for collecting data, to think differently about how traditional market research was conducted, and finally to make experiments a reality at GMPI seeing results and unlocking processes.

CHAPTER 12

Ecosystems: Building an Ecosystem Playbook for Scaling a New Venture

Christine Griffin and John Greco

CO-INNOVATION

It is easy to think that the success of a Corporate Explorer depends only on finding a value proposition that delights a customer by helping solve an important problem. However, most markets are more complex than that; they involve many other players, each with its own motivations, which may or may not align with yours.

There are providers of adjacent products, whom you depend on to make your innovation successful. There are regulators, who are gatekeepers to market access in many areas. There are intermediaries who influence which products get used and which do not, such as doctors or pharmacies in a medical market, systems integrators in technology, or distributors in product markets. All these players have interests and motivations that may or may not align with your own. That means that "ecosystem" relationships can either play a beneficial role – completing a value proposition and helping accelerate customer adoption – or become a barrier to adoption.

Corporate Explorers need a strategy for working with this "ecosystem" that will help customers adopt their product or service. They also need a strategy to access that ecosystem to acquire the capabilities, capacity, and customers to scale their venture. The ecosystem determines success or failure regardless of whether you choose to engage it or not. You need to dig deeply into the motivations of the players to understand what it will take to win their support or neutralize their impact. Ecosystems also provide quick access to the assets and capabilities that are too expensive or time-consuming to build on your own, thus enabling you to scale faster.

The purpose of this chapter is to help Corporate Explorers develop the strategy and structure through which they can act with partners to *co-innovate* and adopt an innovation to deliver a value proposition to the end consumer. We describe six steps they need to take to develop their ecosystem playbook. It illustrates these steps by using case studies derived from the technology giant Analog Devices, and the major U.S. retailer Best Buy. In these examples, the Corporate Explorers accept that they are dependent on others for the success of their innovation. They see themselves as being at the center of a web of relationships in which each partner increases the chances of market success, rather than posing additional risks.

BUILDING THE ECOSYSTEM PLAYBOOK

In 2018, the U.S. electronics retailer Best Buy set its sights on the home health market. They set an audacious ambition to serve five million people in five years, helping them receive care at home using technology.

Best Buy had many assets on which they could rely. As a well-known consumer brand, they were already trusted by consumers. They also had developed a successful in-home support service, the "Geek Squad," which gave them a right to play in the market. However, scaling a new business in the healthcare market involves unparalleled complexity. There is a wide array of players involved, including payors (either insurance companies or government agencies), providers (doctors, hospitals), and myriad suppliers and regulators.

Best Buy started by building a service based on their existing assets and then began adding multiple acquisitions, having spent $2.2 billion on them over four years. Best Buy's footprint in home health expanded as a result of these acquisitions (GreatCall, Current Health, BioSensics, and others). Nevertheless, Best Buy rapidly realized that acquisitions were only one part of the story. Success would involve building partnerships with payors and providers, such as Anthem, Athena Health, and Geisinger. These relationships came as a part of a deliberate effort to build an ecosystem around the Best Buy Health offering. We will review the six lessons derived from the Best Buy story that any Corporate Explorer can apply to increase the odds of success.

Step 1. Identify Today's Value Creation Journey

The starting point on the value creation journey is to decide what steps are involved in creating a customer value proposition (Figure 12.1).

Consider the example of Best Buy's Care at Home solution. Best Buy knew that they had the ability to deliver services to the homes of their customers; however, the customers received medical services through other healthcare providers. These healthcare providers were getting reimbursed by insurance companies, who used different data services to capture information about consumers. In other words, there were a host of services enabling consumers to age safely at home, but Best Buy played no role in delivering any of them.

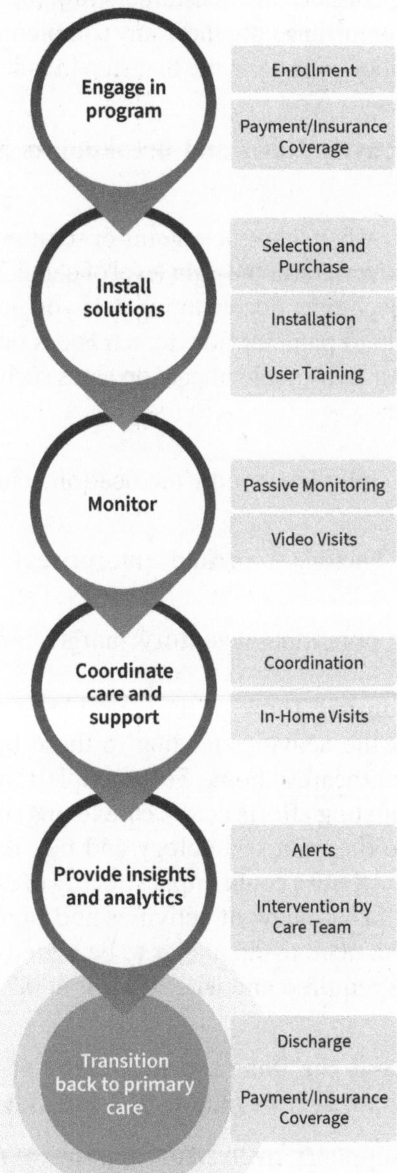

Figure 12.1 Value-creation journey.

Map your customer's journey by starting one or two steps upstream from your intended participation in the journey and extend as close to the end-user as possible (for example, include your customer's customer). Consider how customers buy the product or service and what it takes to use it successfully (for instance, are there any complementary products?). Understanding the end user's value-creation journey is the first step in building an ecosystem playbook.

Step 2. Map High-Level Activity Flows and Breakpoints in the System That Your Solution Could Address

Identify points in the journey where current systems or solutions are broken (Figure 12.2). The hardest part about this step is working at the right level of detail. Too deep, and you're just reviewing a process, spending as much time documenting it as you are thinking about improvement. Too high, and you're not able to pinpoint how to act. Focus on the biggest breakpoints in the system, especially those with a measurable impact on areas such as time, money, or reputation.

Some examples include:

- Healthcare: Lack of compliance with medication schedules; coordination of home health services.
- Factory automation: Factory floor and enterprise IT systems often don't talk to each other.
- Automotive: The cost of holding inventory; margin consumed by dealers.

Circle key breakpoints in red. Think of these problems as part of the "as-is" situation. Work backward to identify the activities leading to these breakpoints. Consider potential breakpoints in delivering healthcare at home. For example, remote devices might be too complex for many to use, coordinating efforts across care teams could be challenging, and urgent interventions would require the right technology and first responders. Imagine how inefficiencies across any of these activities could impact quality of care, cost, and patient outcomes.

Once you have a clear "as-is" view of activities and breakdowns, focus on the "to-be" situation. What activities will need to change or to be added? How will value flow change? Which activities will still be required and who will do them?

Step 3. Map and Understand the Role and Interfaces of Ecosystem Players Who Use and Provide Products or Services Along the Journey

Map the type of users and suppliers involved at each step of the journey, along with a list of specific companies that might make interesting partners or adversaries. Ecosystem participants could play any of the six roles (with some participants having multiple roles):

1. Customer: A company or individual that uses a product, system, or service.
2. Producer: A company that produces a product, or service.

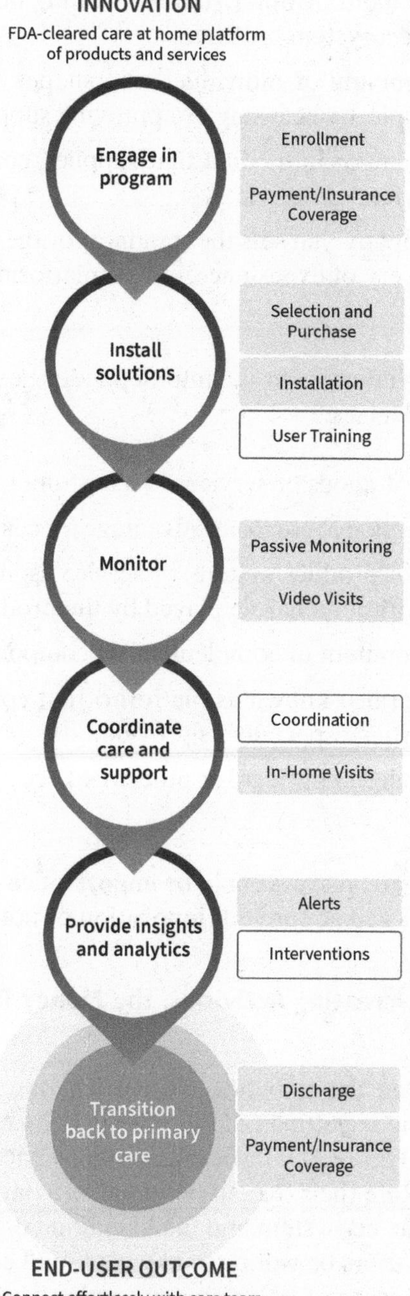

Figure 12.2 Value-creation journey: Breakpoints.

3. Regulator: A government or other standard-setting body that defines technical or legal obligations of ecosystem members.
4. Intermediary: A company or individual who shapes the actions of others in the ecosystem, for example, by licensing or approving suppliers.
5. Integrator: A company or individual that supplies, configures, or integrates products, systems, or services of others.
6. Orchestrator: A company that sets the standard for the ecosystem, through technology advantage, delivery of experience, or as a platform owner (for example, Apple or Google).

Use arrows to indicate relationships and interdependencies between participants. There are six types of interdependencies:

1. Sell to: Direct sales of goods or services to a customer.
2. Sell with: Combines value to create an advantage for customers from a joint purchase.
3. Sell through: Sales of product, system, or service as an integral part of the sale of another company, without any role played by the producer.
4. Co-innovate: Development of complementary components of the innovation.
5. Connect to: Service (also known as platform) that connects buyers and sellers to the benefit of all parties, especially its provider.
6. Comply with: A requirement (legal or otherwise) ecosystem members must comply with to do business.

Note which roles or specific players could be important co-innovators or have power to influence whether end users will adopt your innovation or not.

Step 4. Identify Key Value-creating Activities, the Money Flow, and the Player Motivation

Now that you have identified the activities and participants, follow the money. Where is value being created and who is getting paid to provide it? Complete the detailed Ecosystem Evaluation Template (Figure 12.3) to examine the capabilities, motivations, and risks of each ecosystem player. Rate their overall potential as a partner or threat.

Consider your role in the ecosystem and the likelihood of capturing the full amount of the value created. Will end users be willing to pay you? Will ecosystem partners be willing to pay you? Are there new ways of going to market that expand the value being created within the ecosystem? Can you capture a fair/unfair share of that expanded value?

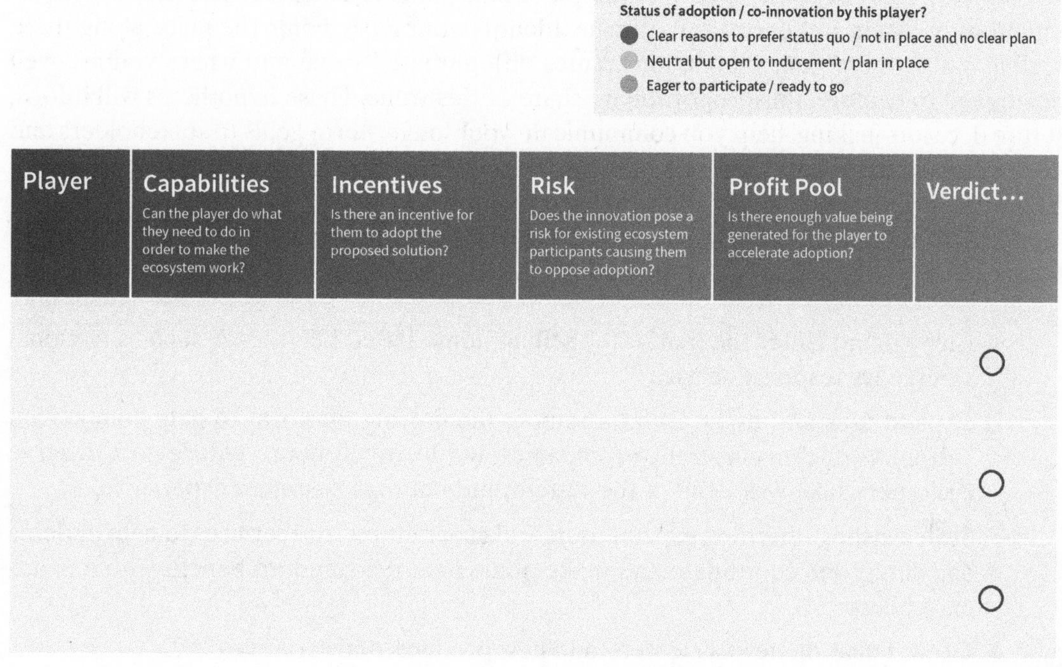

Figure 12.3 Ecosystem Evaluation Template.

Some companies mistakenly believe that they are best positioned to orchestrate an ecosystem and can demand an unfair share of revenue, a situation referred to as an "ego-system."[1] Best Buy's desire to orchestrate "Care at Home" makes sense, as they are well positioned to offer devices, tech services, omnichannel and supply chain capabilities, and a HIPAA-secure platform. To underscore this inclusive approach to ecosystem building, Best Buy Health's CEO, Deborah DiSanzo, insists, "We are not building this alone."[2]

At the end of this step, you should have a good understanding of how value is created and how money flows through the ecosystem. You should also have an idea how you can capture value, who might make a good ecosystem partner, and who might be a barrier to the adoption of your solution. It's time to develop your ecosystem strategy.

Step 5. Build Scaling Path: Plan to Add Capabilities, Capacity, and Customers Needed to Scale (Build, Buy, Partner)

Build a plan that anticipates what capabilities, capacity, and customers you need to combine to deliver your value proposition to the end user. These are defined as:

- Capability: Technologies, products, skills, and business models.
- Capacity: Managing volume through fulfillment, manufacturing, and customer service.
- Customers: Access to install base, channels, sales team, and brand.

Develop early hypotheses about multiple scaling paths you might consider, such as combinations of assets and partners to pursue. Identify your *entry point*, the place along these scaling paths where your innovation creates differentiated value and where you are well positioned to capture a disproportionate share of this value. These hypotheses will inform future decision-making, help you communicate your longer-term goals to stakeholders and partners, and guard against the risk of being overly opportunistic in your approach. Use the Scaling Path Template to illustrate your plan (Figure 12.4).

Best Buy, for example, describes its scaling strategy to win in home health in four steps (Figure 12.5):

1. Entry point: Enter the market by selling home-based healthcare, such as personal emergency response services.
2. Expand uses and users: Build a remote monitoring platform to help commercial customers, such as insurance companies and health systems; reduce cost to serve customers; take waste out of the system; and improve customer experience.
3. Scale existing offerings, expand users and capabilities: Add services to help patients and caregivers coordinate and make home health a standard benefit within insurance plans.
4. Grow: Focus on new customers; add new products and services.

Best Buy accessed customers and monitoring services by acquiring GreatCall. It then added more subscribers, along with new capabilities in telehealth and medication management services, through the acquisition of Critical Signals Technology. Its acquisition of Current Health brought a remote care management platform that connected devices in customers' homes to care providers. It also added new insurers and providers, such as Mount Sinai and the UK's Health System. In 2021, Best Buy Health partnered with Apple to host their Lively app with a live 24/7 assistance feature.

Step 6. Define Your Role

Define your role in the ecosystem. Are you positioned to shape and lead the ecosystem to deliver value proposition, or will you collaborate or follow? Decide whether to leverage assets from the core, build them from scratch, buy them, or partner with them. Identify specific companies which may be attractive partners or targets.

Build your ecosystem and scaling path(s) gradually; you don't have to do everything at once. Treat this process as an *ecosystem playbook* with options and audibles. Start from your entry point and assemble the minimum core assets needed at launch to deliver your value proposition – your minimum viable ecosystem (MVE).[3]

Experiment with the MVE in the market to validate whether your offering and go-to-market approach are working for your customers and your partners. Identify trigger points that tell you when it's time to invest in new assets or try other scaling path options

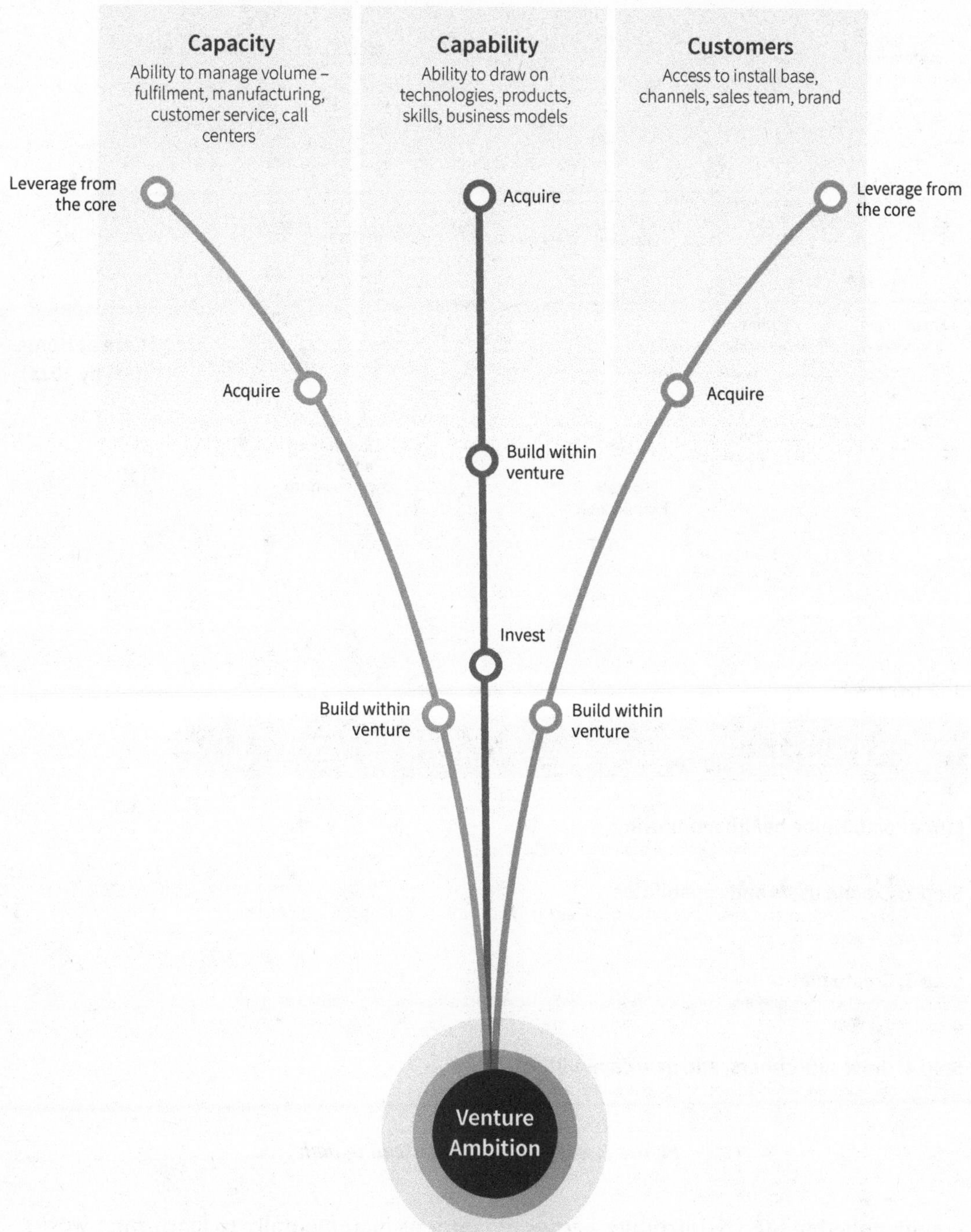

Figure 12.4 The Scaling Path Template.

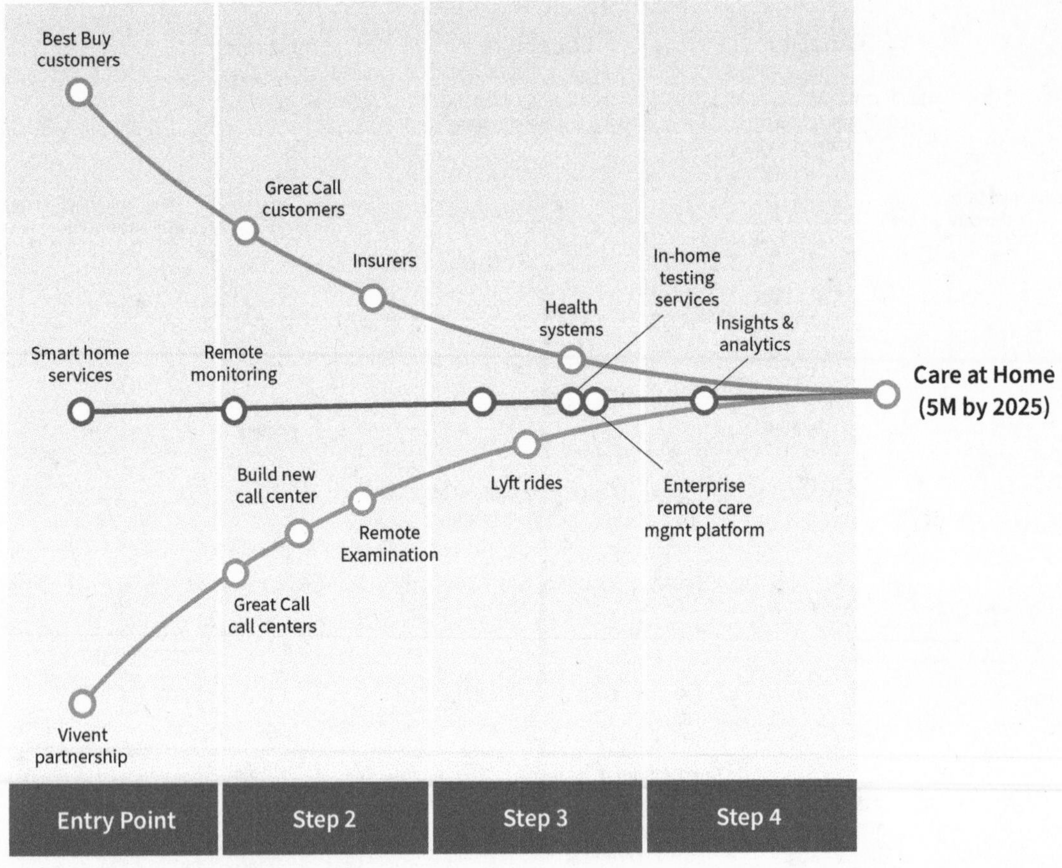

Entry Point: Home health monitoring
Leverage existing assets and partner for home health/safety expertise.

Step 2: Expand users and capabilities
Acquire Great Call- subscribers, connected devices, call centers. Acquire CST- scale monitoring business, insurers. Build new call center.

Step 3: Create platform
Acquire Current Health- subscribers, medical devices, in-home testing, secure shopping. Partner with Lyft, payors and providers.

Step 4: Grow subscribers, add new capabilities
Focus on new customers, Apple Lively app, big data and analytics.

Figure 12.5 Best Buy health scaling path.

you identified in Step 5. Introduce ecosystem options incrementally to learn what works – and then iterate. You will be constantly learning and pivoting, and your ecosystem maps and strategy should continue to evolve.

KEY SUCCESS FACTORS

New ventures need to harness the power of an ecosystem to scale their business. Ecosystems provide quick access to the assets and capabilities that are too expensive or time-consuming to build on your own; they enable you to scale faster. Use a disciplined approach, a mix of art and science, and create five key components to build a winning ecosystem strategy:

1. **The ecosystem playbook.** Build a playbook that anticipates what industry solutions you aim to build and which partners you need. This informs decision-making and helps guard against the risk of being overly "opportunistic" in your approach.
2. **Partner selection.** Find quality partners who would bring brand equity, market presence, sound finances, strategic fit, technology, agility, and know-how.
3. **Resources to succeed.** Commit organizational attention and resources required to win with appropriate staffing and governance.
4. **Measurement.** Progress in increments linked to clear key performance indicators (KPIs), so that you can learn and adapt.
5. **Learning mindset.** Adopt outside-in practices so that you minimize risk of self-reinforcing assumptions. You need to know what your potential partners want from the relationship as it may not be what you expect.

APPLICATION CASE STUDY: NAVIGATING A COMPLEX HEALTHCARE ECOSYSTEM

Analog Devices (ADI) is a global leader in design, manufacture, and marketing of high-performance analog, mixed-signal, and digital-signal processing integrated circuits with revenues of more than $11 billion. In 2013, ADI's CEO, Vincent Roche, and his executive team embarked on a strategy to "move up the stack," seeking to capture more of the value ADI's hardware created in the end markets and ecosystems it served. Digital health was identified as a prime market where ADI could succeed: ADI produced sensors for medical devices and diagnostic equipment and could leverage its design expertise to solve more, and bigger, healthcare problems. ADI identified opportunities to develop solutions addressing the small number of chronic diseases that drive most of the healthcare spending in the United States, such as diabetes and congestive heart failure.

In 2016, ADI recruited Venu Gopinathan, co-founder of a medical device startup and director of Kilby Research Labs of Texas Instruments, to develop ADI's healthcare solutions. Gopinathan initiated the development of a remote monitoring device to predict the need for hospitalization from a chronic disease before its onset, thus improving patient health and reducing medical cost. Although it was clear that the team could deliver the technology, the bigger challenge was the route to market.

(Continued)

The healthcare ecosystem is complex. The goal of most ecosystem players is to bend the "iron triangle" of access, quality, and cost; however, participants' incentives and business models are often at odds. ADI's solution proposed to create value by using data to reduce cost. To capture that value, multiple stakeholders would need to be aligned, some of whom didn't benefit from reducing cost. ADI would also have to navigate a fragmented network of data providers and create value in a situation when health outcomes are highly dependent on patient behavior.

The ADI team conducted a detailed assessment of the value chain and the ecosystem by mapping the participants, the ways value was created, and important breakpoints in the system. It also identified places where ADI's value proposition would be differentiated and defensible. Key to this analysis, says Gopinathan, was to "create a picture of dollars flowing across the system. Chase the dollar and try to determine which ecosystem participants will give you money and why."

ADI identified the need to find ecosystem players who had high prevalence of chronic disease among their patient populations and wanted to reduce costs. This led the team to focus on Medicare Advantage Plans and Accountable Care Organizations, two value-based care entities responsible for their members' medical costs. Gopinathan's team analyzed these groups, looking for gaps in the current standard of care and payment model. They faced a key question: Is it possible to move up the stack to capture more value?

The team chose to move up the stack with a bolder business model but realized that alone, they couldn't deliver a more integrated solution to customers. Therefore, they focused on engaging three strategic partners:

1. Data integrators, who needed to put monitoring data in the right hands at the right time and to enable ecosystem players to communicate effortlessly across workflows.
2. Medical equipment suppliers, who were positioned to assemble, distribute, and set up devices and related supplies.
3. "Last mile" players that can interact with patients and doctors.

By engaging medical device suppliers to assemble and distribute ADI's products, ADI could generate a solution that was easy to adopt by providers and patients. By engaging the "last mile" care providers, ADI could offer a more holistic solution while also overcoming a key adoption barrier.

Partners were critical. However, one of ADI's key learnings was that some activities shouldn't be outsourced. Initially, the team tried to outsource regulatory compliance to consultants. They discovered that without "skin in the game," a shared responsibility for outcomes, and a keen understanding of what ADI wanted to achieve, outsourcing this critical element was not very effective.

The team had to figure out how to make divergent stakeholder business models work, and how to distribute value among partners. ADI found many ecosystem partners trying to claim the bulk of the cost reduction, and others unwilling to share their data. ADI modeled revenues in such a way as to persuade both ecosystem partners and internal advocates how value-sharing could benefit each of the players.

ADI's ecosystem strategy and its commitment to share the value it created has set the stage for an ecosystem that was ready and willing to deliver the value desired by participants.

As the integrated monitoring platform matures, scaling can begin by adding more customers and capabilities to the platform. Gopinathan's advice is, "Don't think about scaling until you are truly ready and know where and how to scale with the biggest impact."

A summary of the ADI team's advice would be as follows:

- Co-develop relationships with executive leadership, so that there is alignment when the big decisions need to be made. This helps sustain momentum and provide the long-term support needed to succeed.
- Follow the money in the ecosystem and make sure you have a compelling reason for other players to give you some.
- Make sure that partners are sharing in the value created and have skin in the game.
- Don't scale too early; wait for the business to mature and internalize all the lessons learned before moving to the next challenge.

CHAPTER 13

Validation: Managing the Journey from Concept to Scale

Ellie Amirnasr and Charles Vaillant

HUNTER STRATEGY

A new business innovation in corporations is just like a venture. Managing it as an operational business or corporate R&D project is a recipe for failure. One common pitfall is applying traditional key performance indicators (KPIs) too early, as it stifles risk-taking and prevents innovation. Instead, we argue in favor of using nonfinancial KPIs that indicate progress at the early stages of new business validation. These serve as a compass that helps the innovation team, stakeholders, and management navigate their way to success. Well-defined progress and success metrics, when combined with the right understanding on how to build a $100 million business, enable business owners to evaluate the actual performance of their business in almost real time.

At MANN+HUMMEL, we used the "Hunter Strategy" concept designed by Christoph Janz[1] to design a growth validation process for our digital ventures focusing on exploration-type business. As a company, we are used to defining many indicators or metrics. However, if everything is important, then nothing is.

We define the three most important KPIs to measure progress toward success. We differentiate between leading and lagging indicators. At the early stages, we track leading indicators, such as number of generated leads; as the business matures, we monitor more lagging indicators, such as conversion rate and customer acquisition cost (CAC).

At the beginning of every stage, we spend time understanding, preparing, and agreeing on KPIs in the growth validation process. This reduces ongoing effort in reporting and communication between the innovation team, stakeholders, and management. Ideally, all the data should be pulled from an existing database, accessible in just one click, and conveniently displayed. At MANN+HUMMEL, we even coined a new term for this: Clickly®.

VENTURE MATURITY

Have you ever wondered why your organization is failing to reach its potential in the developing exploration-type business? Is it because you are incompetent at your job? Or any of the following is true?

- You have painful confrontations about the best approach to a project.
- You face conflicting organizational priorities.
- You are always jumping from one "urgent" project to the next.
- You have the same arguments again and again.
- You find yourself endlessly explaining the same things to clients and stakeholders.
- Your team lacks a clear focus and direction.
- Clients and colleagues expect your team to conform to their way of working.

Companies, just like products, have life cycles of their own. As the company gains traction, it achieves growth in terms of maturity, which is translated into product output, new customers, market share, employees, and, ultimately, value creation.

The time required for a successful business to reach a satisfactory level of maturity (for example, $100 million in revenue) will take several years, depending on the level of effort to build and sell the technology. Moving a venture to this level requires it to go through many learning cycles. You need time for the tech team to "work their magic," and the sales and marketing teams to "date" enough customers to determine if someone is "taking them to the dance." Sales cycles just take time, and people need to be convinced through interactions, demonstrations, and validations.

At the same time, you must have the courage to look at yourself in the mirror and acknowledge that the product-market fit or market traction may just never come, and you are becoming a zombie business (walking dead with no financial and business life in you). This journey requires a balance between patience to learn and being ready to make courageous decisions to change course, pivot, or halt a business.[2]

The venture capital world has created a well-accepted designation for the different phases of a venture: from seed to series A, B, and C. At MANN+HUMMEL, we have studied the corresponding phases of a venture to bring clarity to our internal ventures. We define a few stages of a corporate venture: seed idea, launching a venture, growth, expansion, and maturity.

Our objective in this chapter is to provide clarity with respect to which phase we are in and, therefore, to define what needs to be validated. This will enable us to figure out what to measure, and, therefore, which KPIs to apply.

At MANN+HUMMEL we are hunters and going after businesses with $100 million or more potential. We call them "moonshot businesses."

GROWTH VALIDATION PROCESS FOR CORPORATE VENTURES

Management guru Peter Drucker once said: "What gets measured, gets managed." Depending on the type of business, stage of the business, and business model, what is measured varies. This means that it is possible to have financial or nonfinancial KPIs.

When it comes to corporate ventures and exploration-type businesses at early stages, the primary KPI is rarely revenue. Revenue indicates the value captured, not the value created, and at an early stage, what you want to measure is whether you are *creating* value or not.

The value creation metrics help the team stay focused and navigate through different stages of the business. These metrics enable stakeholders to evaluate team performance and make sure they are on track to achieve a repeatable, scalable, and profitable business.

Now, how do we define the progress and success metrics? There are a few steps you need to take before you define the progress and success metrics for each exploration project.

Step 1: Understand Stages of Corporate Ventures

We define five stages in the life of a corporate venture: ideation, seed, launch, growth, and expansion (Figure 13.1), after which the new business can be called mature.

Ideation. Ideation is the process by which you generate ideas and solutions through sessions such as sketching, prototyping, and brainstorming. The key question here is whether the venture idea is viable and worth developing into an actual business from a corporate standpoint. Four key questions need to be answered before moving on to the next stage:

1. Does the idea align with corporate strategic direction?
2. Do we understand the macrotrends and know the influencers that drive customers' decisions?
3. What is the problem this product or solution is trying to solve, and who is the buyer and user in target customer segment?
4. Did we identify underserved customer pain point or need?

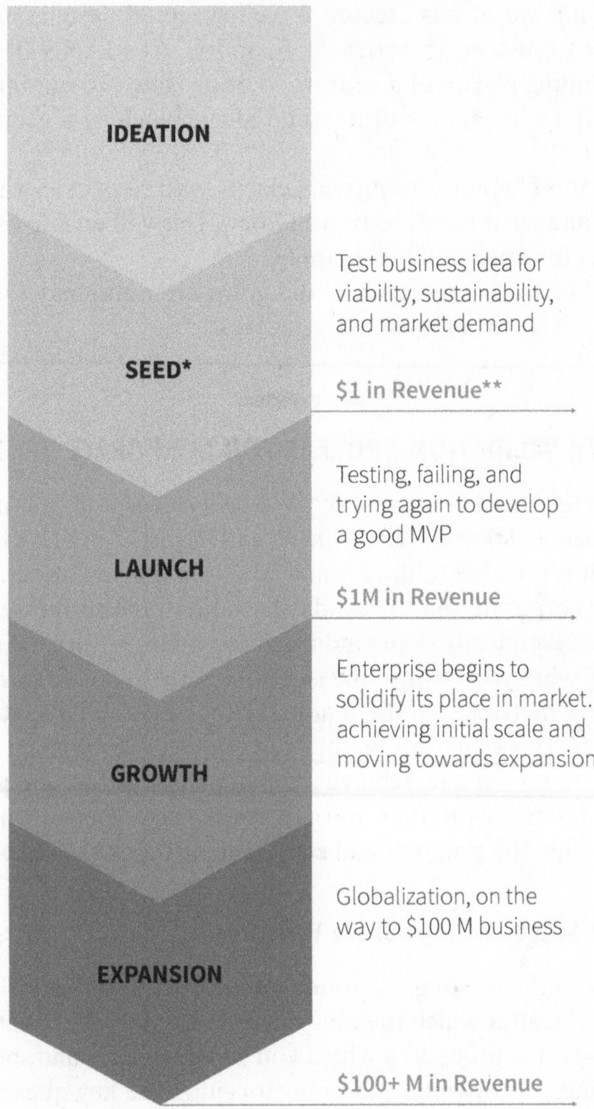

Figure 13.1 Five stages in the life of a corporate venture.

Seed. At the seed stage, you need to answer the following questions, starting with the "Why":[3]

- Why is this a problem today?
- How the problem is being addressed today?
- How does the idea solve the pain points of prospective customers differently from existing solutions?

Forty-two percent of ventures fail at this stage because they did not serve a market need or were not solving a customer pain point. It is critical that at this stage, the venture focuses on identifying the market need clearly and come up with a unique, hard to copy product or solution.[4]

Launch. Is my business repeatable? After validating your business hypothesis and identifying the associated underserved customer pain points, it's time to launch the venture and achieve the product-market fit. You need to start building on the idea by creating a minimum viable product (MVP) and testing it with customers to get feedback.

In this phase, the following steps should be followed:

1. Define your value proposition.
2. Specify your MVP feature set.
3. Create your MVP prototype.
4. Test your MVP with target customers.

By creating the MVP and validating it with target customers, you start to establish a customer base in the target market. At this stage, you should track the leading indicators such as pipeline health and product stickiness.

Growth. Is my business scalable? In this phase, you are working toward scalability of the business. The progress metrics become more quantitative compared to the early stages. At this stage, you should focus on both leading and lagging metrics. We discuss examples of these types of metrics in the next section.

Expansion. Is my business profitable? At this stage, the business expands to a new region and new market segment with similar pain points. Consequently, we can start to add traditional financial metrics focused on revenue and profit.

Step 2: Determine Your Hunting Target

It is crucial to know what type of business you are trying to build. Not every business is the same, and sales cycles are different, depending on the type of business. Are you into consumer goods with a low transaction fee? Or are you into large industrial goods requiring capital investment of millions of dollars? Consumer goods are typically inexpensive and have a short sale cycle, sometimes just minutes. Industrial goods can take years to progress from lead generation to purchase orders. Therefore, the metrics required to build a sizable business can be very different.

We adopted the "Hunter Strategy"[5] concept, which is rather simple and fun to communicate (Figure 13.2). We define each strategy by giving it a different animal type: Elephant, Deer, Rabbit, Mouse, and Fly. For example, if you are hunting for a $100 million business, you will need one thousand customers paying you $100,000 (Elephant) or 10 million customers buying your $10 widget (Fly). This very simplistic analogy allows us to make sure we analyze each business strategy differently, whereas similar ones can use the same approach.

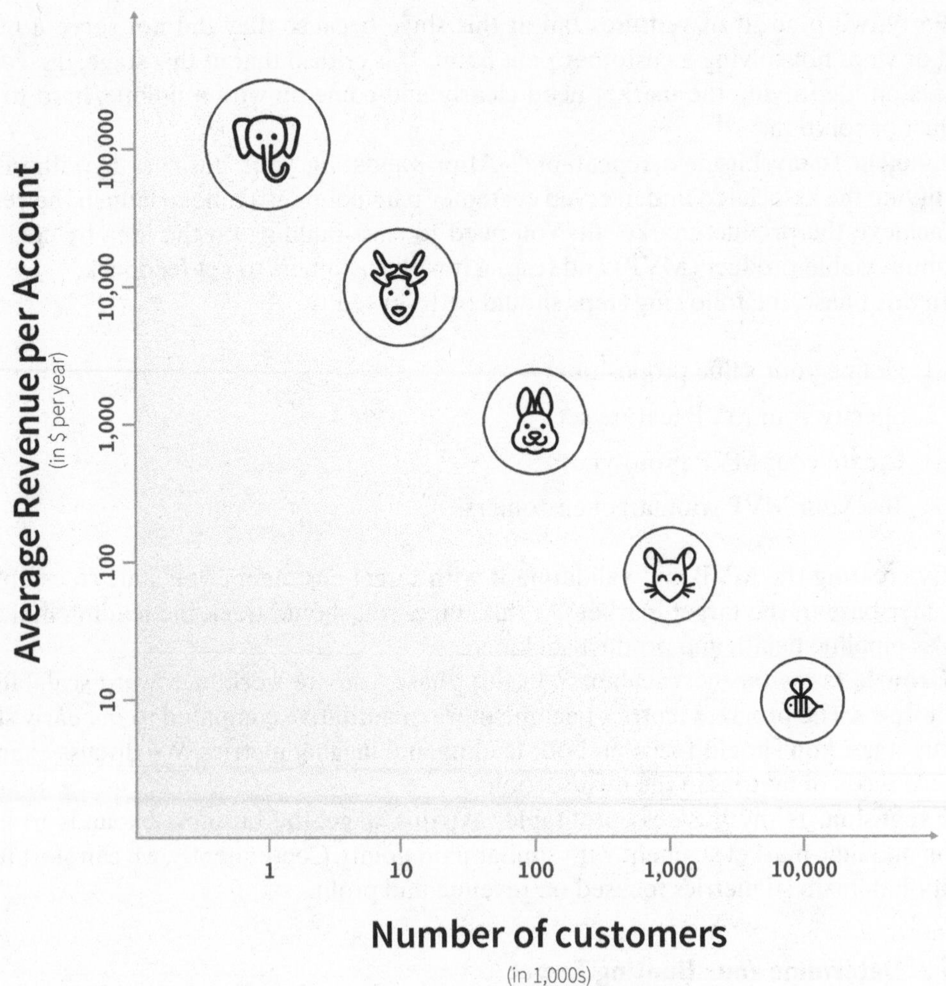

Figure 13.2 "Hunter Strategy" concept: How to build $100 million in annual revenue.

This can help define the needs for your supporting tools and resources, including customer service, lead generation, or the structure of a dedicated sales group.

Step 3: Define Success Metrics for Each Stage

Once you are clear on what "animal" you are hunting for, it's time to define what success means for each life-cycle period: seed, launch, growth, expansion, or exit. This is where the financial metric trap normally takes place. You cannot and should not measure your team performance to a sales objective if you are in the seed or launch phase. At that stage, you are not interested in financial returns because it is very likely that you have not acquired enough market knowledge to have clarity into the business dynamics such as price points, addressable market size, sales cycle, and product-market fit.

Now let's be clear: sales traction is very important from day one. Getting orders from customers illustrates that you can convert a product into value for a customer and receive payment in exchange. This conversion is tangible confirmation that you have a product-market fit – and if you are doing things right, you are engaging customers very early.[6] Of course, at this stage, the product is not yet perfect, but the fact that a customer is willing to use it shows that you are onto something. This is progress. This is the goal. Without it, you are nowhere, except in the innovation theater.

Each phase has a start and an end point. You always know where you start, and you need to make insightful decisions and take actions to achieve the associated level of maturity for that phase. For example, at the end of the seed phase, you want to have clarity on the total addressable market (TAM), and at the end of the launch phase, you want to determine if you have a good product-market fit and if your order intake is growing and accelerating. These are your success metrics; when met, they signal that you have successfully graduated from the current stage and ready to tackle the next one. If you have made it this far, you're confident that you're on track to deliver aspirational goals a few years out.

Step 4: Define Your Progress Metrics

As mentioned earlier, building a business is not a matter of a few months; it will take years to build a repeatable, scalable, and profitable business. Therefore, each phase, while not necessarily having the same duration in length, may last more than a year, often two, possibly three or more. It's clear that not being able to measure the performance of a venture until you reach the finish line (the end of the stage), potentially two years away, is not helpful.

How do you know you are going to make it? How do you know that you are doing the right things? Too often the venture team is convinced they are onto something exciting. It is a type of hype: they love to pitch their products and are addicted to someone telling them how cool their solution is, and that the future is bright. We have seen ventures very excited to have a new very important lead, possibly even a Fortune 500 company! This would dominate any board meeting discussion, as the optimism is contagious. They believe this is it! They are now at the inflection point of the business.

Unfortunately, they are just about to realize, in a few months, that nothing happened. But now, they found an even better lead and the venture rollercoaster starts again. We call this the "venture theater" that leads to "zombies."

The team is not completely at fault because they don't have a tool to help them step back from the daily grind and look at the big picture. The missing piece is the progress metric. Remember, what gets measured gets managed! The progress metrics are measurable parameters that can be monitored frequently and need more than one data point per month. It is highly recommended to define three progress metrics; more than three may add too much complexity. The progress metrics should illustrate directly or indirectly that you are marching toward a successful graduation of the stage (even two years out). It is like using a navigation app on your phone: you get real-time information that you are driving in the right direction and are on track to arrive at your destination even several hours away. Examples of progress metrics include the number of pilots you are running with customers, growth of your core knowledge or IP base, new business partners you are signing to distribute your product, Return on Advertising Spent (ROAS), and many more.

Step 5: Create the Growth Validation Card

Armed with the knowledge of where we are in the business life cycle, what type of business we are hunting for, and having defined success and progress metrics, we are good to go. Well, at MANN+HUMMEL, we realized quite quickly that the approach was relatively academic, and we were missing a simple yet effective way to implement it. We had written the code; now we needed to build the most-user-friendly "app."

We needed a simple tool that every team member, stakeholder, and even a person without any prior knowledge could use to quickly get a sense of the health of the business. We have achieved this goal by creating a one-page live dashboard that displays data pulled from the sales and marketing tools such as CRM and Google analytics, financial and accounting tools, and product and user management tools.

Step 6: What's Your Kill Criterion?

We were almost ready to go.

In a 2021 *HBR* article, Scott Kirsner[7] describes the kill criteria approach to help decision makers know when to "pull the plug." Kill criteria rarely draw attention, and if they exist, they are almost never defined and agreed up front at the start of a business creation.

Senior management likes to talk about the "failing fast" culture, but when management can shut down the corporate venture at any moment with no warning, the team gets insecure and frustrated because they feel blindsided. They assume that all is well until it is not, until suddenly someone decides they need to stop the cash burn. To avoid surprises, you should define and align the kill criteria, so that everyone knows how to read the health status of the venture. With this process, we separate objective from subjective, so there should be zero ambiguity.

Our kill criterion is built into our progress metrics. Since we know we need to drive for speed and fast decision-making, we decided to engineer our kill criteria inside our KPIs. Therefore, if all progress metrics are unsatisfactory, and they have a negative trend for two months in a row, the team gets a strike. After each strike the business goes through a reassessment process. On the third strike, everyone agrees to pull the plug. This means everyone agrees that it is time to stop and refocus the resources on something else. The kill criterion is then simply the lack of progress of the most important factors for a certain amount of time.

APPLICATION CASE STUDY: INTELLIGENT CLEAN AIR MANAGEMENT SOLUTION FOR COMMERCIAL BUILDINGS

A business that emerged from one of MANN+HUMMEL's innovation programs is *qlair*. This business was earmarked as exploratory because:

- It was a new product: replacing a manual process for clean-air management in different segments by introducing Internet of Things (IoT)-based products and services.
- It was a new market: MANN+HUMMEL didn't have immediate access to facility service companies and end customers in the facility management industry.

The seed phase for *qlair* was completed in six months, and it launched its first MVP of IoT product and services for clean-air management. In the first few months of the launch phase, the team realized that they were "Deer Hunters." Based on this information, the team defined their progress and success metrics. Three progress metrics categories were selected: product stickiness, pipeline health, and growth. Five success metrics categories were also selected: traction, market opportunity, growth, product-market fit, and repeatable sales process.

The three progress metrics were defined as follows:

1. Product stickiness: Air quality report open rate
2. Pipeline health: Number of proposals submitted multiplied by the value of the proposals
3. Growth: Number of sensors installed each month

The five success metrics were defined as follows:

1. Traction: Annualized recurring revenue
2. Market opportunity: Number of customer segments covered
3. Growth: 100% year-over-year growth for 12 months
4. Product-market fit: Conversion rate
5. Repeatable sales process: Number of sales partners with 50 or more sensor orders

All the operational data for each KPI was stored in databases using customer relationship management (CRM) software for sales, backend database for product (AWS or Azure), and internal admin database for general operation. To make it easier for the team and stakeholders, we visualized the progress and success metrics using a modular dashboard PowerBI. As mentioned earlier, the goal was to create a tool with which every team member, stakeholders, and even a person without any prior knowledge of the business could quickly get a sense of the health of the business.

In our process, we described that it is important to monitor the health of the business via progress metrics. Therefore, for each performance value we look at two indicators: "Are we meeting the target?" and "Is the trend positive?"

(*Continued*)

The stakeholders should be focusing on constant progress (things are working – they get it!), rather than absolute targets. The absolute targets need to be there, but often our lack of knowledge forces us to make many assumptions, so it is very likely the targets will be missed. Nevertheless, we need targets to motivate the team to be successful (they need a North Star!)

Each of the two indicators are color-coded in green, yellow, and red. Our kill criterion is nothing else than having all progress metrics indicators in the red for several months in a row. In other words, if, for example, for two successive months, the team was far off their target *and* they had no growth and no progress, then everyone should agree that something is not right.

When this happens, the team knows they get a strike. This is not about blaming the team but instead identifying that something we agreed upon has not been realized – the performance is not there, the hypothesis for the business is not validated. They are now on a probation period and are expected to work on an after-action report to evaluate the situation and present it to the stakeholders at the next board meeting.

When the business gets the first strike, the reassessment process starts. In this process, the team goes back and answers some questions from early stages with the knowledge they have today.

1. Reassess the value propositions in the product:
   - Is the product meaningfully differentiated to win?
   - Is the product the right value at the right price?

   Things that help you get to answers at this point are competitive analysis and value curve.
2. Reassess the "go-to-market" strategy:
   - Are we selling the product in the right way, through the right channels, and with the right process?

   Things that help you get answers at this point are to revisit the business model canvas, customer journey (for each channel), and sales.
3. Reassess the team structure:
   - Are we missing key talent? Do we have the right mix of internal as opposed to external resources?
   - Do we operate as a team in an effective way?

   The thing that helps you get answers at this point is peer review (review sprint velocity).
4. Reassess market opportunity:
   - Are we sure customers want this product? Has something changed in the market?
   - Does the opportunity still have $100 million revenue potential?
   - Are we too early? Too late?

Things that help you get answers at this point are third-party market size assessments and bottom-up market size analysis based on all learnings to date.

After answering the key questions, the team can select from the following set of conclusions:

- Stay the course; we are almost there.
- A list of corrective actions to any of the above.
- Full and true pivot to a different value proposition requiring more product type investments (presumably supported by real target customers).
- Lastly, adjust progress metrics.

In this case, the team together with stakeholders decided to take the list of corrective actions and adjust their progress metrics. The stakeholders then reviewed the proposal and decided on the course of action.

The maximum strikes before shutting down the operation in our case is three. However, because of this radical transparent approach, it is very likely that the team on its own would make the decision to pull the plug early. They should not need senior management to demand it.

There is one other alternative to address an underperforming business: to change the team or change the leadership of the team. This is normally difficult for the team to decide on its own and it lies with the supervisory body to make the call.

SECTION III

EXPLORE ORGANIZATION AND LEADERSHIP

CHAPTER 14

Ambidextrous Organization: What It Is, When to Use It

Michael Tushman and Charles O'Reilly

SEPARATING EXPLORE FROM CORE

At some point in their journey, Corporate Explorers need to step outside the existing organization and be given freedom to operate. This means they need an ambidextrous organization – one that seeks to drive organic growth by separating units charged with exploratory innovation from those that run the core (exploitative) business. A growing number of organizations set out to become ambidextrous. Some organizations succeeded, others did not. We have analyzed these cases to identify the elements typically associated with success at ambidexterity. In this chapter, we will describe these success factors and use them to develop practical guidelines that could help managers design organizations in support of the work of Corporate Explorers. A Corporate Explorer can seek to influence to put these conditions in place, but most often a senior sponsor needs to take ownership for this work.

There are four factors favoring ambidextrous organizations that apply regardless of the specific business. While they are by no means sufficient, they are necessary; that is, attempts at ambidexterity are likely to fail without these four factors:

1. **Strategic intent** – A clear strategic ambition that justifies the very need for exploration, including the identification of organizational assets and capabilities that can be used for competitive advantage of the exploratory unit.

This chapter is adapted from Lead and Disrupt, 2021, Stanford University Press.

2. **Aligned senior team** – Senior management commitment and oversight to fund and nurture the new venture and protect it from the pressure of the core (exploitative) business, which can – and, most likely, will – attempt to kill it.
3. **Autonomy and access** – Sufficient separation of the exploratory unit from the core business so that the new venture can develop its own architecture. This also includes the development of the mechanisms for accessing the assets of the core business.
4. **Common values and culture** – A common identity of the exploration and core business units, which helps all involved understand that they are on the same team, with a common purpose of realizing the firm's ambition.

In the following sections, we will describe each of these factors in more detail. But before doing that, let's ask a question that every manager should ask before attempting to build an ambidextrous organization: "Do we need such an organization for the Corporate Explorer to succeed?" The answer to this question depends on the nature of the innovation being pursued.

AMBIDEXTROUS ORGANIZATION DECISION

Ambidexterity is messy. It means pursuing ideas that may not pay off, and pursuing these ideas means withdrawing resources and people away from activities that are likely to provide higher financial returns in the short term. Given the difficulty of managing core and explore in the same organization, why bother? Does the Corporate Explorer really need an ambidextrous organization to succeed?

Imagine that a Corporate Explorer presents a company with an opportunity to move into areas beyond its core. One way to decide whether ambidexterity makes sense in this case is to consider to which extent the realization of this opportunity can leverage existing firm's assets (sales channels, manufacturing, technology platforms, brand, and so on) in a manner that would provide competitive advantage for the new business. Consider the four quadrants in Figure 14.1.[1]

Quadrant I: Not Strategically Important and Not Operationally Related

When the opportunity is strategically unimportant (that is, not intrinsically aligned with the company's existing strategy) and cannot benefit from the company's available resources or capabilities, there is no compelling reason to pursue this opportunity, even if it looks attractive. Under these circumstances, the recommendation would be to spin out the new business into its own entity or sell it to another firm.

For example, Ciba Vision, a maker of contact lenses, developed a drug that combated a debilitating eye disease. However, since this product was sold through different channels, had different regulatory approvals, involved different technologies, and required a different manufacturing process, the company spun out the product to its parent corporation, where it became a successful pharmaceutical product.

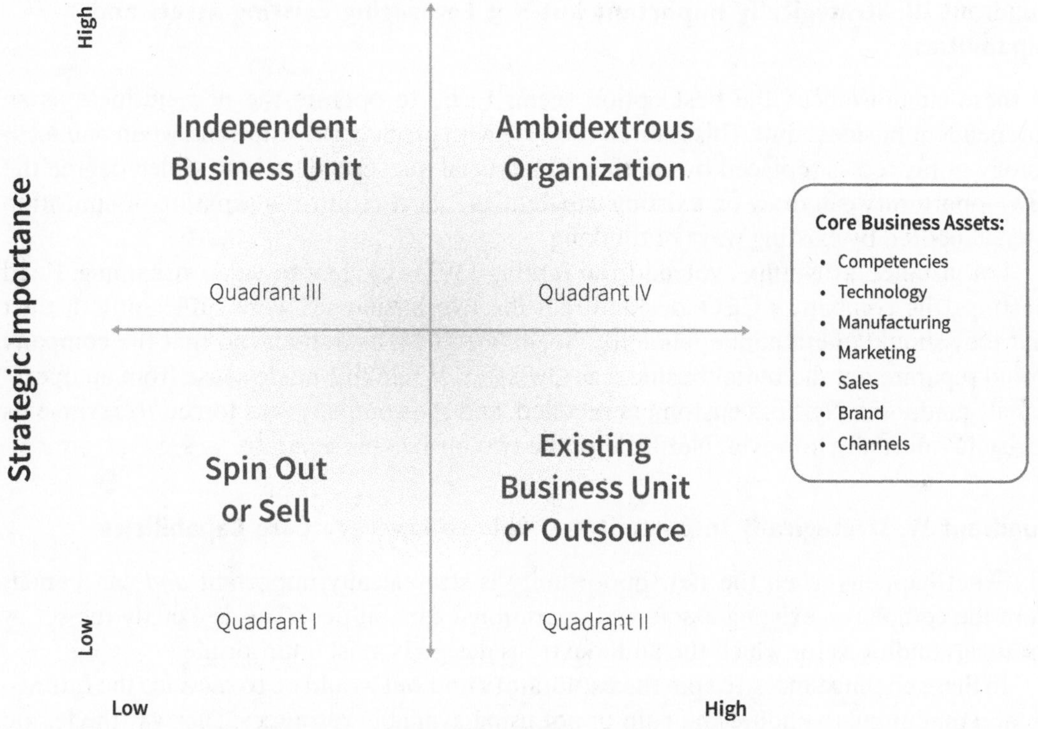

Figure 14.1 When is ambidexterity needed?
Source: Charles O'Reilly and Michael Tushman,
Lead and Disrupt: How to Solve the Innovator's Dilemma,
2nd ed. (Stanford University Press, 2021). Used with permission from Stanford University Press.

Quadrant II: Operationally Related but Not Strategically Important

This condition represents occasions when the new opportunity can leverage the company's current capabilities but is not strategically important. Under these circumstances, it can be incorporated into one of the company's business units or contracted out depending on its value to the company.

For example, a personal computer manufacturer or smartphone maker has the capability to repair defective products. This may be important to some customers but is not strategically important for the long-term success of the whole business. Consequently, the repair of these low-margin items is usually contracted out. Similarly, many internal functions, such as Human Resources or IT, are operationally relevant, but they are hardly strategically important. Under these circumstances, the choice is to continue to perform these functions internally or outsource them to a reliable partner.

Quadrant III: Strategically Important but Not Leveraging Existing Assets and Capabilities

In these circumstances, the best option seems to be to operate the new business as an independent business unit. This is often the case with product substitutions, when one technology or process is replaced by another. The crucial question here is, to which degree the new opportunity can draw on existing capabilities – or it requires a separate organization unencumbered by existing ways of thinking.

For instance, as Netflix evolved from renting DVDs by mail to video streaming, Reed Hastings, the company's CEO, decided that the two businesses were sufficiently distinct that they should operate independently. So, in late 2014, he announced that the company would separate out the rental business as Qwikster. While this made sense from an operational standpoint, Netflix's customers rebelled, and the company was forced to reverse its decision. Internally, however, Netflix kept the two businesses separate.

Quadrant IV: Strategically Important and Able to Leverage Core Capabilities

But what happens when the new opportunity is strategically important *and* can benefit from the company's existing assets and operational capabilities? This is exactly the set of strategic conditions for which the ambidextrous design is most appropriate.

In these circumstances, to spin the exploratory unit out would be to sacrifice the future – or, at a minimum, to endure the pain of not using available resources. This was the lesson Walmart learned in 2000, when it initially spun out its dot-com business, Walmart.com. This move robbed Walmart of the ability to develop digital capabilities, complicating its efforts to compete with Amazon.

If there is an opportunity to leverage the firm's existing assets to create a business that has the potential to be strategically valuable, then there is a need to become an ambidextrous organization. While small firms must place a life-or-death bet on just one or two experiments, larger companies can run multiple experiments, in which failure does not jeopardize the enterprise and may instead increase learning. Some of these firms may develop into important new revenue streams, such as Amazon's cloud computing, or create capabilities vital to the long-term success of the core business.

Becoming an ambidextrous organization is a strategic decision based on the use of existing assets and capabilities to develop a competitive advantage in new markets. It is not simply the extension of existing products and services – or unrelated diversification. Nor is it simply the development of new technology. Ball Corporation entered the aerospace market as a way of driving growth but did so only because its expertise at the interface of metal and glass gave it an advantage over competitors. Fujifilm's entrance into health care was based on its ability to leverage its expertise in surface chemistry, which gave it an advantage over competitors.

FOUR SUCCESS FACTORS

With the commitment to the ambidextrous organization having been made, the sponsor of the Corporate Explorers needs to work to ensure that four success-enabling factors are in place.

Strategic Intent

Every journey toward building an ambidextrous organization must start with a clear definition of the objectives of a new business. To this end, the following crucial questions must be answered:

- Who is our customer? What customer segments do we choose to serve – or not to serve?
- What is our value proposition? Why should customers choose our product or service?
- How will we make money? Where will our profit come from?
- What will we do internally and what activities can we outsource or use ecosystem partners to complete?
- What is the basis of our competitive advantage? How will we defend our profitability over time? Is our advantage sustainable?
- What is the scale of our ambition? How will we know we have been successful?

Asking these questions was a routine practice for IBM's Emerging Business Opportunity Program in 2000–2010; other companies have developed their own approaches. Although different in the details, each of these efforts is designed to identify new business opportunities, validate them, and then scale – all in a systematic and repeatable way.

Each approach explicitly acknowledges the need for organizations to develop a portfolio of exploratory projects. All focus on leveraging a company's existing assets and capabilities to drive new business growth. Each begins with a clear strategic intent and a deep understanding of what assets and capabilities can be used for competitive advantage.

While undeniably messy, an ambidextrous arrangement appears to have an edge over other new business designs. An empirical study of 13 business units and 22 innovations confirms that the ambidextrous organization is comparatively more effective than other popular designs, such as spin-outs and cross-functional teams in promoting successful innovation streams.[2]

Aligned Senior Team

The second key to implementing ambidexterity is the commitment of the senior management to serve as active sponsors, securing funding and providing support to the Corporate Explorer and their new venture. Without active engagement on the part of a very senior leader, exploratory offerings often fall prey to the short-term demands of the mature business. Besides, lacking stable funding, such efforts will inevitably be starved of investments.

For example, IBM had an explicit rule that very senior executives should get involved, offer the right type of oversight, and take ownership of the new venture. Crucially important is that, in this role, leaders need to act like entrepreneurs and not managers of a mature business.

Several business cases were described when the failure of a new venture was attributable, at least in part, to the lack of senior management oversight, which left lower-level leaders of this effort unprotected from the pressure of the larger business. For example, at Cisco, the lack of a dedicated senior sponsor and stable funding resulted in a competition for John Chambers' (Cisco's then-CEO) attention, with the result that many new ventures never received the support and attention they needed to survive.

One needs to emphasize that the explicit sponsorship of growth initiatives is only possible when members of the senior team themselves agree about the importance of both exploitation and exploration – with neither being seen as more important. Without a clear consensus in the senior team about the ambidextrous strategy, there will be less information exchange, more unproductive conflict, and a diminished ability to respond to external change.

Worse, mixed signals from the senior team make the already delicate balancing act between exploration and exploitation even more difficult. Because keeping such a balance is crucially important, a change in the ways the senior management team operates may be required. For example, at IBM, the senior team was rewarded based on companywide metrics, not line-of-business performance. This resulted in the shift of attention from short-term projects (line-of business compensation scheme) to the long-term collaboration (companywide metrics).

If the dissent continues, the senior leader may have no other option as to isolate or eliminate those who oppose ambidexterity. For example, to ensure consensus for his network strategy at *USA Today*, the CEO Tom Curley replaced five of his seven senior managers. At Ciba Vision, Glenn Bradley replaced 60% of the senior team to ensure commitment to his initiatives.

Autonomy and Access

The organizational structure needed to succeed in an exploratory business is very different from that needed in an exploitative one. The very purpose of the ambidextrous format as opposed, for example, to a spin-out is to allow new business to leverage organizational capabilities that would not be available if this business were operating completely independently. And unlike a cross-functional team design, which diffuses responsibility across functions, the ambidextrous design permits both a tighter focus and the opportunity to use resources from the larger organization.

However, for this to work, exploratory units need to be able to create their own alignments. For example, both IBM and Cisco had senior management support for their new business ventures. But while at IBM new business ventures were explicitly encouraged to develop their own architecture, Cisco was less willing to separate out new ventures, often trying to run them as part-time efforts without separate staffing and organizational alignments. The results were different, too: the success of new ventures at IBM and their failure at Cisco.

At the same time, research shows that although the structural separation of the innovation unit is necessary, it is not sufficient for successful ambidexterity. Not only do exploratory units need independence to develop their own alignments, but they also need access to the assets and capabilities of the larger organization. In other words, they need to be both separated *and* integrated. Figure 14.2 illustrates what this seemingly paradoxical arrangement could look like.

Structural separation of units looks conceptually simple but in real life, senior managers often fail to properly implement it. This can leave exploratory units without sufficient resources or at risk of being overwhelmed by mature business. For instance, units may be asked to comply with the demands of the legacy business (such as, for example, financial reporting, IT compliance, purchasing rules, or HR processes) that are difficult to meet due

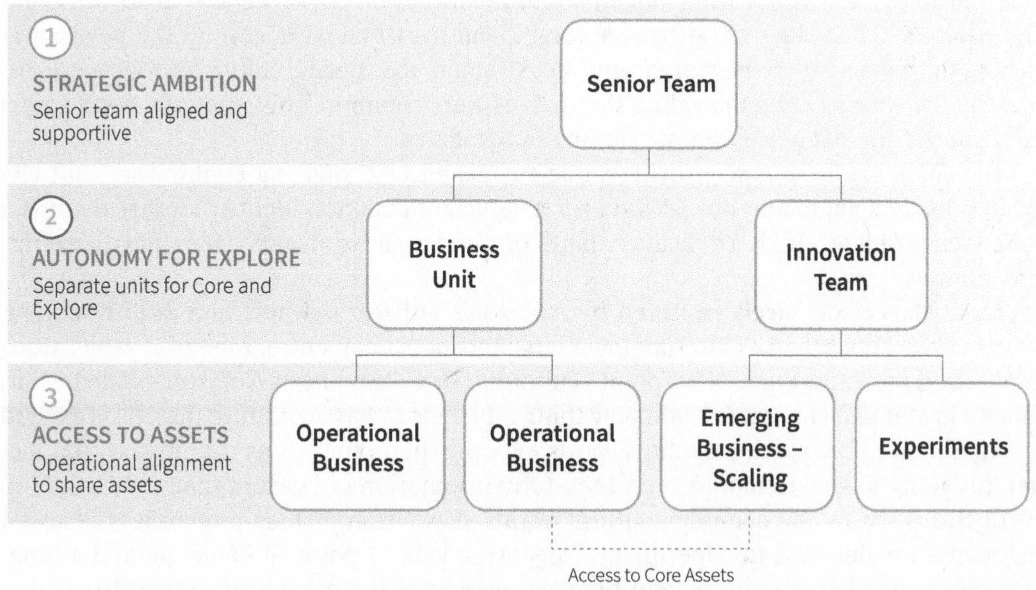

Figure 14.2 Ambidextrous organization design.

to their small size. A top-level oversight is, therefore, needed to make sure that the new venture gets all the help from the mature business that the former requires. Otherwise, the exploratory unit would struggle and lose momentum.

Common Values and Culture

The fourth ingredient needed for ambidexterity to succeed is a shared identity across the explore and exploit businesses. Various units must see themselves as pursuing a common goal and sharing common values. This ambition provides rationale for cooperation between the core and explore businesses that are likely to see each other as a distraction or a threat. The shared values and culture provide the shared operating instructions for that collaboration.

Having "common values" doesn't mean having uniform behavior. This requires leaders to manage a delicate balance between common values and different cultures in the core and explore units. Some values and the associated behaviors must be shared throughout the entire organization – for example, integrity, respect for people, teamwork, and accountability. At the same time, specific norms and behaviors required for other values – such as initiative, customer orientation, innovation, and risk taking – may vary depending on the business.

When *USA Today* introduced an online newspaper for the first time, the print reporters initially saw the online staff as not serious journalists and even as a threat. In their turn, the online employees believed the print staff members were dinosaurs – and both saw the TV news people as a joke. Why should they cooperate with each other? To ameliorate these tensions, CEO Tom Curley talked about the future of *USA Today* as "a network, not a newspaper." The values of fairness, accuracy, and trust that were core to the newspaper became the values for the new organization. Although the specific cultural norms were different in the various units, the values themselves were common. This created a bond across the organization that permitted the sharing of resources.

The challenge here is to provide sufficient distance so that the exploratory unit can develop its own alignment but provide for a sufficient common identity so that there is a shared sense of fate. This is a delicate balance of a common vision and values and differentiated cultures.

This balance was nicely captured by Amazon's Jeff Bezos when, in a 2015 interview, he was asked about the keys to running a large business in an entrepreneurial way.[3] Bezos emphasized the importance of corporate culture: "For a company at Amazon's scale to continue to invent and change, to build new things, it needs to have a culture that . . . is excited by experimentation, a culture that rewards experimentation even as it embraces the fact that it is going to lead to failure . . . A long-term orientation is a part of that."

In Bezos's view, the common cultural norms at Amazon include a relentless focus on customers, a willingness to experiment, frugality, a lack of political behavior, and a long-term perspective. These norms help bind the people of the organization together across disparate units. However, what they mean in a specific unit can vary widely. For example, experimentation in an Amazon fulfillment center is all about incremental improvements and increased efficiency. But experimentation in Amazon's Lab126 is about coming up with new hardware to improve customers' buying experiences.

The most important thing to remember is that ambidexterity requires leaders to be capable of fostering these differences and not letting a rigid adherence to specific rules and norms to suffocate entrepreneurial culture.

These four elements provide the basis for a successful ambidextrous organization that can support Corporate Explorers in their work. Absent any of the four, and ambidexterity is likely to fail, with serious consequences for the new ventures. It is the interplay of these elements that permits exploration to take root in the context of exploitative inertial forces.

One of the most impressive recent applications of the ambidextrous organization was performed at the Japanese materials firm, AGC.

APPLICATION CASE STUDY: AMBIDEXTROUS ORGANIZATION AT AGC

***By Hideyuki Kurata*[4]**

AGC Group is a 115-year-old global corporation headquartered in Tokyo, Japan, with more than $15 billion in revenues. Originally an architectural glass company, AGC's business portfolio has changed substantially since 2015, when our current chairperson, Takuya Shimamura, was appointed CEO. Under his leadership, we have adopted an ambidextrous approach to the company's growth. This separated our business portfolio between core businesses and strategic businesses. In the core business, our goal is to heighten competitiveness and build robust profit foundations. The strategic business is focused on high-growth fields that utilize our strengths to create future growth pillars for the company. When we started this approach, AGC's management team defined mobility, electronics, and life science as strategic businesses, and we continue to grow and expand these businesses through marketing strategy and M&A deals. In FY2021, these strategic businesses contributed approximately 25% of the corporation's profit, and by 2030, we anticipate this will rise to 50% of the overall (Figure 14.3). This is an achievement of which we are very proud and it has also led market analysts to reclassify AGC as a growth stock.

There are several key features to our ambidextrous organization. A key first step was the creation of the business development division (BDD) to be responsible for business incubation through the corporate investment system. The business divisions and R&D divisions send personnel to the BDD to train them to become in-house entrepreneurs, or Corporate Explorers. This system of nurturing businesses and training personnel helps prepare for the eventual handing off of the new ventures to business divisions leads. It also helps to improve the sustainability of ambidextrous management by overcoming various problems such as shortages of personnel for creating new businesses, or misaligned interests, that tend to arise between new business divisions and mature business divisions.

(Continued)

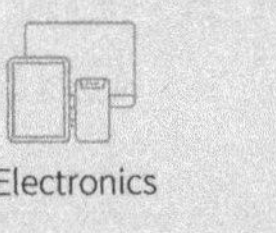

Figure 14.3 AGC group strategy (from the AGC Annual Report, 2022).

One aspect of this system is that new businesses can be developed in an incubator, meaning traditional rules that apply to established business in AGC, for example, in terms of risk or return, do not apply to these businesses. This gives them the freedom to operate and grow, while still being able to leverage AGC's finance and corporate strengths. Then, if successful, they can later be scaling in the core businesses.

AGC comprehensively evaluates businesses based on criteria that include resilience to market changes, asset efficiency, growth potential, and carbon efficiency; it makes decisions on how to allocate management resources; and then it draws up business strategies and investment plans. Over the long term, it is imperative that we maximize economic value and social value while pursuing our business portfolio strategy. In our core businesses, we are focusing on technological innovations to reduce greenhouse gas emissions in the manufacturing process while increasing the ratio of higher-value-added products. In strategic businesses, since carbon efficiency and asset efficiency are high, AGC is keen to spur further growth, which will translate into the creation of a more sustainable business portfolio.

Of the three businesses designated as strategic businesses, the life science and electronics businesses were the first to embark on growth trajectories. In the biopharmaceutical CDMO (contract development and manufacturing organization) in the life science business, AGC has been contracted for drug development projects through to commercial production with a combination of single-use bioreactors (SUBs), which can handle many kinds of strains in small lots, and stainless-steel cell culture (SUS) bioreactors, which are suited for large-scale projects. The company is executing measures from a long-term perspective with the objective of reaching ¥200 billion (USD1.5 billion) in net sales from fiscal 2024 to fiscal 2025, by strengthening competitiveness in the field of cutting-edge gene and cell therapies. In the electronics business, AGC is expanding the use of photomask blanks for EUV lithography in the semiconductor production process. AGC plans to double its production capacity in fiscal 2022 and again in fiscal 2024, in a bid to tap into demand in this growing market. Both of these hugely successful and promising businesses originated in the BDD.

In R&D, we have adopted ambidextrous development. "Right-handed" development refers to the innovation of existing production technologies and basic technologies and to the development of new products together with our customers. This involves working closely with customers and catering to their needs. This type of development uses a forecasting approach in which current conditions are the starting point of projections and improvement measures. "Left-handed" development, by contrast, is based on back casting, which begins by anticipating future trends and then undertakes the initiatives and new business creation needed to adapt to these trends. The goal of left-handed development is to open up new markets by redefining existing production technologies and fundamental technologies (Figure 14.4).

AGC's history includes many examples of both types of development. An example of right-handed development is AGC's use of architectural glass production technologies and basic technologies. Using these technologies, we developed Low-E glass, which is a highly functional double-glazing glass that has heat-insulating and heat-shielding properties. As for left-handed development, the development of automotive glass and glass for cathode-ray tubes enabled forays into the automobile and television fields.

Balancing the two approaches is the key to advancing ambidextrous development. Important though right-handed development is to meet the needs of customers, this approach alone will not allow us to adapt to major changes in society. My role as CTO is to allocate management resources between right- and left-handed development and encourage researchers to tackle both near- and long-term development challenges. I am committed to achieving an optimal overall balance between them.

Encouraging employees to take on new challenges is a fundamental aspect of the organizational culture at the AGC Group. Adapting to industry and market changes, the history of the Group is one of constant creation of new applications for materials, and a spirit of taking on challenges is essential to innovation. Our founder, Toshiya Iwasaki, impressed upon employees the importance of challenging themselves, stressing the words "Never take the easy way out, confront difficulties." As a result, throughout our history, AGC has

(Continued)

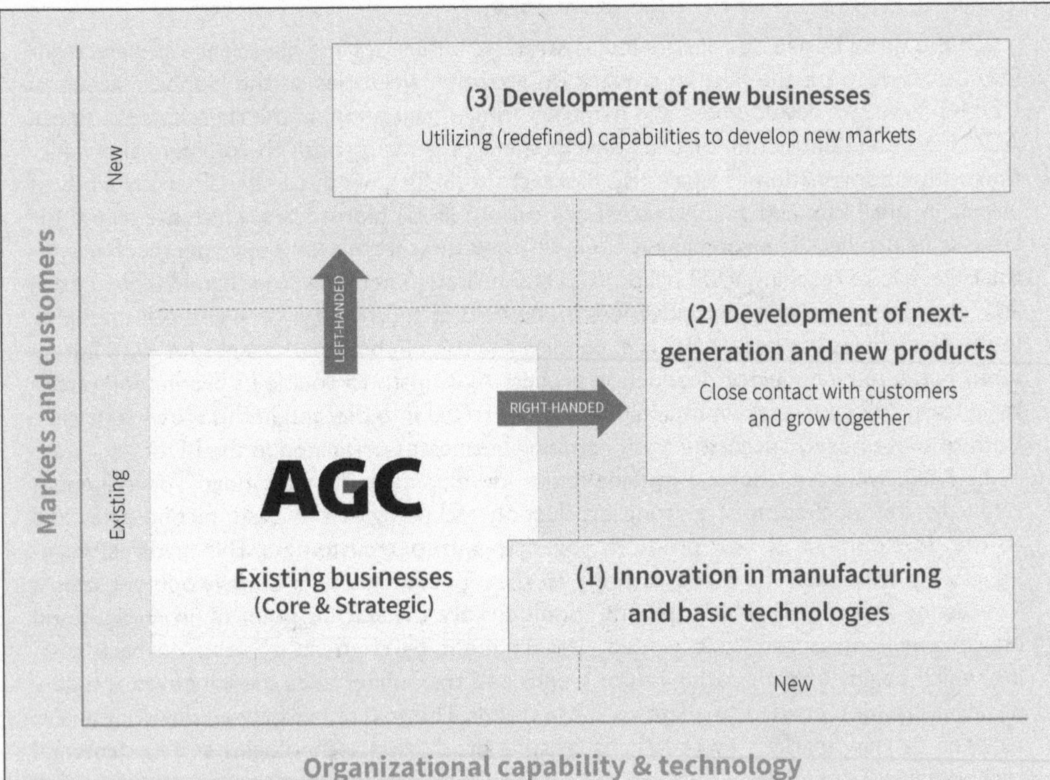

Figure 14.4 Ambidextrous R&D approach (from the AGC Annual Report, 2022).

contributed many meaningful developments and advances in our industry, which have played an important role in society.

The accumulation of such achievements has shaped the current organizational culture of the Group. At the center of these achievements has always been the contribution of our people. AGC has a large group of talented, diverse individuals who function as one team, with a unified purpose of achieving our mission of using our unique materials and solutions to make people's lives better around the world. Dialogue is key to preserving this organizational culture. Through dialogues with business divisions and employees, management has continued to champion that learning from challenges and experiencing failures is good. The culmination of successes and failures from facing challenges in our management systems and organizational culture is an irreplaceable, intangible asset that facilitates the continued improvement of corporate value for the AGC Group today and will continue far into the future.

CHAPTER 15

Explore Unit: How to Build a Team for Exploration

Christine Griffin, Erich Kruschitz, and Andrew Binns

RHYTHM OF EXPLORE

Ambidextrous organizations, like the one at AGC described in Chapter 14, separate the work of Corporate Explorers from the rest of the business. This gives the Explorer autonomy to operate outside existing corporate rules, while remaining close enough to the core business to leverage corporate assets to scale a fledgling business.

However, separation alone is not enough. The explore unit is also managing a business with a different operating rhythm. The existing business is seeking to optimize performance within a set of known variables. In contrast, a Corporate Explorer's task is to de-risk the company's investments in future growth opportunities. It requires a different organizational approach to manage the exploratory operating rhythm.

There are five elements to designing an organizational approach for an exploratory unit:

1. **Purpose.** What is the explore unit expected to achieve; what is its ambition?
2. **Resource allocation.** How are exploratory units funded?
3. **Decision making.** How will the organization make decisions about capital and resource allocation?
4. **Team.** How do you structure the unit and recruit a winning team?
5. **Operating model.** What does the team do; how does it structure its work?

This chapter offers guidance on how to answer these questions and provides the example of SanusX, an explore unit set up by the European insurance company, UNIQA.

PURPOSE

One of the most impressive characteristics of successful entrepreneurs is that they see a bigger opportunity, not just the immediate one to generate revenue. We all know that Amazon started as an online bookstore, undercutting the existing business of bricks-and-motors retailers with an e-commerce model. However, the key decision that laid the groundwork for the firm's success was that Jeff Bezos planned his logistics operation for a much larger business that would span multiple retail categories. He set his ambition to the scale of the opportunity, not what he thought he could achieve in the short term.

The default for corporate managers is the reverse: they are schooled in setting achievable goals; to underpromise and overdeliver is considered a virtue. However, the lesson of Bezos and others like him is that you need to set an ambition that is equal to the scale of the threat or opportunity of disruption. This should guide all further decisions you make about the scope of activities for the venture, the partnerships it needs, its resources, and value proposition.

For an ambition statement to be useful, it needs to be aspirational (that is, to have a clear goal), logical (to provide a strategic rationale), and emotionally compelling. At the venture level, it helps include a financial metric, for example, $100 million revenue by 2030. This helps get everyone's attention to the scale of the task and makes it clear what the Corporate Explorer is expected to deliver.

The size of the aspiration should reflect the scale of the opportunity and should be big enough to create anxiety, even a little fear. This is about exploring beyond the business that you have today. However, it should not be within the current planning horizon, as it is not a goal in the sense of a key performance indicator or other metric. It helps if there is a nonfinancial metric involved as well that captures the impact the venture will have on the world. For example, Best Buy Health's ambition is to serve five million elderly consumers by 2025, or SpaceX's goal is to make humans interplanetary.

RESOURCE ALLOCATION

Funding an explore unit from within an annual expense budget is very challenging, because the timeframes are extended beyond the paybacks that firms are used to dealing with, and the outcomes are uncertain. Often, firms try to manage this conundrum by fitting the explore unit into the existing financial budgeting process on the assumption that this will provide rigor for managing the investment.

This is a flawed assumption. For example, one firm we worked with had invested over a billion dollars in exploring new areas of growth. The new ventures it created were asked to define annual budgets for revenue and expenditure, just like the existing business units. The finance team eventually accepted that the revenues would be zero, but still insisted on a firm expense budget. The result was made-up goals and nonsense business cases. Worse still, the ventures were expected to spend their budgets or risk losing them next year, thereby forcing them to make unnecessary hires and spend on unwanted equipment. An extreme case perhaps, but one that highlights how the annual plan is not fit for this specific purpose.

Corporations need to adopt an approach to managing financial resources that synchs up with the experimentation practices of the explore business. This means funding in small increments, disbursed when the venture needs them, not against an artificial calendar.

There are several mechanisms that firms can use to align resource decisions more directly to the needs of an exploratory venture.

- **Budget autonomy.** At the top of any Corporate Explorer's list is budget autonomy. They want to operate with the same freedoms as an entrepreneur. We agree, though we would add that it is vital to also replicate the scarcity most startups experience. Corporate Explorers need an ability to spend because without this ability, they cannot develop meaningful incubation experiments. They may also need to bypass company procurement rules that are set up for large spends on a competitive bid basis, whereas all a Corporate Explorer needs to do is to spend a few hundred dollars to run a simple online test – so, budget autonomy, but also scarcity. Successful, large businesses spend money in a way that a startup never would. This forces startups to make careful choices about how to learn what they need to know, without overcommitting themselves. Corporate Explorers work best when they operate in the same conditions. It also helps them guard against developing a reputation for waste that can be turned against them when opponents try to cut budgets.
- **Milestone based.** Venture capital firms fund new startups through a series of funding rounds: series A, B, C, and so on. The entrepreneurs go to the market and seek either more funds from existing backers or recruit new ones. They use evidence of what they have achieved so far and make commitments to what they think they can achieve in the next round. This basic structure is the one that established companies adopt to manage early-stage ventures, with an investment board, as described later, making the choices about when to release funding at different milestones.
- **Multiyear commitments.** Corporate Explorers need funding committed over multiple years far more than they need a specific dollar amount. This arrangement enables them to scale the venture to the opportunity, rather than having to deliver short-term results that justify their existence in the annual budget cycle. This requires the finance team to commit to a number—even a lower one than the Corporate Explorer wants—over multiple years, without further intervention.
- **Out-of-cycle funding.** Even with a multiyear commitment to funding, a Corporate Explorer may find that the allocated budget fails to keep pace with what is needed

to respond to the market opportunity. Sometimes, market adoption of innovation is much faster than anticipated, often because of unexpected external events, such as a global pandemic. That makes it vital to have someone in the C-suite with the capability to commit funds out-of-cycle, so that the opportunity is not lost. At IBM, the emerging business opportunities all had the ability to request "emergency" funds from the senior vice-president for strategy. It was a modest amount, but it did enable innovation teams to pursue customer opportunities that might otherwise have been lost.

DECISION MAKING

These are useful mechanisms for allocating resources to exploratory businesses. However, you also need a way to make decisions about what resources are allocated and when, without spending too much time on this. Time is a critical resource for innovators, and large companies' decision making is notoriously slow. We advocate putting in place a simple governance approach as early as possible in the life of a new venture, so that the discussion about *how* we make the decision is separated from *what* decision we need to make. Explore governance has three different bodies or decision-making units involved:

1. Senior leadership team (SLT): The top managers of the corporation or management board in European firms.
2. Investment board: A subset of managers delegated to manage explore investment portfolio on behalf of the SLT or the board. In some instances, this is the same as the SLT.
3. Explore unit leaders: Corporate Explorers and their team with responsibility for a new venture or a portfolio of ventures (Table 15.1).

Firms may also appoint an advisory board that includes managers drawn from inside and outside the company. This acts as a "shadow" board of directors for an individual venture, providing guidance and insight to the Corporate Explorer. However, it is not a decision-making body.

Table 15.1 Explore decision-making bodies.

	Senior Leadership Team	Investment Board	Explore Unit
Purpose	Owns growth ambition and portfolio strategy decisions	Manages portfolio investments	Manages ventures, proposes hunting zones
Membership	Senior team or management board	CEO, CFO, CTO, Strategy Chief	Explore unit leader

Table 15.2 Explore business decision rights.

	Senior Leadership Team	Investment Board	Explore Unit
Ambition	D	C	C
Budget	D	C	C
Hiring and Firing	I	I	D
Capital Allocation	C	D	C
Explore Unit Goals	I	C	D
Pursue, Pivot, Stop	I	C	D

These three bodies need to make six different types of decision, including on issues that extend beyond resource allocation.

1. Long-term ambition for the explore venture
2. Allocation of budget
3. Hiring and firing an explore team
4. Capital allocation to enable acquisitions
5. Goals for the next 12–18 months (or some other relevant timeline)
6. Pursue, pivot, or stop judgments of individual projects

However, it is best to think of these decisions as not being made in isolation from one another. Each decision-making body has a role in each decision. We usually define three roles: they *decide* (D), they are *consulted* (C), or they are *informed* (I) (Table 15.2).

TEAM

A new venture adds new team members rapidly as it moves from the ideation into incubation phase. Corporate Explorers wrestle with questions: "What team members do I need?" "What sorts of skills should they have?" "Do I hire from inside the corporation or go outside for entrepreneurial or domain-specific talent?"

Here are some guidelines for answering these questions based on our experience. An Explore unit should include the following roles:

- Venture leadership, to own the venture and its vision, to develop a compelling business case and scaling path, and to inspire the team.
- Market analysis, to identify and evaluate emerging trends and new market spaces.
- Customer discovery, to identify and validate high-value customer problems by conducting in-depth research.

- Venturing and M&A, to identify and secure investments and alliances that enable the venture to scale.
- Product management, to commercialize and manage new offerings through business experimentation techniques.
- Organizational culture, to lead agile practices that sustain a pace of discovery and learning (also see following section, Operating Model).

Figure 15.1 lists skills, experiences, and attributes especially needed at the early stages, when the team focuses on ideation and incubation. As ventures mature, the explore unit may start to add individuals with specific technical or operating experience (for example, CTO, operations, sales, and customer service).

ROLE	SKILLS	KEY EXPERIENCES	ATTRIBUTES				SKILLS/KNOW		
			Adaptable	Customer Oriented	Courageous	Collaborative	Domain Expertise	Technology	Inn. Methods
Venture Leader (Product Managers)	• Build and inspire a cohesive team • Craft a compelling business case • Decision-making (fast/agile vs. perfect) • Build strategic alliances and partner strategy • Scale new businesses	• Team Leader • Start-up/business builder							
Market Analysis	• Identify and profile new market spaces: competition, size, attractiveness • Track emerging trends and connect the dots	• Market research, particularly in emerging categories							
Customer Discovery	• Customer empathy, ability to articulate high-value problems • Rigorously conduct hypotheses-driven experiments • Fuel work with a constant flow of ideas/insights	• Design thinking • Ethnographic research • Hypothesis-driven analytics							
Venturing/ M&A	• Research and analytic skills, financial modeling • Decision-making, particularly @ investment and alliances • Communication	• Start-up or incubator • Corporate venturing • Portfolio management							
Product Marketing	• Market research, analytic and technical skills • Pricing, packaging, customer acquisition/mgmt. strategy • Communications – messaging, positioning, collateral	• New product launch • Role as "voice of the customer"							
Culture & Org	• Strong social network inside and outside Core • Challenge legacy mindsets • Conflict resolution	• High conflict situations • Courageous challenger							

Figure 15.1 Explore unit members' skills.

A word of caution: there is a temptation to hire quickly. The euphoria of getting budget approval for a new explore unit encourages some Corporate Explorers to build up the team right away. We find that sometimes, teams start too fast without enough clarity on the opportunities they will pursue. If this is the case, adding more people will only dilute the team's focus.

OPERATING MODEL

Traditional organizational structures with departments and functions are good when there is a multiyear mission with a goal. You give someone responsibility for leading the group and let them run with it. Projects are more flexible, with teams assembled to deliver on a specific goal (e.g., desirability, feasibility, viability), usually within a set timeline. Explore teams are constantly learning—experimenting, validating, pivoting, and often, stopping new ventures.

Explore units need to be able to spin up a new team or decide to disband one within a short timeframe if milestones are not met. This gives the explore unit a different feel, more like a software startup than a traditional business. Indeed, the agile software development movement has informed many of the practices that are most useful for leading an explore business team. We refer to this arrangement as *exploratory business sprints,* which run through ideation, incubation, and scaling of a new venture. The key features of exploratory business sprints are as follows:

Teams. Appoint a team of not more than four people (at first) focused on a discrete hunting zone or opportunity. Some teams add an innovation coach to help teams implement methodologies, such as design thinking or agile. During the ideation phase, these teams can be part-time, but as the opportunity moves into the incubation phase, the teams become larger, and it is critical to have all or most of the team working full time on the venture.

- **Cadence.** Create short time frames within which the team does its work: for example, a 90-day cycle split into three 30-day sprints. This creates momentum by ensuring that there is constant pressure to get to the next sprint with something tangible accomplished.
- **Scopes.** Each sprint needs a clear definition of what the team is expected to achieve. What is the result or outcome? Is it data from an experiment, validation of a customer need, or optimal pricing? The sprint sponsors should sign off on the scope, so that there is complete alignment on the task. However, a scope should not dictate how to deliver the outcomes; this is the work of the team.
- **Rituals.** A key to successful sprints is to create an environment for learning, in which successes and failures are openly discussed, so that they can form a basis to judge the viability of a new venture. Key rituals create this environment. Such rituals can include *kick-offs*, at which sponsors and teams negotiate the scope for the next sprint;

daily stand-ups, when teams describe key actions and help needed; and *retrospectives*, during which teams share feedback on how the way the team is operating is affecting the quality of outcomes.

- **Decision making.** Reporting on outcomes, not activities, focuses attention on the decisions that need to be made. Did a venture validate or refute a hypothesis about the customer problem, value proposition, or some other element of the business design? If it did, what does this mean for its desirability, viability, and feasibility as a venture? Making decisions in the sprint process – not in a typical corporate back room or hallway conversation – is critical to creating this learning environment for teams.

Establishing an explore unit gives the explorer autonomy and resources to operate outside existing corporate rules, while remaining close enough to the core business to leverage corporate assets to scale a fledgling business. Additionally, the unit's different operating rhythm – sprint teams using an agile approach to experimentation and operating in disciplined cycles, and an investment approach based on milestones – ensures that the unit does not invest ahead of learning. These principles were realized at SanusX, an explore unit set up by the European insurance company, UNIQA, featured in the Application Case Study.

APPLICATION CASE STUDY: SanusX

by Erich Kruschitz

UNIQA Insurance Group is one of the leading insurance groups in Central and Eastern Europe with approximately six billion euros in revenue and over 22,000 employees. Operating in 18 countries, it provides property, casualty, life, and health insurance to around 16 million customers. UNIQA's ambition is to transition from "insurer" to "carer," to enable individuals to live safer, better, and longer lives. In 2020, UNIQA established a separate unit, SanusX, to explore opportunities to help create a healthier society and become a "holistic healthcare provider" reaching 100 million euros revenue by 2025. I (Erich) was chosen to lead SanusX.

Innovation Portfolio: Defining SanusX Purpose and Scope

At SanusX, the focus is on the "why" of what we are doing – not only from a financial point of view (or a shareholder perspective), but from the point of view of the individual employees and working teams. Our vision is to create a healthier society. This guides our ambition, motivation, internal discussions, decision-making processes, and unit goals. This top-down approach started with classic vision and value workshops involving executives, managers, and external advisors, including a physician, a nurse, a mental health professional, and people familiar with healthcare regulations.

This energized the first 10 SanusX employees. People felt connected to the mission. Early work aligned the organization around the explore unit's purpose, scope, and hunting zones.

In its first year, SanusX implemented an objectives-and-key-results (OKR) framework[1] to anchor the vision and mission in outcomes that the organization could understand and support. Every individual goal (objectives, key results, key actions) not connected to our overall mission and vision was eventually dropped.

Decision Making: Deciding on the Management System of SanusX

From the beginning, SanusX had autonomy to manage resources independently of other parts of UNIQA. We had little, if any, connection to the core functions like IT, human resources, and finance, meaning that SanusX could move quickly outside of the usual corporate routines. It also meant we had to manage these tasks ourselves, giving SanusX a much stronger identity as a corporate start-up. A governance structure was put in place to guide decision making (Table 15.3). Progress was formally reviewed quarterly with UNIQA's CEO and Supervisory Board.

Table 15.3 SanusX business decision rights.

Decision	UNIQA Board	UNIQA CEO	SanusX CEO
Decision 1: UNIQA strategic objective of emerging business and budget	D	C	C
Decision 2: SanusX strategic objectives	D	C	C
Decision 3.1: Allocate SanusX resources	I	C	D
Decision 3.2a: Allocate UNIQA capital large investment	D	C	C
Decision 3.2b: Allocate UNIQA capital medium investment	C	D	C
Decision 3.2c: Allocate UNIQA capital small investment	I	C	D
Decision 3.3: Invest beyond annual budget	D	C	C
Decision 4.1: Pursue, pivot, kill for ideate/incubate	I	I	D
Decision 4.1: Pursue, pivot, kill for scaling	C	C	D
Decision 5: Hiring decisions SanusX	I	I	D

I reported directly to Andreas Brandstetter (UNIQA CEO), but also had a fixed monthly slot at the UNIQA executive board meeting to solicit strategic insights. Also, once a quarter, the board was invited to visit the SanusX office for the SanusX team to report its progress directly to the shareholders. This direct feedback mechanism strengthened our connection to the core business.

(Continued)

Going through a structured decision process to stop a project is key. There is a limited number of projects you can scale (at SanusX, we limited the number of parallel teams to five). It is always hard to give up an idea you ideated and incubated as a team. However, if you don't stop projects, you miss out on the learning part and will lack the capacity to start new, more promising ventures.

Operating Model: Structure Unit

The blueprint for SanusX management system was the Netflix model "no-rules rules."[2] A crucial component was the high talent density and the concept of freedom and responsibility for every team member. SanusX put a lot of effort into having the best person at every position. Team members had the authority to act quickly and independently in the best interest of the company. On the flipside, everyone had to take responsibility for their decisions and was accountable for them.

SanusX had a flat structure for the first two years: two managing directors with "squads" of three to five people working on specific topics (Figure 15.2). This included a product owner, a coach, and innovation catalysts (people who work actively on the offering). Budgets were agreed quarterly with the managing directors, and squads had the authority to spend the money as they decided. Squads benefited from centrally managed SanusX services, such as marketing, finance, M&A, HR, and IT. The services were designed to help squads succeed.

As the unit evolved and more teams (and subsidiaries over time) moved to the scaling phase, the structure morphed from squads to operating teams.

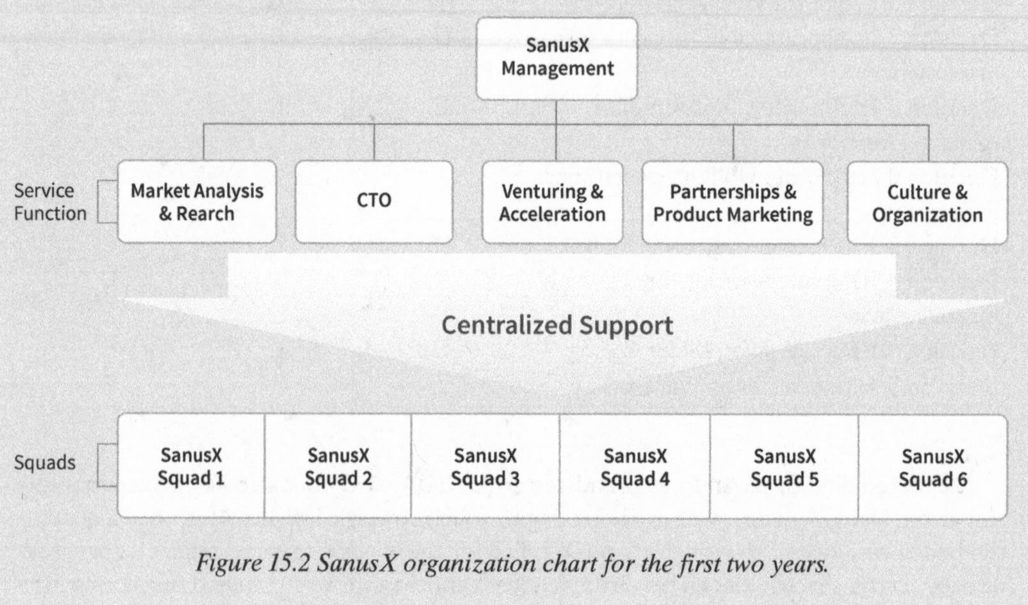

Figure 15.2 SanusX organization chart for the first two years.

Resources: Hire a Winning Team

SanusX's first hire was an international human resources manager with strong recruiting experience and the right mindset to build the SanusX culture. Sourcing the right entrepreneurial talent was a challenge, exacerbated by the fact that SanusX was founded in April 2020, during pandemic lockdowns. The manager had to completely rethink the hiring process, and developed several approaches to find great talent:

- Applicants developed and presented explore case studies to the whole SanusX team. Anyone on the team had a right to "veto" any candidate.
- In the interview rounds, SanusX engaged a psychologist who specialized in getting people "out of their comfort zone" (for example, by asking them to sing in front of a group). It was insightful to see the candidates in this environment; more interestingly, the candidates were excited about this approach, and this reflected positively on the SanusX brand.
- Together with a VC and instructor at INSEAD, SanusX launched an intensive seven-week program called the "SanusX Entrepreneur-in-Residence Program." The program guided business school students through a complete ideate, incubate, and partial scaling process. Students regularly pitched their ideas to executive panels. The program quickly became popular among students in the healthcare arena, and within the first three years, the program had applicants from the top European universities like Cambridge, Oxford, INSEAD, London Business School, and Imperial College London.

SanusX has new team members hired from outside and team members from UNIQA, such as myself. The switch from a corporate culture to a corporate start-up culture is sometimes difficult. We found that it was easier to integrate people from the legacy business once we had established SanusX's new corporate start-up culture.

Core Business: Creating the Connection to Leadership

SanusX benefits from having a visionary CEO, Andreas Brandstetter. It was Andreas who motivated and inspired UNIQA to adopt the ambidextrous approach and enter the "caring industry." Now, Andreas and the UNIQA board had the task to "spread the word" for the whole company and secure further executive support.

They invited the top eighty UNIQA managers (the "We Inspire Group") to a one-week immersive executive education program at Harvard Business School. The goal of this program was to understand how to build an ambidextrous organization, to leverage assets from the core, and to participate in designing the most important parts. Four key success factors contributed to strengthening our relationship to the core business leadership.

1. A clear strategic intent that justifies the need for exploitation and exploration, including the explicit identification of those organizational assets and capabilities that can be used for competitive advantage by the exploratory unit.
2. Senior management commitment and oversight to nurture and fund the new venture and protect it from those who would kill it.

(Continued)

3. Sufficient separation from the core so the new venture could develop its own structure and processes, and the careful design of the interfaces needed to leverage critical assets and capabilities from the core, including criteria to decide when to either drop the exploratory unit or integrate it back into the organization.
4. A vision, values, and culture that provide for a common identity across the explore and exploit units, helping all involved see that they are on the same team.

We collectively rated the UNIQA/SanusX execution for the first six months, and concluded that we were doing well on sufficient separation and vision, and values and culture. At the same time, we needed to do a better job of defining a clear strategic intent and on securing senior management support. That led to Andreas and me inviting the executive board to a half-day offsite meeting to align the core business and the explore unit. At the center of the discussion were key factors needed for a successful attempt at ambidexterity as we had learned it from O'Reilly and Tushman.[3]

We further defined improvement opportunities and terminated some projects. This exercise created a more collective ownership between the broader UNIQA team and SanusX. For SanusX, it also created stronger access to core assets. Similar workshops with the We Inspire Group provided valuable insights and much stronger alignment between the core and explore teams.

UNIQA is a public company and, as such, needs to publish quarterly results. Therefore, explaining the ambidextrous approach to investors was crucial. It helped that I held the role of head of Group Finance at UNIQA for many years before moving to SanusX. I also kept regular contact and a strong relationship to the CFO, Kurt Svoboda, and his team, enabling budget issues to be addressed collaboratively and quickly.

Operating Cadence: Ensuring Disciplined Exploration Approach

SanusX started with a huge ambition and a small team. At the beginning, it would have been beneficial to be even more rigorous in limiting the number of new projects. If you are in an exploration unit of a large corporate, many start-ups and small companies will approach you with "billion-dollar ideas" and partnership offers. You will have to make decisions about what to do and, more importantly, what not to do. Introducing a disciplined approach to exploration was not a one-time exercise but a continuous process. Staying focused is hard when you are getting bombarded with ideas from internal and external sources.

The most powerful framework we used was the OKR framework, which demanded every individual goal be connected to mid-term goals, mission, and vision. SanusX built an OKR dashboard in Excel and Mural, and the squads used it to manage their progress. After implementing the OKR framework, we eliminated many ongoing initiatives that did not align to overall goals. Team motivation and speed of exploration increased significantly. OKRs are built around a "purpose pyramid" connecting ambition to specific goals.

Another practical approach was the "systematic garbage disposal," a tool initially developed by Malik[4] and reused for SanusX purposes. Once a year, during the SanusX off-site, the team brainstormed the following question: "Of all things we are currently doing, what wouldn't we start today if we weren't already doing it?" The amount of slack the team identified and eliminated every year was remarkable.

The SanusX way of working was built around executing a disciplined and fast-learning exploration approach. In 2021, we had four squads working in three-month cycles split into one-month sprints. Every cycle consisted of the following:

- Setting goals (defining hypothesis and objectives and key results for the next three months), which were discussed and approved by the SanusX leadership team.
- A monthly sprint checkpoint, at which squads discussed the progress with the leadership team in focused, 45-minute sessions, either asking for further support or pivoting to other ideas based on learnings.
- An hour-long report to the leadership at the end of three months to discuss what the squads had learned.
- A one-week reset phase following the report, during which the squads discussed next steps based on the learnings of the past three months. For each initiative, squads recommended a "start-stop-continue" decision to the broader SanusX leadership team.
- Decision point, at which the SanusX leadership team considered the squad's recommendation of how to approach the next wave. A strict rule of "using our resources to achieve our vision and mission" was followed at this point. Often this led to stopping certain initiatives to focus on the most promising ones before beginning the next goal-setting phase.

Three years after its founding, SanusX continues to operate as an ambidextrous unit, ideating, incubating, and scaling new ventures. The autonomy, discipline and passion of the unit has SanusX well on its way to the bold ambition to become a "holistic healthcare provider" reaching 100 million euros revenue by 2025.

CHAPTER 16

Strategic Diversity: Selecting and Developing Corporate Exploration Teams

Richard Robertson

EXPLORE TEAMS

Corporate Explorers are a unique breed of professionals who can recognize the innovation capabilities within corporate structures and utilize the available resources to start up new initiatives. Enabling them to do so is their ability to understand both the formal, structured, and rigid processes of corporate environments as well as the more informal, flexible, and fast-moving environments of start-ups. As a result, Corporate Explorers can navigate all the necessary phases of strategic innovation and growth: from ideation to incubation, scaling, maturation, and transformation.

However, even the best Corporate Explorer won't be able to do everything alone. They need a founding team to build a new venture. To do this, Corporate Explorers must be able to successfully identify and select the talents they need to help them execute their vision and priorities.

Building high-performing teams that have the optimal composition to successfully take on complex challenges is an ongoing priority for every organization. Many concepts, frameworks, and assessments have been developed to aid in this challenge. The available tools deal with many different aspects of team building, ranging from personality profiles, communication styles, and skill and integrity assessments. These are most definitely critical characteristics to be looking at, and gathering information about them is invaluable.

However, one aspect in maximizing team performance is often overlooked: *strategic diversity*.

STRATEGIC DIVERSITY

I will define strategic diversity by using an analogy. Think of a soccer team with our Corporate Explorer as the coach. He or she has one straightforward objective: to build a team that will outperform all other teams in the championship.

One question that the coach can and should ask is, what type of personalities and communication styles the team needs. For instance, a team filled with extraverts will behave differently from a team of introverts and will require a different type of guidance. Similar questions could be asked around communication styles and skill levels. As stated, these are critical questions to ask when trying to build the team that is most capable of delivering on the coach's vision.

However, those aspects alone will not tell us much about whether this team has a winning collection of players. To get maximum performance out of each of our players and the team, we need to know what type of players we need and who will perform best in each position. We can all agree that our team needs a variety of talents to win. After all, a team consisting of only strikers or defenders will rarely win a match, and if they do happen to win one, the next team will quickly adapt its strategy.

The same is true for a business team. We need to know what types of contributions are needed to achieve specific business objectives. Some will need to be explorers driven by a compelling passion to develop new ways of doing things; others will be optimizers energized by bringing structure and delivering repeatable results.

Given the rapid pace of change in a new venture, the balance of explorers and optimizers will shift frequently. There needs to be optimal strategic diversity to support different phases of growth in the venture – and that means knowing what the team needs at each phase, and who will deliver that.

GROWTH CURVES

One useful approach to visualize how a company moves through different growth phases is to use the so-called growth curve (also referred to as the S-Curve; Figure 16.1).

The first phase is the ideation phase. Here, growth is still slow, and the focus is on innovation. Very few structures are in place, and the dynamics can be described as flexible and fast-moving, but also insecure and unproven. This phase requires people who are highly exploratory in nature, people who thrive in unfamiliar and unknown situations and think in opportunities instead of risks, and who would rather move too fast than too slow.

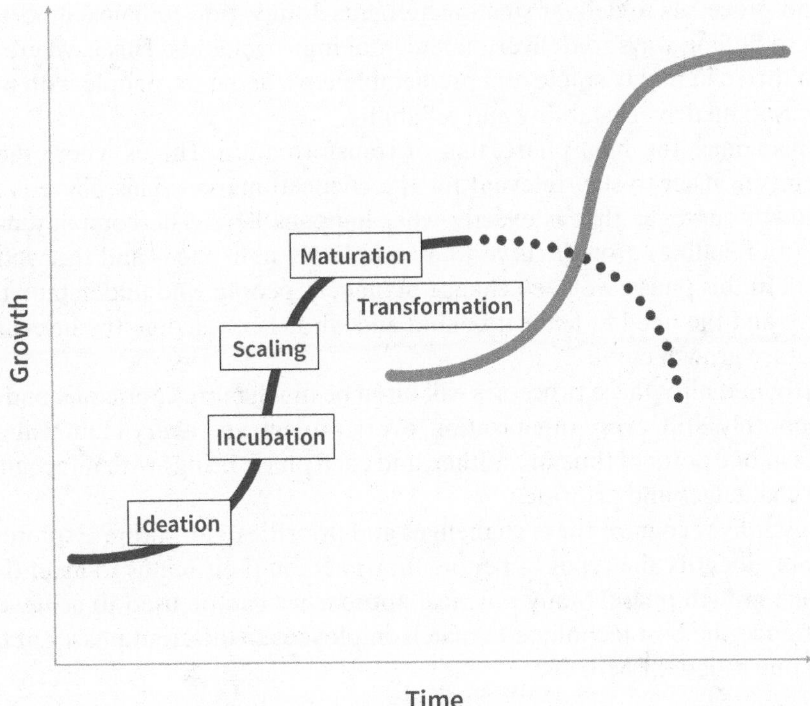

Figure 16.1 The growth curve.

The second phase is the incubation phase. This is the phase in which the focus starts to shift from creating the product to testing it with real customers. Incubation is not about generating new concepts, but rather about learning, in a structured way, regardless of whether the concept aligns to the customer's needs, or whether the customers will buy and use the product. This phase requires people who are great at translating ideas into testable prototypes and minimum viable products (MVPs), people who are practical and data driven.

The third phase is the scaling-up phase. This is where the focus moves to operational activities aimed at ramping up sales and production. Investments are directed at creating repeatable processes for serving customers, such as an efficient delivery structure. More people are hired, more formal agreements are made, more processes are put in place, and the organization grows at a rapid pace. Here, the need is for "can-do" people, who are highly operational, love to roll up their sleeves and deliver concrete results, and who don't mind a more predictable environment.

The fourth phase is the phase of maturation, where other offerings enter the market, and price competition may become intense. The focus here is on profits, on squeezing existing products and processes to deliver small increments. Innovation remains important, but its focus shifts to finding ways to deliver incremental improvements. This is where one needs people who thrive in highly stable and predictable environments, people with a deliberate mindset focused on driving stability and reliability.

After this comes the final phase, that of transformation. This is where the company needs to reinvent itself to stay relevant for the changed market. This phase is also called jumping growth curve, as that is exactly what happens here. The company moves from its existing (and ending) growth curve to a completely new one – and the whole process repeats itself. In this phase, we need change managers, people who understand the current growth curve and the need to leave it behind and who also welcome the insecurity of yet-unknown future growth curve.

Obviously, in reality, these processes will often be much more capricious, and things will rarely go smoothly. Still, every organization, every project, and every team will go through these phases at one point of time or another, and each phase brings with it recognizable and predictable challenges and priorities.

To successfully recognize these challenges and priorities, Corporate Explorers must be able to reliably identify the types of people they need on their teams to meet the requirements of each growth phase. Many practical approaches can be used to achieve that, but, in my experience, the best technique to match employees to different phases of the growth curve is the one called AEM-Cube.

HUMAN BEHAVIOR

Think about human behavior along three dimensions: attachment, exploration, and managing complexity.

Attachment reflects whether people are more attracted to interactions with people or with content or things. People-attached professionals identify easily with others and focus heavily on other people's emotions, states, and well-being. People who are strongly people-attached tend to focus on sales, customer service, and human relations; or they simply like being a member of a large group or community. They are great with other people but may find it harder to apply processes or take an analytical approach to problem solving.

Content-attached professionals have a strong affinity for everything to do with content (things, data, numbers, processes, physical objects, or electrons). They get excited by working with this content, discussing it, understanding it, and engaging with it. Being content-attached tends you toward products and technical tasks. This is where we find inventors, entrepreneurs, scientists. These people, often praised for their brilliance, perhaps lack a natural connection to other humans.

Exploration refers to how people deal with and contribute to change. Some people are highly exploratory, whereas others are more focused on optimizing. Exploratory professionals are instinctively drawn to change and renewal. They can't help thinking outside existing rules and prefer to frame the world as rich with opportunity, not with risk. They can be impulsive or even reckless in their relentless drive for change, seeing it as an end in itself, rather than one with a purpose or desired outcome.

Optimizing professionals are at home in more structured and predictable environments. They are not against change but do need to know why, how, and when the change is going to happen. They have a more patient and deliberate way of doing things and bring stability and reliability to the team. As a result, they can at times be perceived by others as being reactive or lethargic.

Finally, the **managing-complexity** dimension describes how people deal with complexity. People are either more specialized or generalized in the way of doing things. A specialist likes to go in-depth to deliver a contribution. They spend a lot of time developing their own unique knowledge and skills and will often strive to deliver a contribution to their domain that exceeds others.

In contrast, a generalist will take a broader approach. They focus more on the big picture, oversee larger systems and processes, and integrate people and ideas necessary to optimally deal with these. The implication of this dimension is that the generalist has a high comfort with ambiguity, being willing to see problems as complex and multifaceted, whereas the specialist is keener on complicated challenges that they can solve.

The value of these three distinctions is that it helps us predict which team can give its best contribution on the growth curve. A team of high exploratory, content-attached specialists has a better chance to generate a breakthrough product. However, they may be at a disadvantage when engaging with customers, whose needs and preferences they must understand and accommodate. This is strategic diversity in action: Does the composition of the team match the requirements for its position on the growth curve?

These distinctions are useful on their own but have even more power if we can measure a team's preferences. This can be done by the AEM-Cube, a time-tested tool that identifies people's natural position on the three dimensions and, therefore, predicts the strategic contribution that they can provide to the team[1] (Figure 16.2).

While taking the AEM-Cube assessment, team members answer a set of 40 or so questions. The results are then rendered in a format that shows where they sit relative to one another in terms of their preferences.

However, the reality of working on a team is that we do not always do what we are best at; instead, we adapt and start becoming defenders when we are better at midfield. This is captured by a second questionnaire that positions the team members along the same three dimensions of attachment, exploration, and managing complexity; however, this time, the members of the team rate one another's contribution to the team. The difference between the two positions, self-assessment and assessment by others, reflects the tension the team may be experiencing in its ability to manage the growth curve. If many people play out of their position, this tends to indicate there is a team performance problem looming.

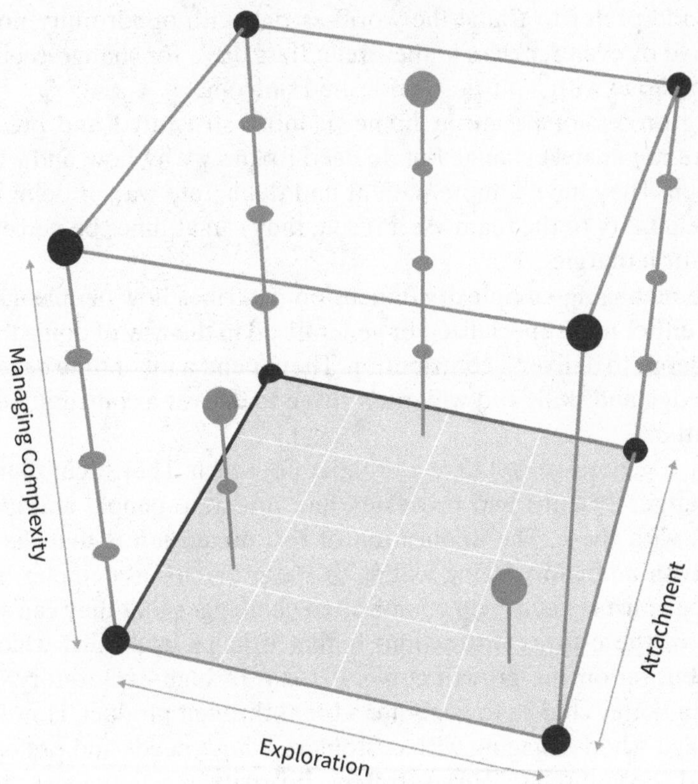

Figure 16.2 The AEM-Cube assessment.

IMPLICATIONS FOR CORPORATE EXPLORERS

Strategic diversity is a lens Corporate Explorers can use at any time for examining the performance of exploration teams. It connects human behavior to the stage of development of the venture, thereby helping to make choices about how to assemble, lead, and develop the venture team.

Selecting team members to fit the venture's current needs means listening for information about a candidate's preferences at interview. It is possible to tell where people sit on the three dimensions just from listening to them. Ask candidates to describe their previous jobs in detail, ask them to imagine they are narrating a scene in a movie, what did people say, what happened next, and so on. Their preferences will be clear from how they tell the story. Do they talk mostly about technical achievements, such as contribution of tools or processes? Or, are they describing the personalities and contributions of their colleagues? Similarly, when scaling a venture, listen for evidence that they like to bring structure to chaotic situations, that they are people who would play a linking role between the low S-curve explorers and the process-focused optimizers.

As the team develops, it can get stuck; every time it tries to make progress, it gets the same result. The problem could well be a lack of strategic diversity. There are several common breakdowns to watch out for:

- *Lack of measurable outcomes from experiments*: A team doesn't seem to understand how important it is to have tangible evidence – this implies not enough content-attached people on the team with an orientation for data.
- *New idea loop*: The team constantly tries to search for new possibilities, instead of scaling the ones it already has. This suggests too many explorers and not enough midcurve people with the ability to bring structure.
- *Concept trap*: A team likes to talk concepts, like business models and strategies, and does not go deep into the mundane details of issues like product design. This implies a team skewed too heavily to generalists. A healthy balance between specialists and generalists will enable a team to deal better with complex challenges.

These imbalances – and many others – affect the performance of the team throughout the life of a venture. However, they particularly matter at key inflection points. When a venture's funding is approved to scale it to the next level, it is important to ask if the team is growth-curve ready. This is an execution risk that Corporate Explorers can anticipate and manage. It also requires some self-awareness from the Corporate Explorer. Have they hired people in their own image and is that the cause of the problem? It is common for Corporate Explorers and entrepreneurs to rely on people with whom they are personally close, who share the same vision, but who may share the same biases. They need to look in the mirror, ask whether this may be a cause of the problem.

Just knowing that human behavior tends to align people with different roles on a growth curve is useful insight for Corporate Explorers. They can use it straightaway to make decisions about the venture team. They can also add rigor to these choices by using a tool like the AEM-Cube to assess the team. Assessing the team at kick-off, annually, or just when problems occur, can create an ongoing dialogue about how the team's composition fits its current task.

APPLICATION CASE STUDY: CHANGING HORSES MIDSTREAM

In 2007, one of the world's leading healthcare application developers set up an ambitious innovation program. The company realized that its innovation capabilities were lagging those of its competitors. The company was facing the classic challenge that many leading corporates face: an overload of bureaucracy and regulations stifling disruptive innovation and hindering change. The company set up a program to create new ventures to be run as independent startups to prevent them from getting bogged down by the corporate machine.

(Continued)

One initiative was to develop and bring to market a digital pathology scanner. In 2007, the field of digital and computational pathology was still in its infancy, and this venture was set up to launch a truly disruptive product. Most pathology analyses were completed in an analog manner, meaning that people had to physically examine the samples one by one. This was a slow and time-consuming process, and sharing the results was even more difficult. The scanner was designed to process hundreds of samples automatically at the same time and share them globally for further analyses, when necessary, dramatically decreasing the time, energy, and costs of these analyses.

The director of the company's human resources appointed an innovation manager to help make this vision a reality. The innovation manager showed all the characteristics of a true Corporate Explorer: he understood the corporate culture of the company, and he knew how to navigate it and leverage the available resources. At the same time, he was also familiar with the needs of a disruptive startup in terms of people, communication, and culture.

His first job was, of course, to outline the startup's strategy. This was followed by locating available resources within the company, both in terms of finances and know-how. He also needed to find the right mix of people to navigate the startup into the next phases of its growth cycle.

The Corporate Explorer used AEM-Cube to gather data on the team members chosen for this initial phase. As the team develops the technical prototype, this phase demands a strong exploratory focus. The Corporate Explorer staffed the team with people strongly oriented to exploration.

As the AEM-Cube predicted, the team performed excellently. The scanner was tested and delivered on time, and initial feedback was very positive. Everything seemed to be going great.

Unfortunately, the project took a turn for the worse as it moved to scaling. In 2011, there was a sudden rise in customer complaints. Execution stalled, and tensions started to grow within the team.

How could all this happen after an extended period of highly successful strategic execution, especially given that this was practically the same team that had performed so well in the beginning? How could this team suddenly start to falter without any clear warning signs?

The answer was that the strategic challenge had changed but the team had not. As the business scaled, there was a shift toward production, delivery, and customer service. Instead of a team of exploratory leaders focused on content, the venture needed more optimizers capable of bringing structure and repeatability.

A new AEM-Cube assessment, unfortunately, confirmed this assertion: the team's strategic diversity was the same as at the inception. It was still staffed mostly with people with a strong exploration dimension, but very few, if any, people with strong optimizer dimension. In other words, the team's existing strategic diversity didn't correspond to the venture's current growth phase.

Going back to our soccer analogy, this is like asking a group of pure strikers to focus completely on defense. It's not that they cannot do it; it's that they will perform suboptimally in an area they do not feel particularly comfortable in or passionate about.

The group of exploratory, content-focused professionals were now asked to be patient and sociable with customers. They had to deal with political undercurrents within their client's companies. They were asked to deliver results in the areas they had little experience in and did not feel energized by. And even though they were trying, results were inevitably suboptimal. No wonder that people were becoming frustrated and angry!

Running a new AEM-Cube assessment has allowed the Corporate Explorer to "change horses midstream," so to speak. By making necessary corrections in the team's staffing, the misalignment between the team's strategic objectives and its strategic diversity has been corrected. The venture's strong performance soon returned.

There are three lessons for Corporate Explorers from this case.

First, change is inevitable. As a new venture grows and matures, each new growth phase brings its specific challenges and priorities.

Second, strategic diversity matters. It is critical for a Corporate Explorer to know what challenges the venture is currently facing, and which specific member of the team can contribute to meet each challenge.

Third, a Corporate Explorer should always be ready to change a winning team. Once the venture successfully completes its current growth phase, new challenges and priorities will emerge. Only by adjusting the composition of its team can the venture succeed in the next phase.

CHAPTER 17

Leading High-Stakes Conversations: Getting the Senior Team Onboard

Alexander Pett and Kristin von Donop

SENIOR TEAM COMMITMENT

Getting and sustaining senior-level commitment to innovation is at the top of every Corporate Explorer's list of key success factors. The typical corporate approach to this is to have a good-news story to tell – positive customer feedback, technical achievements on the product development roadmap, new partners signed up. However, the good-news story approach is a trap. It lowers tension in the senior team, making it harder to talk about substantive issues, resolve tough problems, and get authentic agreement.

Corporate Explorers need to be able to create productive tension in senior teams so that when they have tough issues – like resource conflicts with core business units, channel conflicts, budgetary constraints – they can discuss and resolve them openly.[1] Creating productive tension means understanding enough about conversation dynamics to know when tension is lacking and having a repertoire of interventions to make it happen. This chapter offers guidance on how to do this.

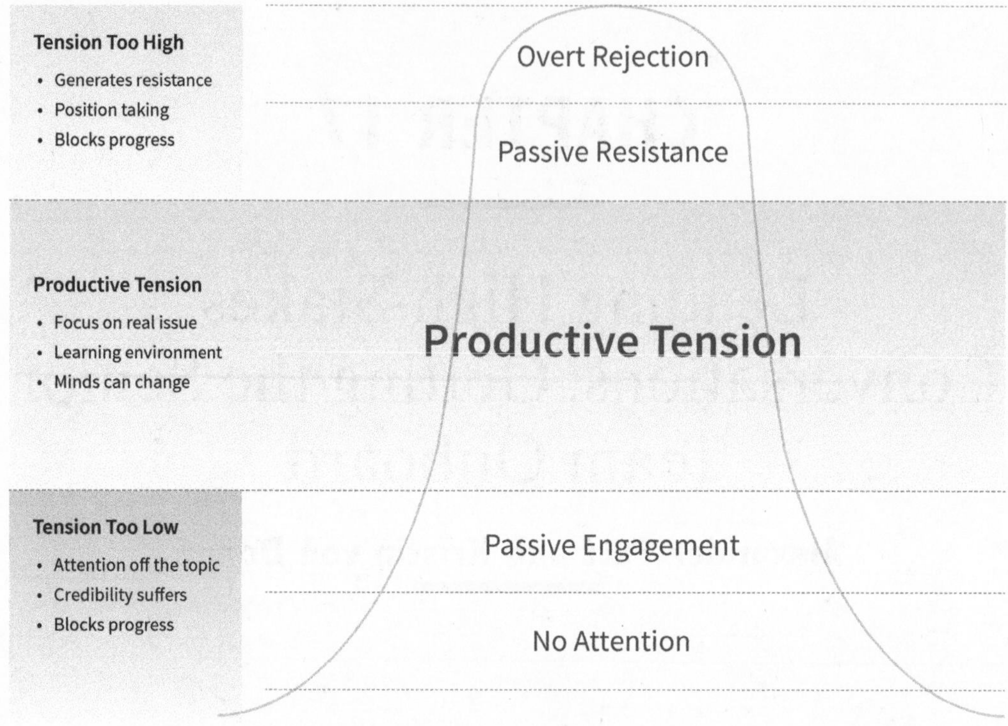

Figure 17.1 Understanding productive tension.

VALUE OF TENSION

Anyone with experience presenting to a senior management team remembers leaving the meeting dissatisfied. They were listening and seemed to support what were you saying, but somehow you are just not sure. They were very polite, although they asked some tough questions; somehow, they seemed to be pulling their punches. It was like the real conversation was not happening. In the weeks that followed, it became clear you did not really have the senior team support that you were seeking.

This is a common problem for Corporate Explorers who are often pushing the boundaries of corporate policies, looking for exceptions to rules, taking the company into new market areas, or developing different capabilities. There is also a high probability that there is real conflict between what the new venture wants to do and the interests of members of the senior team. The sales leadership may be nervous about the new venture approaching customers. Business units may protest that they are encroaching on their turf. Marketing may want to control the new venture's brand identity.

Few of the issues faced by the Corporate Explorer get solved by having a low-tension conversation that fails to address the real issues. They also do not get solved if there is a full-on argument, with shouting and lots of emotion. In Figure 17.1, you can see that low tension can lead to passive engagement or no engagement at all. Passive engagement is a challenge because it can look like positive engagement. Low tension typically means that there is no real attention to your proposal. High tension is problematic at two levels: passive resistance can look like engagement, but opposing views can remain hidden, or resistance can be created in the way the conversation is being handled. With overt high tension, it is more obvious there is disagreement, which will prevent progress unless handled appropriately.

What the Corporate Explorer needs to do is hold a conversation in what we call a zone of productive or constructive tension. This is the zone where there is sufficient candor to name the most important issues and then work on them openly, no matter how contentious they might be. There are three key skills needed for productive tension. You need to *create* tension, *control* it in the discussion, and *close* effectively. We provide some how-to recommendations for creating a zone of productive tension, controlling this zone, and closing off conversation in a way that maximizes momentum (Figure 17.2).

The techniques are practical and should be useful to any Corporate Explorer. However, applying them can be harder than it seems. Most adult human behavior is driven unconsciously. We do not think moment to moment about how we are going to act; it's reflexive. Under pressure this reflex becomes stronger, and the gap between what we intend to do and what we actually does widen. As a result, despite our good intentions, we do not achieve the outcomes we want. So, in addition to the positive advice, I describe some of the pathologies that can emerge and how to recognize them so you can intervene and change the course.

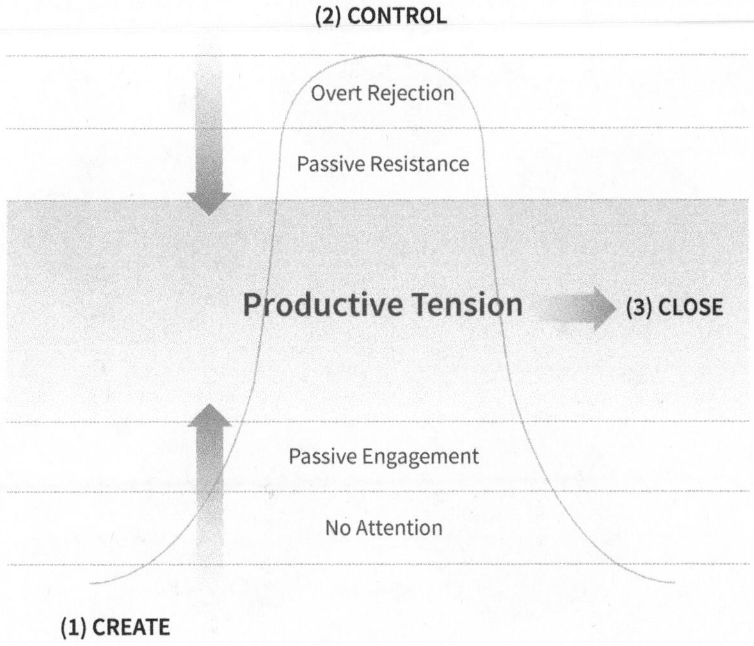

Figure 17.2 Adjusting tension to maintain dialogue.

CREATE: GETTING THE CONVERSATION INTO THE ZONE OF PRODUCTIVE TENSION

Your first task is to create a "frame" for the conversation that makes it possible to include the high-tension topics (Figure 17.3). Start by having a clear answer to the question, "What is our conversation for?" It is for exploring possibilities, enrolling colleagues into a new initiative, working through tough trade-offs, or creating agreements for investment or action.

State your purpose so your stakeholders know how to be involved. "The purpose of this conversation is to get your agreement on. . ." Or, "The purpose of this conversation is for me to ask for your help in addressing some barriers to progress that have emerged." Frame the "for" right out of the gate. This gets the attention of a group, sets expectations for the sort of conversation that you are going to have and, most importantly, why you need to have it with this group specifically. Tension falls if the people in the room do not understand what is personally required of them. It is easy for a Corporate Explorer to focus on what matters to them, rather than attending to the question of why it matters to the audience What is at stake for them?

See the framing as an equilateral triangle. At the base is all the knowledge and insight that supports the conclusion you want the stakeholders to understand. It is easy to fall into the trap of framing the conversation backward and start with these data. Productive tension

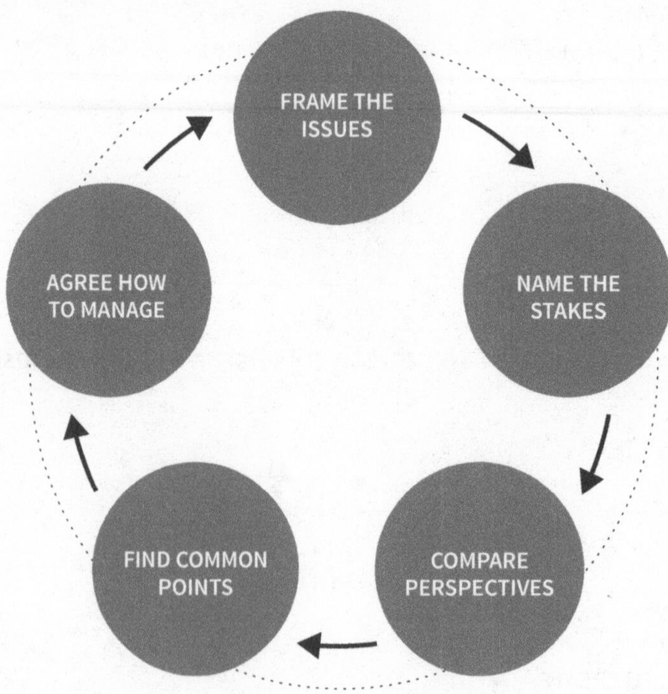

Figure 17.3 Create tension.

requires you to start with the point of the triangle and expand briefly. Explain the "what" of your proposal in a sentence and then illustrate briefly "how" you formed this perspective. This sets you up to describe the implications of your data – "What if we do and what if we don't?" This needs to include not only the implications that matter to you, but also those that connect with the primary concerns of your stakeholders. How will it affect the strategic priorities that matter to those in the meeting?

Having framed the issue, you need to invite comments so that you can compare perspectives on the problem: "How do you see these issues?" or "What is your perspective?" This step sounds simple, but it is the most likely to be skipped as our human reflex action takes over and causes us to overstate our opinions. Corporate Explorers are, by their nature, usually heavily invested in the proposal, with all the data on hand. The risk is they overshare, and the attempt at framing is a long, slow introduction, resulting in low tension in the room, which leaves executive team members in varying states from listening to switching off. Critically, the moment of productive tension is lost, with the credibility of the proposal potentially undermined by the quality of the introduction.

Once you have the issues on the table, it is possible to find common points, areas of shared analysis, and focus the discussion on how to manage disconnects between the different needs. Now, you are in a high-tension conversation about the real issues.

CONTROL: KEEPING THE CONVERSATION IN THE ZONE OF PRODUCTIVE TENSION

Once you have tension, you need to manage it, using different techniques to both increase and decrease the tension to stay in the productive zone. The most obvious challenge is giving the discussion a clear focus. Senior leadership team members are typically confident in their own opinions and like to share their thinking. This means that there will be many opinions in the room at once. It is easy for the Corporate Explorer to lose control of the discussion as it becomes "cluttered" with too many issues to resolve, and it drifts toward low tension because the conversation does not have a clear purpose.

One tool that can help in this situation is the Four-Player Model, which describes the dynamics of a conversation (Figure 17.4). The Harvard psychologist David Kantor identified four different actions that happen in a meeting.[2] He goes as far as to say that these are the "only" things that can happen.

These actions are: *move,* a proposal or an assertion with action; *follow*, the completion or support of the move; *oppose,* a challenge to the move; and *bystand,* a comment or question about how the discussion is being organized. Here are examples in simple terms:

Move – It is time for lunch.

Follow – I agree.

Oppose – No, we have more work to do.

Bystand – We can vote on it or just follow the loudest voice in the room!

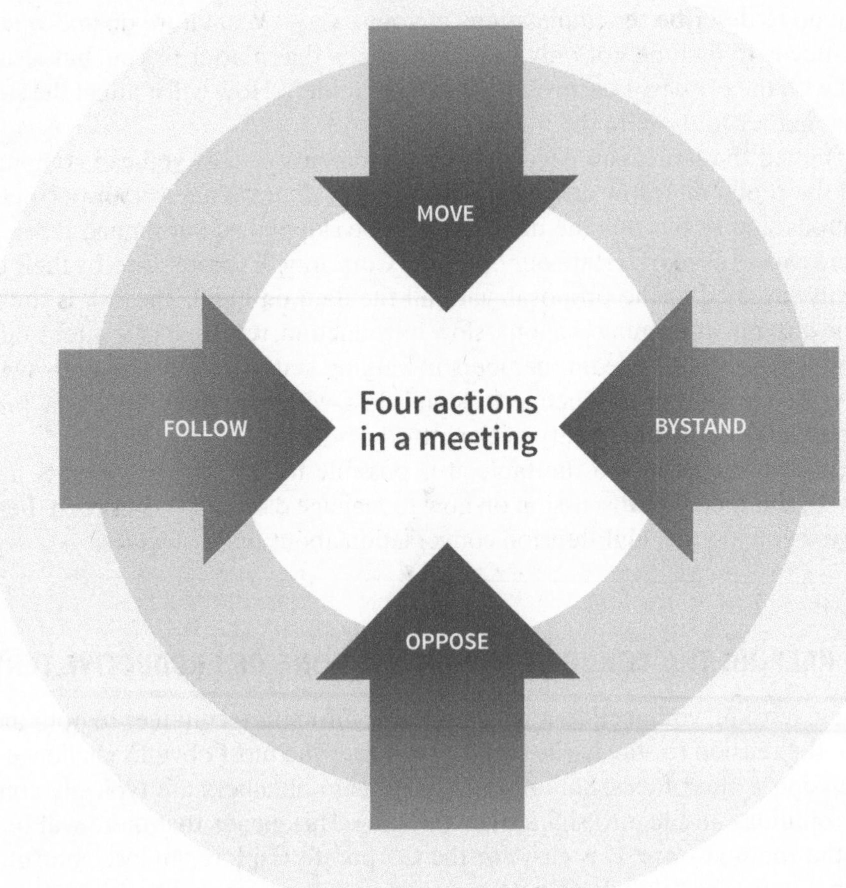

Figure 17.4 Four-Player Model.

You can increase tension in the room by making a move that names the issues, for example, "We need to address the conflict that exists over account ownership between the sales team and the new venture. What do you think?" This invites someone to state an oppose.

Oppose is vital to your success. Before you can create genuine agreement, you first need to surface all areas of real or potential disagreement so that you can seek common ground and resolve the issues. The Corporate Explorer needs to move between both modes, ensuring that the tension remains high enough to get the real issues discussed. Corporate Explorers need to demonstrate openness to disagreement, displaying the learning mindset that they use to lead business experiments.

Inquiry reduces tension by opening the conversation to alternative viewpoints – seek to understand the oppose, to find out what sits behind the opposition so that you can find a way to bridge the gap between alternative perspectives. Remember, to create an agreement, you need to find the disagreement in the room first so it can be dealt with. If a stakeholder disagrees with a proposal, Corporate Explorers need to be genuinely interested in the concern, ready to explore it with open questions so that they can understand concerns.

The alternative to this is "position-taking," where the Corporate Explorer stakes out their position and shows no interest in the alternative perspectives. The discussion gets stuck in move–oppose, with people taking sides in the discussion. A lack of openness can also trigger passive or active resistance. If stakeholders don't feel heard, they will make their case more assertive, risking to increase the tension. People can usually handle being disagreed with, but they object to not being listened to.

If you get stuck in either situation, the best path of action is to "bystand" by calling out what is happening. "We are stuck, I have not properly understood your objection and I am trying to sell you on my point of view because I am deeply vested in success. Can we start again? I would like to better understand your objection to what I propose." It can be a high-stakes play, but it is the one that is more likely to reduce the tension in the moment and thereby open the possibility for resolving issues productively.

You can quickly diagnose what is happening in a conversation by counting how many questions get asked and how many are answered. When these numbers are low, that implies the conversation is stuck in move–oppose; there is no real dialogue happening. You can change this dynamic by checking with the questioner, "What do you think when you hear my answer?" or "To what extent have I answered your question?" Explorers need to be acutely sensitive to hearing and responding directly to questions. They are usually in a lower power position in the room, and with many questions coming at once key points from potentially sympathetic stakeholders can go missing. This is high-stakes stuff that is not done as well as we like to think. In one executive team meeting, I counted 80 separate questions asked of Corporate Explorers; only 38 got an answer.

CLOSING TENSION

The goal of a meeting with a senior leadership team is to resolve a matter of importance, which means getting to closure on an action. However, if you try to jump to a conclusion too quickly, then you risk getting the inauthentic close that I described at the beginning of the chapter. Often, in the face of a disagreement, we can simply jump to the action stage to try and get the proposal "across the line." It is like a sudden rush for the touch line. This action often results in too-high tension because it appears dismissive to those who were challenging the proposal. High tension at this moment usually generates resistance and can undermine the credibility of the presenter.

The discipline is to not jump ahead to force commitment and change, but to engage stakeholders in recognition of the value of the proposals and to deal with the alternative or additional points of view early and openly. Premature moves to action tend to stall progress, often spiking the tension too high.

Think of a conversation as traveling along a path with distinct stops or turns along the route. You can label these as clarity, recognition, commitment, and change.

- **Clarity:** Are you and your stakeholders clear on the purpose of the conversation in a way that creates productive tension?
- **Recognition:** Have you created recognition of the proposal – its value and implications – and worked through differences?
- **Commitment:** Have you got agreement for a proposal? Have you tested for buy-in, identified the barrier to progress at this point so they can be tackled early?
- **Change:** What action is needed to make progress?

The final recommendation relates to the change phase of the dialogue. Make sure expectations and commitments are clear between you and your stakeholders. Be explicit about what is going to happen and when; who is involved; and when you will next present to or engage your stakeholders. It sounds so simple, but this act of closing is crucial to ensure expectations are aligned, and it helps your credibility.

Failure to confirm to specific actions, such as who has responsibility for these actions and when this will return to the team, can be a missed opportunity that means a loss of momentum or even reputation. If you return to the leadership team and fail to show the progress the stakeholders were expecting, it could be because the expectations had not been aligned at the previous meeting.

PRODUCTIVE TENSION TECHNIQUES

The task of keeping senior leaders aligned with the work of a new venture never ends. The same is true for entrepreneurs. They must work tirelessly to raise capital, then to keep different funders aligned, even when they have conflicting agendas. The life of a Corporate Explorer is different and, perhaps, more complicated, but the fundamental need of aligning funders is the same.

Corporate Explorers who learn to manage these relationships with authenticity and transparency are much more likely to succeed than those who deploy the "good-news" story. They must raise the level of productive tension so that senior leaders are reminded how easy it is to unintentionally kill explore. The trick is to do this without sounding like a spoiled teenager, always complaining about not getting enough attention! Here are techniques that Corporate Explorers have used to raise the level of tension in their conversations with senior managers:

1. **Self-assessment:** For example, one Corporate Explorer gave his senior leadership team a *Harvard Business Review* article that listed six key success factors for growth initiatives. He then invited them to self-assess the organization's support for the new venture team. The senior leaders found the same weaknesses that the Corporate Explorer had diagnosed. But because it was the team's assessment, they were less defensive than they might have been if he had just presented the analysis himself.
2. **Experiment rituals.** Use a rigorous approach to experiments in which the new venture states clear falsifiable hypotheses (for example, customers will buy our new product at this price). Then, instead of reviewing data, you review how many hypotheses were proved true or false. This contrasts with the usual approach of just presenting data that are supportive or confirming of your proposals. It makes conversations more transparent and transforms review meetings into an open forum for confronting barriers to progress.
3. **Advisory boards:** Bring outsiders into the mix by forming an external advisory board for the venture. These could be leaders from target customers, potential partners, entrepreneurs, or retired executives without a stake in the outcome of the Corporate Explorer's work. Their independence will allow them to raise issues that an insider might struggle to.
4. **Peer comparisons:** Although "best practices" are anathema to explore, an external benchmarking review of your situation (in comparison with peer companies) can get previously undiscussable issues on the table with senior leaders.
5. **Education workshops:** Executive education sessions can create a forum for lifting managers out of the day-to-day routine and inviting them to confront bigger issues. At IBM, the Strategic Leadership Forum was a vehicle for aligning middle management support for the Emerging Business Opportunity program.
6. **Retrospectives:** Instead of allowing the new business to be reviewed with the same cadence as existing businesses, make sure that the big issues are always on the table. One client uses a strict 30-day sprint approach to implementing experiments, which brings the project teams and sponsors together for evidence-led reviews.

These are all techniques real Corporate Explorers have used. The power to create, control, and close productive tension is in your hands and with it the ability to secure and sustain senior leadership support.

APPLICATION CASE STUDY: STORY OF AN INTERNATIONAL ENERGY COMPANY TOLD BY THE CTO

In a mature and very successful energy company, we faced a predictable future in our core business, but perhaps with diminishing returns – not enough to threaten our existence but certainly enough to consider alternative future scenarios. It was decided that an innovation division was needed to pursue opportunities that were adjacent or alternative, using the skills honed through many decades of core business success. This new division was also designed to provide a high level of service to the core business.

The Problem

The problem started with this separation. The core faced a predictable, but, from a certain perspective, unexciting future, and a bright new expanding division created the perfect environment for high-tension interactions. Only by addressing this tension would both divisions be able to flourish and support one another. However, as will be explained, the classic process of transformation didn't alone resolve the inherent tensions. We faced issues of low productive tension resulting in no real progress being made, and high-tension problems of inappropriate lines being drawn and defended. Too late, I began to operate on productive tension. The transformation timeline was too long, and we lacked genuine stakeholder alignment in the early stages by not more explicitly surfacing disagreement and working through it.

Transformation Phase 1

The first phase of the transformation was to translate the Mission Vision Purpose of the company into the role of the new division, which was then shared with key stakeholders. Straight away, players in the core business showed high-tension moves. I misdiagnosed this reaction as being caused by a need for more guidance, so I accelerated the next step of the organizational design to include some guiderails.

These guiderails included the principles of organization design that the new division would adhere to, including the need for "a license to operate" provided by the core site. I innocently believed that the subject was a topic for the next phase. This new guidance was interpreted as applying more control and not as recognizing the concerns of these site-based stakeholders. Had I acknowledged at this point that the initial discussion had gone from a low-tension presentation to a high-tension complex move, I would have dwelt on the fundamental topic and raised acceptance of the division's responsibility rather than focusing on a need for more clarity on the license to operate.

Transformation Phase 2

In the second phase of the transformation, the guiderails were established in a good collaborative environment, where all players made simple transactions (such as "I don't think that centralization is the end ambition," or "I agree it should follow when it adds value through clear accountability or efficiency").The design principles were agreed upon, with an assertion that centralization would be pursued only where it adds value through ensuring clarity of roles or from cost efficiency.

In the initial reaction, behaviors were good and collaborative, and players were making simple noncomplex transactions. However, later reflection showed that this phase was too low tension, and the real issues were not being addressed. Each committee member saw their own idea presented as the solution, because the plans didn't define the proposal clearly enough.

Transformation Phase 3

In the third stage of the transformation, we focused on organizational design and RASCI Responsibility Matrix (RASCI). So, following the agreement on scope in Phase 1 and the rules of engagement in Phase 2, Phase 3 sees the organization being designed in parallel with the RASCI descriptions. Again, it was a very collaborative environment, with simple transaction questions and answers. Now, it appears we have full agreement, but while none of the tension in Phase 1 has reappeared, it also has not been addressed and was now spilling over into other areas.

Transformation Phase 4

Phase 4 was about execution. Now, as the new division started its first steps on its value-adding journey – creating processes and indicators, recruiting, and job evaluating – the cracks started to show.The core began to hunker down and protect its boundaries, and the new division created strategies on how to penetrate these bunkers and trenches.Tensions were suddenly high, and behaviors became complex.

In phase 1 the low-tension discussion meant that the issues in the team were unaddressed and so resurfaced as high-tension disagreement in Phase 4 with the team members retreating to their silos.

Our Solution

We created a test environment for the two divisions to experience the new relationship, which led to the belief in the value of cooperation and shared results. Five high-profile projects were selected, teams from both divisions allocated, and shared project success criteria were agreed.

For example, an R&D recycling facility was to be tested: it was targeted to become 60% more capital efficient than the previous solution and markedly more flexible.The core players could see the tangible benefit of being included, and the new division players saw progress on their specific project. Now the tensions were not too low as something tangible was happening, and yet not too high, either, as both sides saw the benefits in real terms of the collaboration.

(Continued)

Behaviors experienced were now follow–move or oppose–move or even more simple single moves. Tangible real discussions were held on the need for a license to operate and the need for a more transparent supporting structure.

My Leadership Reflection

Due to my lack of productive tension we lost three to six months, and unhealthy tensions grew markedly, strengthening silos and undermining actions. In the end, only by creating a test environment in which we also ran theoretical "test drives" could we create the right productive tension to get all involved to discuss openly, surface disagreements, and work on creating alignment.

Observing the high-tension start phase and the low-tension mid-phase should have sounded the warning bells. Without observing these tension states in the transformation, we would still be struggling with progress. Recognizing high tension is somewhat easier: emotions are high, moves are complex, red lines are drawn. However, more importantly, the low-tension periods were more damaging to the transformation. Spotting the low tension is harder as this can look like a well-behaving team. Creating alignment, therefore, requires intentionally creating and staying in the productive-tension band.

CHAPTER 18

Leadership Movement: Enrolling Others in the Work of Transformation

Kristin von Donop and Yaniv Garty

EXPLORER AS CHANGE AGENT

Corporate Explorers often start as lone advocates of change inside an organization. They see a potential area of growth and champion building the capabilities to pursue it. They cannot do this alone. Implementing innovation and change on a scale relies on others adopting new ways of working to succeed in the future. The Corporate Explorer's task is to generate excitement and galvanize action about new opportunities. We refer to this as a leadership movement: getting others to join and to create the future today by figuring out what is needed and how to build the capabilities for long-term success.

This chapter is a guide to building a leadership movement that cultivates a shared commitment to success. The key to this approach is starting with early adopters and then involving more people to build a movement that implements change at scale. Corporate Explorers are enrolling people in the work of changing the organization's processes, skills, and most importantly, its behaviors.

BUILD A MOVEMENT

In Mark Twain's classic nineteenth-century novel, Tom Sawyer is given the chore to paint a white picket fence. It was a daunting task for a boy who would rather be playing with others. He figures out how to get his friends and other kids in the neighborhood to help him get the job done. Tom did not have a command structure to achieve his goal. He enrolled people in a movement committed to realizing a shared purpose.

This is the toughest task for the Corporate Explorer: to get others to help align the organization around the new venture. As a new unit or venture starts to scale, Corporate Explorers move from a sideshow to real competition for resources and attention inside organizations. Because they demand people to work and think differently, they encounter resistance to change, making it harder to win support. The demands of day-to-day work exert far too strong a force to overcome with persuasion alone. People may listen to a PowerPoint pitch, but this does not lead to change.

Just like Tom Sawyer, Corporate Explorers need to multiply their energy by enlisting others in the work. This is what we mean by leadership movement: a semiformal group of leaders that carry the innovation message, acting together to experiment with new approaches, and implementing what they learn.

A leadership movement is similar to a social movement that mobilizes a diverse group to unleash energy to change the *status quo*. Both movements engage a broad network of people with different expertise, gender, and seniority to achieve a shared goal. They take a collaborative approach, anticipating that everyone recruited has something to add. That does not mean movements have to be consensus-driven, only that problems are more effectively addressed by bringing together multiple perspectives.

Importantly, movements take organizations on a change journey. It is not an event. There is a beginning, a middle, and an end in every journey. These are not staged one-off "leadership conferences." Movements should not be overdesigned or -produced, but instead emphasize discovery and learning. The secret to building momentum is to allow space for people to self-organize so that they take ownership of co-creating the future.

There are three primary steps to building a leadership community: enroll the membership, engage the community, and embrace the resistance.

ENROLL MEMBERSHIP

A movement needs a cause, a shared project, or goal to achieve. The first chapter of this book described how a strategy manifesto can provide a statement of intent. An alternative is to provide a shared methodology or language for change. In the early 2000s, IBM built a leadership movement behind its transformation into a solutions company using a language for strategy execution that it learned from Professors Mike Tushman and Charles O'Reilly.[1]

Then, a movement needs to recruit people to the cause. Start by making a list of all key groups of players (for example, managers in a function or unit); select the people who may sign on as an active ally (Table 18.1). Some of these will be peers or leaders with a similar perspective and set of interests. These are the Corporate Explorer's *allies*, people they can rely on to be active in providing support. Allies have influence and authority in

Table 18.1 Roles in the leadership movement.

ROLE	DEFINITION	PURPOSE
Allies	Peer or manager with influence and authority	Help solve problems for the Corporate Explorer.
Advocates	Peer or manager	Speak positively about the venture to others.
Ambassadors	Peer or manager	Engage with blockers to try to resolve difficulties.
Angels	Senior executive/sponsor with ability to secure resources	Authorize the new venture, hold the Corporate Explorer accountable.

the organization. They provide access to resources, and they can help solve problems on Corporate Explorers' behalf.

Then, there are *advocates*. These are people who will speak positively about what you are doing and why it is important for business. Reputation is a precious thing for a new venture. It is easy to earn a reputation for being profligate with money or high-profile failures. You may code these as learning, but gossip can quickly turn them into liabilities, unless actively countered by advocates. Help your advocates understand the ambition and ask them to tell the real story. Reward them with your gratitude and by being helpful in return. These relationships help you endure the low points and celebrate the achievements.

Corporate Explorers also need *ambassadors*, people who have relationships with senior managers, particularly those who may not currently support the innovation and change agenda. Finally, and most importantly, Corporate Explorers need to find an *angel,* someone who is willing to commit resources to back the project.

However, even when the angel is the CEO, that does not guarantee success. There are too many examples of CEO-mandated transformations that fail because they elicit an allergic reaction from the organizations that they lead. Only founder CEOs have the power to direct their organizations; most are just the person with the most influence. There are silent killers in the organization who can frustrate any top-down mandate for change. You need to build a movement around the transformation goals to overcome organizational inertia, but you cannot direct people to change.

ENGAGE COMMUNITY

In marketing, we talk about finding "early adopters" for a new product. That is what allies, advocates, angels, and ambassadors are for the leadership movement. These are the people who buy into the movement early on and give it momentum. It may also be sufficient for some Corporate Explorers, helping them neutralize corporate antibodies sufficiently to make progress. However, many Corporate Explorers have an agenda for a more fundamental shift in the business – such as adopting digital capabilities, experimenting with new business models, becoming customer-centric. Achieving these sorts of goals means engaging a wider community as active participants. That involves giving people a task that they find motivational, that they feel capable of achieving, and have license to accomplish. Here are some examples of ways we and colleagues have helped build leadership movements.

- **Formal, multiday events.** At companies like IBM, Intel, and Analog Devices, we have seen leaders use highly collaborative workshops to transfer ownership of a transformation effort from a group of managers – the Corporate Explorer and their Angel – to a wider community. As in the case from Intel we share below, these workshops have the task of diagnosing the barriers to implementing a strategic ambition and developing a plan to close them.
- **Sprints.** The agile sprint method organizes work in short cycles, which helps balance attention between the day-to-day demands of execution and scaling innovation. It gives small, semi-autonomous teams the license to experiment with new ways of working and to learn which has the most impact; the method also creates accountability to implement changes. The discovery in sprint teams teaches people how to walk the path and transform the way the organization operates. This is vital because what it takes in one organization to transform is different from what is needed in another.
- **Newly hired managers.** Tap into the wisdom of executives with less than two years of tenure with the company. They bring a fresh perspective about what is possible.
- **Cross-business-unit exercise.** Invite colleagues from other parts of the organization to explore new markets or technologies. Engage external experts to stimulate ideas. Focus on soliciting their ideas and feedback about potential growth areas.
- **Learning and development.** Create a training workshop that uses your innovation as a case study and engages the group to identify solutions. Find out who is enthusiastic about the opportunity and how to keep them involved.

A community needs vitality, and that means pruning membership. Support the new people and help them integrate into the community. Pay attention to who is doing work and to those who aren't. Some people may want to be a part of the work but do not commit the time. Avoid letting them "wither on the vine" and instead thank them for their support and keep them updated. They may end up being future advocates. Let them go, and make room for new people to join the work. We will see this work in the Intel case study that follows.

Engage many. As U.S. President Theodore Roosevelt once said, "Force the bystanders to get in the arena."

EMBRACE RESISTANCE

All Corporate Explorers will face resistance—and blockers. This resistance is likely to come from senior managers in the core business, who may need to give up something to help the new venture succeed or who have nothing to gain from its success. Their first reaction may be to protect what they have in case change represents a threat. They do not need to be active saboteurs or opponents to be blockers; this is not about having good or bad intentions.

Identify potential *blockers* by mapping the key stakeholders around the innovation. Map these players based on two criteria (Figure 18.1). The first is their ability to block new ventures or to enable their access to assets and resources. The second is their support for innovation. Unless there is evidence of support, it is better to assume that stakeholders are neutral or even opposing. It is not smart to assume support from someone with the ability to derail the work of the Corporate Explorer and the leadership movement.

Get curious about what blockers are interested in and the nuance of their objections. The more you understand what the blockers are protecting, the more able you are to discover what it would take for them to be invested in the movement's success. Here is an example of the value of curiosity.

A technology team developing an innovative new application at a biopharma company was concerned about what would happen when they engaged their colleagues in regulatory affairs. The application had a clear benefit that would reduce diagnostic uncertainty and monitor treatment efficacy for doctors and patients with debilitating diseases. However, the regulatory unit had a long history of blocking medical-device innovation, and many on the tech team feared involving them too early in the process for fear that the project would be shut down. In the end, the team decided to use the same customer discovery techniques they had deployed in developing their innovation. The members of the team interviewed potential blockers, particularly the head of regulatory affairs, and discovered how hard it was to stay ahead of the evolving government standards for medical software. It was, therefore, easier, given restrictions on the regulatory team's headcount, to oppose than to support such projects. As a result, the tech team on-boarded a member of the regulatory team as an "extended" team member so that that member could learn the intricacies of the regulatory process. The innovation team had to slow down on some plans but ultimately gained a committed advocate and invaluable resource.

Listening to the concerns of blockers helps to unhook us from our own assumptions. When meeting resistance, be curious and engage others. Follow these steps:

- **Identify your assumptions.** What is the story you tell yourself about the opposition to the innovation and changes you see as essential? Make this an empathy exercise. Write your opponents' "jobs to be done," then their gains and pains. Ask your allies

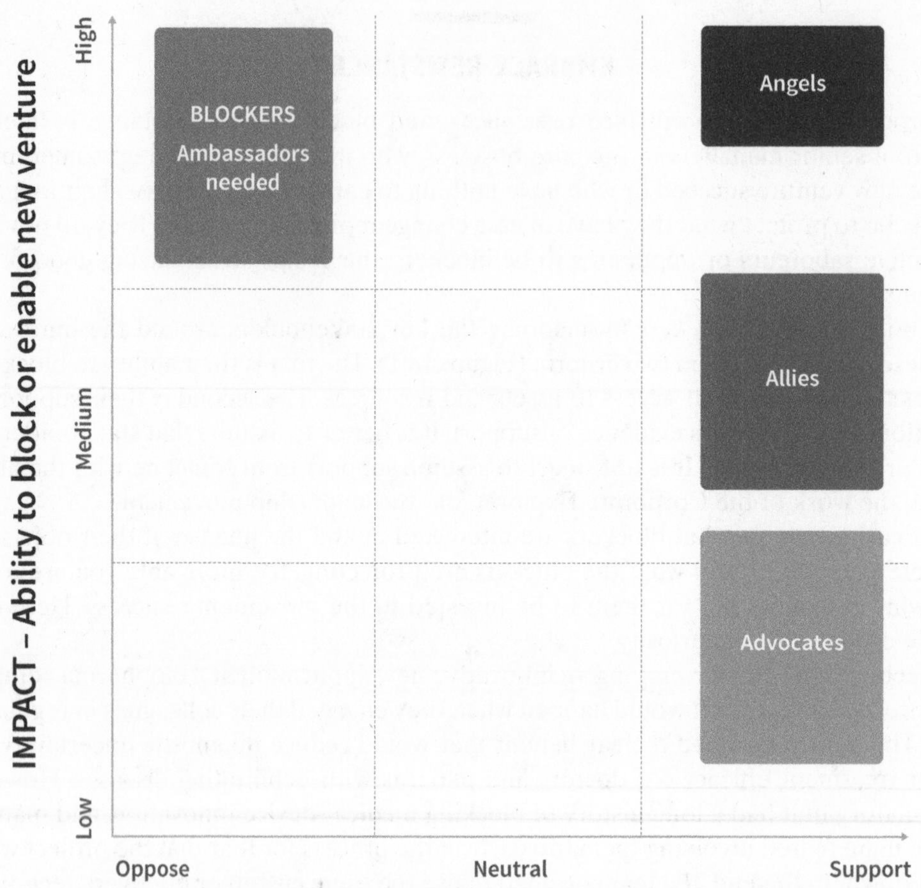

Figure 18.1 Mapping stakeholders.

to share an insight. Find out who influences your opponents' opinions. Add these influencers to your list of important stakeholders.

- **Test your assumptions.** Learn about the pains and gains of the blockers. Discover how it relates or competes with the innovation and change you are advocating. Be open to discovering if there are ways to address their concerns.
- **Enroll the opposition.** Invite blockers to be a part of the discovery, where they can learn how to be successful with you. They may reconsider.
- **Enlist the ambassadors.** Engage the ambassadors when your efforts in enrolling the opposition do not work. Ambassadors are the ones that can describe what you are doing and the logic of the ambition. Their formal or informal authority can help to neutralize the opposers.

TRIGGER A HERD INSTINCT

When you involve a community in the process of change, you create a social movement that signals it is okay to break with legacy approaches. It also creates a container for resistance to surface, be understood, and be addressed. Develop a better understanding of resistance, and you will become more adept at recognizing it and learning how to manage it.

Humans are social animals, highly responsive to the signals about whether they fit into a group. We like to fit into a group. When we see others adopt a behavior, then we like to conform. This is just evolutionary biology, "Humans learned it is safer to belong to a group and not hang out as easy prey waiting to be eaten."[2] A leadership movement makes it safer to adopt the new rules, making it okay to break with convention and adopt a new way of working.

APPLICATION CASE STUDY: INTEL WIRELESS COMMUNICATION SERVICES 2013

How does a semiconductor organization serving the wireless market reinvent itself to meet a 10-fold growth in demand and respond to the challenge of rapid innovation? One approach is to get independent business units to work together to increase the organization's adaptability. That's what happened at Intel's Wireless Connectivity Solutions (WCS).

One of us (Yaniv) was general manager for WCS at the time.

The Challenge

Our chips provide connectivity solutions for a magnitude of segments, with the PC market being the primary one. We have been looking to become the market leader in connectivity, enabling smart and connected devices around the globe, and grow both our top line as well as our operating margins.

We had a clear understanding of where the market was heading and about the products to deliver. We needed to evolve our technology offering and operating model, foster innovation, increase product development, improve product margins, and reduce time to market. The market we were in was about to go through a once-in-a-decade transformation, so a change was imminent if we wanted to succeed in achieving our goals. In a market that involves fierce competition and rapid change, our success depended on adaptability at scale. We needed to proliferate wireless solutions to various technology platforms with the same resources that previously delivered only a few products in the past. At the same time, we had to improve on all performance vectors simultaneously.

It was less clear how we were going to address the magnitude of demand and the technical complexity at the same time.

(Continued)

We were organized in a functional structure with core technology teams matrixed with other teams that implement solutions, take them to the market, and provide services across all projects. We existed within a large corporation and relied on a lot of people who did not directly report into our organization. There were a lot of dotted-line relationships.

We faced an array of challenges. Managers within the functional teams did not respond to the challenges outside their organizations. This created an environment favoring local optimization instead of a united outcome.

This reality troubled me, my chief operating officer, my head of human resources, and a handful of others. We knew we had to integrate the teams to meet rising demand and scale, while fixing our financials, leapfrog on our technology offerings, and serve new markets.

Some of the questions we wrestled with were:

- How do we align methodologies to address the magnitude of technical complexity and high volume and significantly shorten the time to market?
- How do we proliferate the movement across segments and market opportunities?
- How do we develop state-of-the-art technology and products with a stable investment of capacity while looking for opportunities to even reduce the investment profile?
- How do we tackle these questions in a way that strengthens the confidence of our teams to continually evolve?

I knew there was enormous potential for collaboration between the teams inside and outside the organization if they embraced a common goal without knowing the exact details of the journey. We needed to learn by doing to reveal the map.

When I discussed the situation with my direct reports, there was more than some apprehension; people were saying: "We are swapping an engine while the plane is in midair." The unknown was about how to unlock the potential and do this in a way that takes the challenges from their amorphic form into a set of well-defined, cross-organizational solutions.

Phase 1. Align

The first step was to create alignment with my senior team. I told my team we had to accept that we didn't have the answer, and that I don't have all the answers. Some held an old belief that leadership is telling people what to do. Instead, I told them our role is to discover what will work alongside our teams. We needed to unearth and unleash the potential of the collective. This should not be confused with replacing our decision making and creating a high-accountability operation.

After much debate about the challenges, we prioritized five critical gaps to close out of a list of more than 20. The gaps focused on a specific dimension of the product development process. We had to improve how we approached design, verification, integration, managing capacity, and innovation. I selected five leaders to be the executive owners for each of the topics—most, but not all, fully embracing this approach.

Phase 2. Enlist

We selected close to a hundred people from within the organization and supporting teams and assigned them to one of five teams. In addition to our senior team, we included their direct reports, a handful of top change agents, and included some people who were known to be "naysayers" within the organization.

We invited the five teams to a three-day strategic leadership forum to kick off the work. The forum combined large group discussions and team working sessions.

There was a certain degree of cynicism coming into the forum. At first, there were many who wanted the leadership team to tell them what to do. I told them: "If I knew the answer, I wouldn't waste your time here and instead tell you in a short email." Some people took it as a sign of weakness. I told them my job as GM was to prioritize the questions we need to answer and help us address them.

Thanks to the candor of the teams, their analysis brought the inhibitors to the surface. My direct reports and I were not spared their criticism. They told us how we were getting in the way and shared some unkind comments. It was hard to hear but the sincerity was refreshing. They were becoming more comfortable in sharing upward feedback, and that was encouraging. The strategic leadership forum created momentum and focus.

Not too long after we started, the five teams became known as the place to be. The attention these teams got, and the progress they began to make, caught the attention of many. I got inquiries and had to explain to people why they weren't part of the work instead of convincing them to get involved. It was FOMO (fear of missing out) in action.

Phase 3. Sprint

The teams implemented the plans in 90-day sprints. The sprints gave us an iterative approach to experimentation, to run pilots, to fail fast, and scale. It gave us the discipline to try something and learn from our collective successes and failures. It provided a needed structure for instilling change.

We reconvened every 30 days to review progress, share what was learned, discuss challenges, and agree on course corrections. People learned to walk the path of the unknown without being afraid of how it was going to turn out.

I also emphasized the social nature of the solutions. I helped people to be curious when they encountered resistance within their teams and with others in the organization. They needed to face resistance head on, rather than avoid it.

Using the sprints helped us sustain momentum, instill positivity, and create shared accountability for our success. More and more people got involved and it became the place to be if you wanted to work on an organization challenge. We ran sprints for more than 18 months until it became second nature, and there was no longer a need for a structured process.

(Continued)

Phase 4. Impact

We achieved several positive impacts. The teams delivered measurable improvements to our volume, customer satisfaction, product quality, cadence of product introductions, financials, and technology leadership. Over time, some of these KPIs improved by a magnitude of three to more than five, and we eventually outperformed our own goals.

I'm mostly interested in the capability we built. We were having the right conversations about the issues we faced. We transformed our DNA. The most enduring changes were cultural.

The teams went into the trenches together, built chemistry, and developed trust. Team members become more adept at communicating perspectives and concerns. They also learned how to engage and challenge me along the way.

The boundaries between the silos became more permeable. Everyone was looking at the organization as a system and not defending their respective silos. We learned to prevent some of the next challenges from occurring.

Success was contagious. Our attrition decreased and retention was at an all-time high.

These changes lasted for years to come. We learned how to create bigger changes together. We created a broad network of change agents.

Years later, I moved into a different capacity within the organization. Others have also found new career opportunities (mainly within the broader organization). Even a decade later, people within this organization still refer to the same principles earned during our journey. Even people who were not part of the team then use the organizational language we developed and adhere to these same principles as if they had been there.

CHAPTER 19

Organizational Culture: The Silent Killer of Exploration

Charles A. O'Reilly III

CORE AND EXPLORE

Conceptually, the logic of ambidexterity is simple: to be successful, core and explore businesses require different architectures (people, structures, metrics, and culture), so they need to be set up as separate units – one for exploit and another for explore. This is straightforward but not necessarily easy to do in practice. The need to manage different organizational architectures brings with it significant challenges for leaders. Do we have the resources to set up separate units? Can we use different metrics and rewards? Will the existing systems allow us the independence needed to pursue very different strategies (e.g., finance, purchasing, legal, HR)? While these demands are difficult, perhaps the biggest silent killer of ambidexterity and the most difficult challenge for many leaders is the need to develop different cultures across the core and explore units.

The culture needed for success in a mature business typically emphasizes predictability, efficiency, incremental improvement, and compliance with procedures and processes. Being successful in an explore business requires almost the opposite – with an emphasis on autonomy, speed, experimentation, taking risks, and rapid adjustments to changes. The cultures required are completely different. Trying to manage an exploration venture with the culture of a core business is a recipe for failure.[1] How can a leader do both? This chapter illustrates how this can be done – how leaders can shape and change the cultures in their organizations. But to do this we need to begin by being clear about what culture is and what it is not, how it operates, and how leaders can manage it. Once we are clear about these issues, we then illustrate these by showing how Satya Nadella, the CEO of Microsoft, has been able to change the culture of a 130,000-person organization.

CULTURE AND CULTURE CHANGE

The evidence for the importance of organizational culture is impressive. A recent study by Deloitte surveyed more than 7,000 executives and reported that 94% believed that culture was important for business success.[2] A similar survey of 2,200 executives conducted by PwC found that 93% said that culture was important – and that executive interest in culture was increasing dramatically.[3] Other studies report similar results.[4] The good news is that there is widespread appreciation among senior managers of the importance of organizational culture as a source of competitive advantage.

The bad news is that these studies also highlight a serious problem with the management of culture. For instance, only 19% of the Deloitte study respondents believed that their organization had the right culture and 96% of the PwC participants believed that some change to the culture was needed – and less than half the respondents felt that their firm did a good job in managing the culture. A study by the Institute of Corporate Productivity showed that only 15% of companies said that their culture change efforts have been successful.[5] This suggests a paradox: senior executives believe that organizational culture is a critical concern, but most are failing at managing and changing the culture needed to adjust in a fast-changing world. The reason for this disconnect often starts with the abstract ways leaders think about culture. If culture is to be managed and aligned with strategy, we first need to define it in a practical way.

Based on our research and experience, we have a managerially useful way of thinking about organizational culture. Rather than thinking about it as something vague, like values or purpose, a more practical way to think about culture is as a social control system that operates in organizations through the *norms* (or social expectations) that are shared.[6] From this perspective, culture can be seen as *the pattern of behavior that is reinforced by people and systems over time.* This view conceives of culture not as a lofty set of abstract values or something vague like "the glue that holds the organization together" but, rather, as something manageable. It is simply those behaviors that are rewarded formally by systems like money and promotions or informally by the approval of our colleagues. Thinking about culture in this way allows us to diagnose it (understand the existing patterns of behavior), manage it (align it with strategy) and, when needed, change it.

CREATING AND CHANGING CULTURE

If organizational culture is the pattern of behavior defined by norms and values, what can leaders do to shape and change them? There are five common mechanisms or levers that leaders in all strong culture organizations use. These levers are based on the underlying psychology that occurs in settings where there are very clear expectations for the "right" way to behave, making it difficult not to comply.[7] These five key levers (the LEASH model) include: (1) leader actions, (2) employee involvement, (3) aligned rewards, (4) stories, signals, and vivid illustrations, and (5) HR system alignment. Each of these levers is a way for leaders to send signals to their employees about the pattern of behavior that is needed to execute a particular strategy.

1. *Leader Actions* (Leash)
   Most people want to fit in and be accepted by their group or organization. To do this, they pay attention to their leaders. They listen to what they say and watch what they do. They try to figure out what they think is important so that they can be successful. They note where their bosses spend time, what questions they ask, what they like and dislike, and what they see as high priorities. They use this information to decide how to act, what to pay attention to and what to ignore, and how to be seen as a good employee. In this sense, leaders are signal generators communicating to the organization, which in turn helps employees interpret how they should act. When leaders are relentless and consistent in how they behave and in sending the same message, employees quickly learn how to act. Leader behavior and communication is the first, and perhaps most important, lever for leading culture.[8] The Institute of Corporate Productivity study of culture change cited earlier found that in 89% of the successful change efforts, the CEO was the champion and provided the time and resources needed to make it successful.[9]
2. *Employee Involvement* (lEash)
   Strong culture leaders typically encourage social activities and ceremonies to build ties among organizational members. They emphasize intrinsic as well as extrinsic rewards (being a part of the group is a reward itself) and use group approval to signal group membership. They may even involve families, friends, and clients in these activities. The underlying psychology is what is referred to as *incremental commitment*: every time we make a choice to behave in a certain way, we become invested and increasingly feel a sense of ownership – especially when choices are visible to others.[10] This increases psychological ownership. For example, at Microsoft there is a three-day annual company-wide hackathon in which more than 18,000 people participate. At First Republic Bank, a strong culture company, there are three-day semi-annual Culture Carrier Roundtables in which a cross-section of employees participate and become cultural ambassadors reinforcing the company's customer-centric culture. Participation in shaping the culture increases our commitment to it.
3. *Aligned Reward Systems* (leAsh)
   Few people would disagree about the fact that what gets measured and rewarded gets done. This is true for the behaviors that define a company's culture. Are the behaviors needed for the culture really being rewarded – or are leaders talking about what's important and rewarding something else entirely? Leaders in strong culture organizations ensure that the reward system is precisely aligned with the

expected behavior. Clearly money is an important motivator, but it is not a very good way to shape culture. Instead, leaders in strong culture firms are more likely to use recognition, approval, status, and promotion to signal compliance with the norms. Sometimes these symbolic rewards (e.g., employee of the month, certificates of appreciation) can seem trivial, but when they are awarded with sincerity, they can act as powerful reinforcement of the culture. The big risk in many organizations is that the formal reward system (e.g., money and promotion) may not be aligned with the desired behaviors. When leaders claim, for example, that teamwork or innovation is important but employees see others who are not team players getting ahead, or if those who try to innovate and fail are punished, then they quickly form the belief that their leaders are either out of touch with reality or, worse, manipulative.

4. *Stories, Signals, and Symbols* (leaSh)
   Strong culture organizations typically are very clear in communicating how they expect people to behave, sometimes even signaling that the organization is not for everyone, and perhaps only special people will succeed (e.g., "The few. The proud. The Marines."). These messages are relentlessly communicated through stories that provide vivid and emotional illustrations of employees whose attitudes and behavior exemplify the culture. They celebrate these individuals and often make heroes of them. For example, for the past five years at Microsoft the regular Friday senior leadership team meeting always includes a story of a Microsoft employee who did something extraordinary that reflected the cultural values of a growth mindset ("researcher of the amazing"). Other organizations use phrases, slogans, or terms that are special to the organization and reinforce membership and inclusion (e.g., "Googlers," "All for one and one for all"). These symbolic actions signal to employees what the culture looks like.
5. *HR System Alignment* (leasH)
   The final lever for creating and changing culture is a carefully aligned HR system that recruits, selects, trains, rewards, and promotes people who behave consistently with the cultural norms. For example, strong culture companies often have multiple steps in their recruitment processes (e.g., Google, Southwest, Bridgewater, and Cypress Semiconductor). New employees are selected based as much (or more) on their fit with the firm's cultural values and behaviors as they are on their technical skills or experience for the job. Then, employees are explicitly trained in the new expected behaviors. Those who deliver results and fit the culture are rewarded and promoted. Those who perform well but don't fit the culture are eliminated.

These five mechanisms are based on the idea that to shape culture leaders need to send strong, consistent signals about what attitudes and behaviors are expected. By consistently sending the same messages about expected behaviors, getting people involved, providing vivid illustrations of the culture, and visibly selecting, socializing, and rewarding those who live the values, leaders help employees understand what it takes to succeed. Over time, these expectations can become embedded in the organization such that new employees quickly understand what is expected of them. The power of these mechanisms can be seen in how Microsoft has been transformed over the past few years.

USING THE LEASH MODEL: CULTURE CHANGE AT MICROSOFT

In February 2014, Satya Nadella, a 22-year veteran of Microsoft, was named as its CEO. He inherited a 130,000-person company with a confrontational, highly individualistic, political, and internally competitive culture that feared failure. Microsoft was far removed from its glory years and headed toward irrelevance. Although profitable, each of the company's three core businesses (Office, Windows, and server software) was under existential threat from the shift to mobile devices, cloud computing, and the rise of Google and Amazon. Recognizing the cultural challenge, Nadella, in his first address at the 2015 shareholder's meeting, said that "Our ability to change the culture is the leading indicator of our future success."

Since his appointment, Microsoft has been transformed. Its stock price has increased 6× and it became only the second firm to reach a one-trillion-dollar valuation. Nadella, along with his chief people officer, Kathleen Hogan, has led a relentless campaign to transform the culture. Under the banner of a "growth mindset," he has emphasized learning, taking risks, and embracing failure. He put Microsoft's cloud business (Azure) at the heart of this effort, eliminated the Windows division, made Office products available on the cloud (Office 365) and Apple iPad, and integrated sales and engineering.

How did this happen? To show that Microsoft was transformed, let's apply the LEASH model and the five levers described previously. Keep in mind that the underlying mechanism of action – how culture is developed and changed – is based on getting very strong, consistent signals to employees about those behaviors that are needed to execute the firm's strategy and those behaviors that are inconsistent and not desired. Each of the five levers is designed to do this.

1. **Leader Actions**

   Upon being named the new CEO, Nadella needed to signal to both his leadership team and all 130,000 employees that Microsoft would be a different place. Two early signals that this was a new Microsoft was his announcement that Microsoft would provide Office for Apple's iOS and his embrace of open source (Linux) – which the previous CEO, Steve Ballmer, had labeled as a "cancer." His constant message was "mobile first, cloud first." This was an intentional effort to change the culture. He embarked on a nine-month effort to "listen" to the employees and engage them in a process to define the new culture. This included intensive senior leadership team (SLT) discussions, focus groups, town halls, videos, and consultation with experts to identify what needed to change and what didn't. This effort culminated in a meeting of the 180 corporate vice presidents, where 17 teams distilled these data, and resulted in a commitment by the leadership team to a "growth mindset." Nadella then wrote a memo to all 130,000 employees outlining the new approach. He formed a "culture cabinet" to monitor the change effort and suggest further changes. More importantly, he then cascaded this into the organization. This included defining the manager's role as modeling the new culture, coaching subordinates, and caring for them.

2. **Employee Involvement**
   To promote a sense of psychological ownership, Nadella involved employees in dialog meetings, feedback sessions, surveys, offsite meetings, town halls, and daily pulse checks. For instance, focus groups were held with millennials and nonmillennials, current and former employees, engineers and nonengineers, as well as by gender and geography. Kathleen Hogan described this effort as designed to "learn about their experience, the culture they desired, and what they were passionate about preserving from our history, and what we needed to leave behind."[11] The intent was to help identify what needed to change and what didn't, hone the meaning of growth mindset, identify the behaviors that characterized it, provide examples of how it worked or didn't, and offer feedback. This effort also included the use of organizational network analysis to identify the key influencers – and to make sure they were involved in the change effort – often becoming ambassadors for the new culture.
3. **Aligned Rewards**
   The third lever for shaping culture is the use of small rewards to make salient the desired behaviors. Perhaps the most powerful of these was the change in the performance management system from a ranking system in which managers were forced to identify 10% of their employees as low performers and rewarded individuals for undermining their competitors. In its place, they emphasized three dimensions of performance: (1) individual accomplishments, (2) contributions to others, and (3) the ability to leverage others to promote "One Microsoft." This included specifying the behaviors required and changing the metrics from individual to shared measures. For instance, in the new Microsoft, sales were measured not simply on booking revenue but on customer success. People who demonstrated a "growth mindset" were valued, even if they had fallen short in some areas. A new process for promotion to corporate VP was instituted that included a specific "culture interview" to assess how aligned the person was with the culture.
4. **Stories, Symbols, and Signals**
   Beyond management words, actions, and rewards, employees want visible evidence that the new culture is important, preferably evidence that evokes some emotion. Visible actions by senior managers, language, and symbols are an important way to convey these changes. For example, Nadella replaced the word "Windows" with

"Azure" and continually spoke of "cloud first and mobility first." Initially, this didn't mean that people agreed with this view, but there was no denying that senior management was serious about it. A similar symbolic event took place during the first offsite with Nadella and his senior managers. Instead of standing at a podium and reviewing slides, they sat casually on a sofa and talked openly about their purpose for being at Microsoft. After making a public mistake, Nadella publicly apologized and used the opportunity to reinforce the idea of a growth mindset, saying, "I need to be comfortable with confronting my own fixed mindset. We're always going to be imperfect. The question is, are we working to close that gap?"[12] He emphasizes the need to construct a consistent narrative and to overcommunicate, using both traditional and nontraditional methods.

5. **HR Alignment**
   The final lever for driving culture change is one that is sometimes overlooked – making sure that all the HR processes reinforce the new desired behaviors and do not reward the old ones. The danger here is that the old systems and processes that were appropriate for the old strategy are allowed to continue in the new regime. Beyond changing the performance management system, Nadella and Hogan centralized all training on a new platform, providing the training and tools for 27,000 managers to inculcate the new culture, and modifying the recruitment and selection process to be more inclusive, including sourcing candidates from a broader set of universities and shifting the emphasis from screening out candidates to screening them in. This meant changing the onboarding process and training interviewers in unconscious bias, defining what inclusive behaviors looked like, and offering more inclusive hiring tools. Hogan also redefined the talent management system so that promotions were based on a growth mindset and living the Microsoft values.

CONCLUSION

What can we learn from the culture change effort at Microsoft? Two lessons seem important. First, as shown in Figure 19.1, this was a highly integrated effort that included a top-down (e.g., consistent top leadership actions, memorable messaging, aligned rewards, and the allocation of time, attention, and resources) and bottom-up (e.g., employee participation, feedback, celebrations, and the identification and recognition of cultural heroes) approach. Importantly, the leaders defined this effort as a journey, not a destination. Nadella says, "I'm very, very careful not to paint this as some sort of destination we will reach."[13] As Kathleen Hogan notes, culture change is a *process*, not an event. The challenge is to stay focused on the culture change and not lose focus or become distracted, because the minute this happens the mixed signals from senior management will degrade the attention to the desired behaviors. Even after eight years in the job, Nadella remains relentless in reinforcing the growth mindset.

LEVERS FOR CULTURE CHANGE (The LEASH Model)	MICROSOFT
1. **Leader Actions** - that signal the required new attitudes and behavior; and what isn't acceptable	• Spent 9 months "listening" - SLT meetings, focus groups, surveys, town halls, videos, and culture experts. What needs to change and what doesn't? • Offsite with 180 Corporate VPs, training for 27,000 managers
2. **Employee Involvement** - in social activities, ceremonies, and feedback, that promote psychological ownership	• Focus groups, dialog meetings with employees, surveys, pulse checks, 3-day hackathon for 18,000 • Don't change everything, build on the strengths and honor the past
3. **Aligned Rewards** that emphasize status, recognition, approval and promotion - but not big money	• Changed performance management system to emphasize collaboration • Promotion to Corporate VP includes a "culture interview" • Performance based on shared metrics rather than just individual accomplishment
4. **Stories and Symbols** - of the new culture through stories, symbols, heroes, and language	• Develops a consistent narrative for the culture change and constantly over-communicates, a "Growth Mindset" • Senior meetings start with a culture "story" • Nadella publicly acknowledges his mistakes
5. **HR System Alignment** - to include recruitment, selection, training and promotion	• Changed the performance management system to collaboration and growth mindset • Centralized all training to emphasize growth mindset – "manager in a box" training (27,000 managers) • Used Human Resource Business Analytics to monitor the culture change

Figure 19.1 Levers for culture change: The LEASH model.

A second important lesson has to do with the integrated use of all five levers in the LEASH model. Each separate lever is a way to signal to members of the organization which behaviors are desired and valued and which behaviors are not. Each can work by itself, but there is a multiplicative effect from aligning all five. Put yourself in the position of an employee who sees and hears senior managers consistently emphasizing and demonstrating a particular pattern of behavior, who has participated in defining these behaviors, who can see others being rewarded for their behavior (or, sometimes more powerfully, can see others failing because they are not behaving in the correct way), who can see memorable examples of the behavior, and whose HR practices reinforce these. Under these circumstances there is little ambiguity about how to behave.

The conclusion is not complicated: culture, the pattern of behavior that is reinforced by people and systems over time, results from the signals that are sent through each of the five levers. When these levers are aligned, employees can see and feel what the "culture" looks like and understand how they should behave. Their choice is either to comply, fit in, and maybe succeed – or to not comply and be excluded.

IMPLICATIONS

Culture *can* be managed, but it requires leaders to *consciously* choose to encourage different patterns of behavior across explore and exploit units. The danger is that unless leaders are careful, the dominant core culture will be unconsciously transmitted to the explore unit – and this almost always kills the new venture. We have seen this mistake too often. A leader embraces the idea of ambidexterity and establishes an explore unit with the mission of developing new businesses. But the leaders of this business sometimes bring with them the culture that made them successful in the old business where real risk taking was to be avoided and compliance was rewarded. Or, as the new unit attempts to leverage assets from the core business, the dominant core culture resists the new ways of working and demands compliance with old ways of doing things. In this way, culture can be a silent killer of ambidexterity.

APPENDIX FRAMEWORKS

APPENDIX I

01	**CONTEXT** (250–300 Words)	
02	**CHALLENGE** (500–600 Words)	
03	**AMBITION** (300–400 Words)	
04	**STRATEGIC CHOICES** (250–300 Words)	
05	**EXECUTION** (250–300 Words)	
06	**NEXT STEPS** (250-300 Words)	

APPENDIX 2

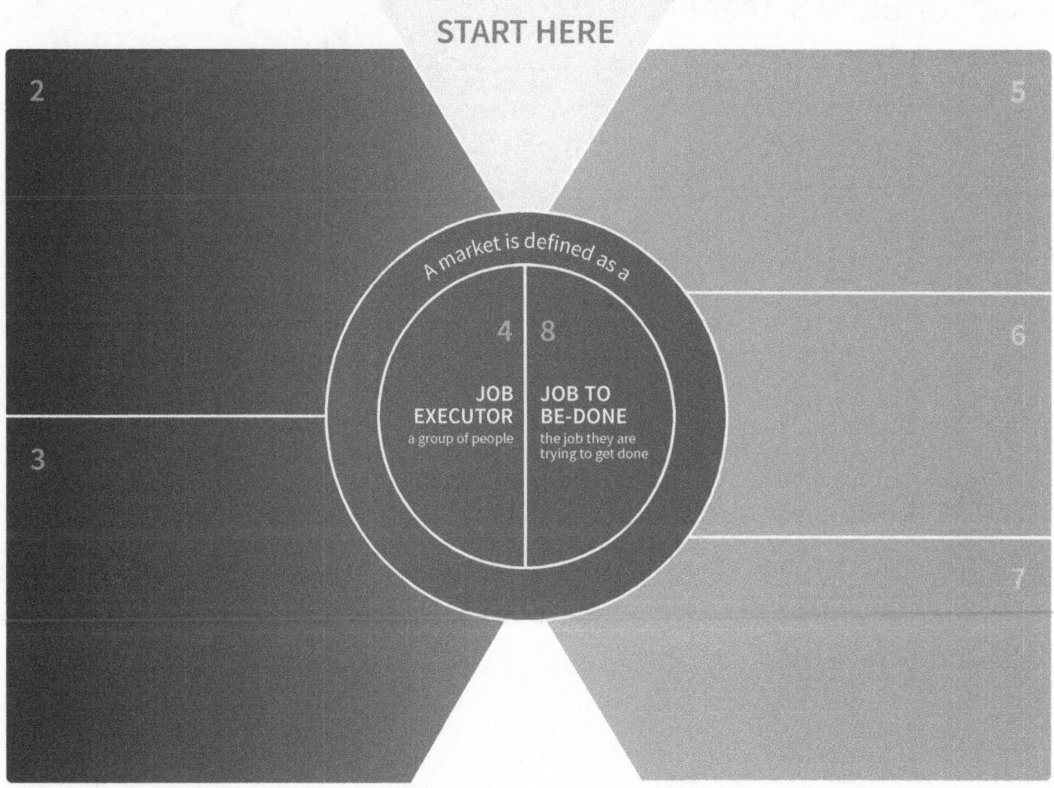
START HERE
2
3
5
6
7
A market is defined as a
4
JOB EXECUTOR
a group of people
8
JOB TO BE-DONE
the job they are trying to get done

APPENDIX 3

Opportunity Screener

			OPPORTUNITY?	EVIDENCE
SUFFICIENT OPPORTUNITY?	Size of Market	Number & Strength of Competing Solutions	Total = Size X Improvement	
	3 = Large 2 = Medium 1 = Small	3 = Few 2 = Some 1 = Many	9 = High 4 = Medium 1 = Low	
END USER "HAIR ON FIRE" PAIN?	Frequency of Task	Time & Frustration to Do Task	Total = Frequency X Frustration	
	3 = Large 2 = Medium 1 = Small	3 = Few 2 = Some 1 = Many	9 = High 4 = Medium 1 = Low	
SOLUTION OWNABILITY & DELIGHT?	Available & Ownable Solution	Solution Improvement vs Current Solutions	Total = Ownable X Improvement	
	3 = Large 2 = Medium 1 = Small	3 = Few 2 = Some 1 = Many	9 = High 4 = Medium 1 = Low	

APPENDIX 4

Value Proposition Assessment

	FUNCTIONAL		EMOTIONAL		SOCIAL
OVERSHOT					
DELIGHTFUL					
GOOD ENOUGH					
NOT GOOD ENOUGH					
	Shoes Securely Fastened	Fast/Easy Process	Encourages Child Development	Feel Like a Good Parent	Fashion

★ New Value Proposition

● Existing Solution

APPENDIX 5

Critical Assumptions Matrix

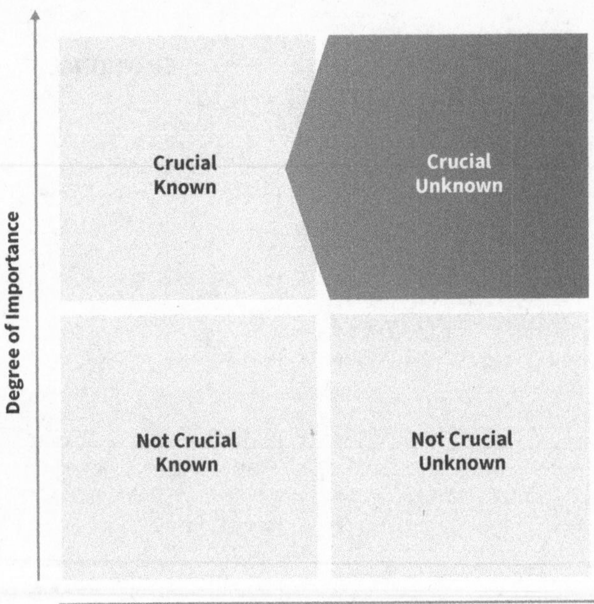

APPENDIX 6

Experiment Card

ASSUMPTION	
LEARNING OBJECTIVES	
HYPOTHESIS (If testable assumption)	SAMPLE SIZE (If testable assumption)
EXPERIMENT METHOD	
EXPERIMENT LENGTH	
EXPERIMENT PLAN	

APPENDIX 7

Ecosystem Assessment

Status of adoption / co-innovation by this player?

- **Clear reasons to prefer status quo / not in place and no clear plan**
- **Neutral but open to inducement / plan in place**
- **Eager to participate / ready to go**

Player	Capabilities Can the player do what they need to do in order to make the ecosystem work?	Incentives Is there an incentive for them to adopt the proposed solution?	Risk Does the innovation pose a risk for existing ecosystem participants causing them to oppose adoption?	Profit Pool Is there enough value being generated for the player to accelerate adoption?	Verdict...
					○
					○
					○

APPENDIX 8

Explore Unit Members' Skills

ROLE	SKILLS	KEY EXPERIENCES	ATTRIBUTES				SKILLS/KNOW		
			Adaptable	Customer Oriented	Courageous	Collaborative	Domain Expertise	Technology	Inn. Methods

APPENDIX 9

Leadership Movement Analysis

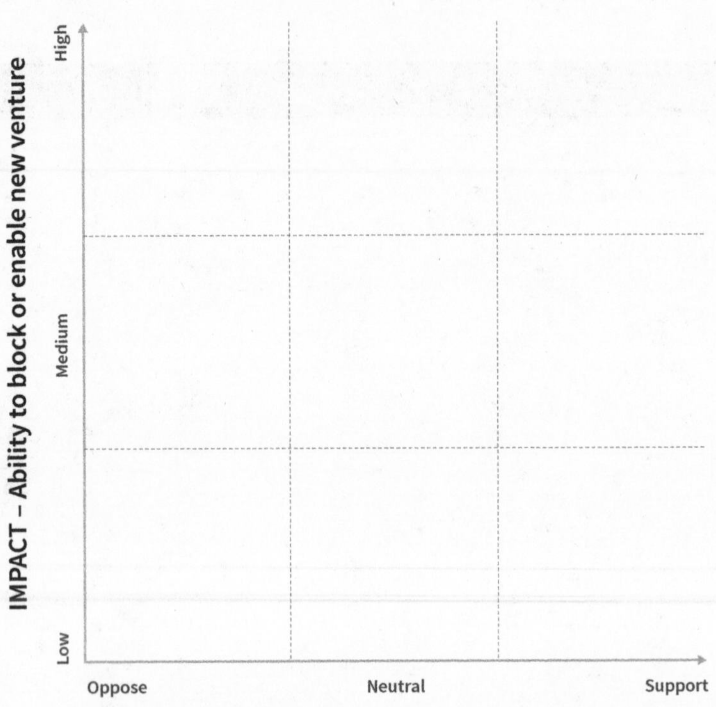

LIST OF FIGURES AND TABLES

Figures

Tables

NOTES

PREFACE AND ACKNOWLEDGMENTS

1. A. Binns, C. O'Reilly, and M. Tushman, *Corporate Explorer: How Corporations Beat Startups at the Innovation Game* (Wiley, 2022).

CORPORATE EXPLORATION: INSIGHTS FROM THE FIELD

1. A. Binns, C. O'Reilly, and M. Tushman, *Corporate Explorer: How Corporations Beat Startups at the Innovation Game* (Wiley, 2022).
2. Mike Beer is Cahners-Rabb Professor of Business Administration, Emeritus at the Harvard Business School.

CHAPTER 2: HUNTING ZONES: SELECTING WHERE TO EXPLORE

1. A. Wilkinson, *The Creator's Code: The Six Essential Skills of Extraordinary Entrepreneurs* (Simon & Schuster, 2015).
2. A. Binns, C. O'Reilly, and M. Tushman, "Leading Disruption in a Legacy Business," *MIT Sloan Management Review* 63, no. 3 (Spring 2022).
3. Charles O'Reilly and Michael Tushman, *Lead and Disrupt: How to Solve the Innovator's Dilemma,* 2nd ed. (Stanford University Press, 2021).
4. *The Economist*, "Cutting the Cord," October 7, 1999, https://www.economist.com/special-report/1999/10/07/cutting-the-cord, and *Los Angeles Times,* "405 Million Mobile Phones Sold in 2000, and Makers Still Get Stung," January 10, 2001, https://www.latimes.com/archives/la-xpm-2001-jan-10-fi-10497-story.html.
5. O'Reilly and Tushman, *Lead and Disrupt*.
6. AGC Annual Report 2022, https://www.agc.com/en/company/agc_report/index.html.

CHAPTER 3: OUTSIDE-IN: OVERCOMING TOXIC ASSUMPTIONS WITH MARKET INSIGHT

1. Pogo, comic strip character, https://library.osu.edu/site/40stories/2020/01/05/we-have-met-the-enemy/
2. P. Senge, "Mental Models. Putting Strategic Ideas into Practice," *Planning Review* 20, no. 2 (March–April 1992).
3. G. Hamel and C. K. Prahalad, *Competing for the Future* (Harvard Business Review Press, 1996), and D. Sull, "Why Good Companies Go Bad," *Harvard Business Review* (July/August 1999).
4. D. Leonard and J. F. Rayport. "Spark Innovation Through Emphatic Design," *Harvard Business Review* (November/December 1997).
5. G. Stalk, Jr., K. Pecaut, and B. Burnett, "Breaking Compromises, Breakaway Growth," *Harvard Business Review* (September/October 1996).
6. I. C. MacMillan and R. Gunther McGrath, "Discovering New Points of Differentiation," *Harvard Business Review* (July/August 1997).

CHAPTER 5: FROM EXPLORER'S INSIGHT TO OPPORTUNITY STORY

1. J. Dyer, N. Furr, and M. Hendron, "Overcoming the Innovator's Paradox," *MIT Sloan Management Review* 62, no. 1 (Fall 2020).
2. A. Binns, C. O'Reilly, and M. Tushman, *Corporate Explorer: How Corporations Beat Startups at the Innovation Game* (Wiley, 2022).

CHAPTER 6: IDEATION FROM WITHIN: HOW TO GENERATE BREAKTHROUGH IDEAS FROM WITHIN LARGE CORPORATIONS

1. N. Machiavelli, *The Prince*, translated by George Bull (Penguin Classics, 2003).
2. K. Krippendorff, *Outthink the Competition: How Innovative Companies and Strategists See Options Other Ignore* (The Strategy Learning Center, 2022).
3. K. Krippendorff, *Strategic Narratives and Competitive Advantage: Do Winners Speak Differently?* (Abo Akademi University Press, 2014).
4. K. Krippendorff, *The Art of the Advantage* (The Strategy Learning Center, 2007).

CHAPTER 7: IDEATION FROM OUTSIDE: A STEP-BY-STEP GUIDE TO CHALLENGE-DRIVEN INNOVATION

1. S. Hill and A. Bingham, *One Smart Crowd: How Crowdsourcing Is Changing the World One Idea at a Time* (Independently published, 2020).
2. S. Johnson, *Where Good Ideas Come From: The Natural History of Innovation* (Riverhead Books, 2011).

3. A. Bingham and D. Spradlin, *The Open Innovation Marketplace* (FT Press, 2011).
4. Johnson, *Where Good Ideas Come From.*
5. Bingham, and Spradlin, *The Open Innovation Marketplace.*
6. T. W. Malone, *Superminds: How Hyperconnectivity Is Changing the Way We Solve Problems* (Oneworld Publications, 2019).
7. Bingham, and Spradlin, *The Open Innovation Marketplace.*

CHAPTER 9: GET OUT OF THE BUILDING: HOW TO GATHER CUSTOMER DISCOVERY DATA WITH INTERVIEWS

1. M. Granger Morgan, B. Fischhoff, A. Bostrom, and C. J. Atman, *Risk Communication: A Mental Models Approach* (Cambridge University Press, 2002).
2. G. Guest, A. Bunce, and L. Johnson, "How Many Interviews Are Enough? An Experiment with Data Saturation and Variability," *Field Methods* 18, no. 1 (2006).

CHAPTER 10: VALUE PROPOSITIONS: USING VALUE FLOWS AND DESIGN CRITERIA MAPS TO CREATE CUSTOMER DELIGHT

1. H. West, "A Chain of Innovation: The Creation of Swiffer," Research-Technology Management (May 2014).

CHAPTER 11: BUSINESS EXPERIMENTS: DE-RISKING EXECUTION SPEND THROUGH EXPERIMENTS

1. A. Binns, C. O'Reilly, and M. Tushman, *Corporate Explorer: How Corporations Beat Startups at the Innovation Game* (Wiley, 2022).
2. A. Maurya, *Running Lean: Iterate from Plan A to a Plan That Works,* 2nd ed. (O'Reilly Media, 2012).
3. A. Binns, "How Not to Invest Ahead of Learning," Change Logic blog, February 14, 2022, https://changelogic.com/blog/how-not-to-invest-ahead-of-learning/.
4. The Durant Guild, GM (China) Investment Co., Ltd., https://www.durantguild.com/cn/en.
5. D. Toma, and E. Gons, *Innovation Accounting: A Practical Guide for Measuring Your Innovation Ecosystem's Performance* (BIS Publishers, 2022).
6. Binns, O'Reilly, and Tushman, *Corporate Explorer.*
7. SAIC General Motors Corporation Limited (SAIC-GM) is a joint venture between GM and SAIC Motor that manufactures and sells Chevrolet, Buick, and Cadillac brand automobiles in Mainland China.
8. To be noted that, due to a limited number of GMPI resources, a subset of potential solutions coming out of the ideate discipline was prioritized for incubation based on their foreseen innovative aspects and business potential.
9. For example, the value proposition team learned through experiments that another customer segment than the one initially targeted for their vehicle subscription solution should be given priority.

CHAPTER 12: ECOSYSTEMS: BUILDING AN ECOSYSTEM PLAYBOOK FOR SCALING A NEW VENTURE

1. R. Adner, *Winning the Right Game: How to Disrupt, Defend, and Deliver in a Changing World* (The MIT Press, 2021).
2. Best Buy, "FY22 Results and Investor Update," March 3, 2022, https://s2.q4cdn.com/785564492/files/doc_financials/2022/q4/Best-Buy-Investor-Event-March-2022.pdf.
3. Adner, *Winning the Right Game*.

CHAPTER 13: VALIDATION: MANAGING THE JOURNEY FROM CONCEPT TO SCALE

1. C. Janz, "Five Ways to Build a $100 Million Business," 2014, https://medium.com/point-nine-news/five-ways-to-build-a-100-million-business-82ac6ea8ffd9.
2. P. Hillenbrand, D. Kiewell, R. Miller-Cheevers, G. Springer, and I. Ostojic, "Traditional Company, New Businesses: The Pairing that Can Ensure an Incumbent's Survival," McKinsey & Company, June 28, 2019, https://www.mckinsey.com/industries/oil-and-gas/our-insights/traditional-company-new-businesses-the-pairing-that-can-ensure-an-incumbents-survival.
3. S. Sinek, *Start with Why: How Great Leaders Inspire Everyone to Take Action* (Penguin, 2011).
4. CBI Insights, "The Top 12 Reasons Startups Fail," August 3, 2021, https://www.cbinsights.com/research/report/startup-failure-reasons-top/.
5. Janz, "Five Ways to Build a $100 Million Business."
6. P. Thiel and B. Masters, *Zero to One: Notes on Startups, or How to Build the Future* (Crown Business, 2014).
7. S. Kirsner, "Don't Let Financial Metrics Prematurely Stifle Innovation," *Harvard Business Review* (March/April 2021).

CHAPTER 14: AMBIDEXTROUS ORGANIZATION: WHAT IT IS, WHEN TO USE IT

1. Charles O'Reilly and Michael Tushman, *Lead and Disrupt: How to Solve the Innovator's Dilemma,* 2nd ed. (Stanford University Press, 2021).
2. M. Tushman, W. Smith, R. Wood, G. Westerman, and C. O'Reilly, "Organizational Design and Innovation Streams," *Industrial and Corporate Change* 19 (2010).
3. *Foreign Affairs,* "The Man Who Sells Everything: A Conversation with Jeff Bezos" (January/February 2015).
4. Hideyuki Kurata is Representative Director, Executive Vice President, CTO, General Manager of the Technology General Division, and General Manager of the Business Development Division at AGC, Inc., global corporation headquartered in Tokyo, Japan.

CHAPTER 15: EXPLORE UNIT: HOW TO BUILD A TEAM FOR EXPLORATION

1. J. Doerr, *Measure What Matters: OKRs: The Simple Idea That Drives 10X Growth* (Penguin Random House, 2018).
2. R. Hastings, and E. Meyer, *No Rules Rules: Netflix and the Culture of Reinvention* (Penguin Press, 2020).
3. O'Reilly and Tushman, *Lead and Disrupt*.
4. F. Malik, *Managing Performing Living: Effective Management for a New World* (Campus, 2015).

CHAPTER 16: STRATEGIC DIVERSITY: SELECTING AND DEVELOPING CORPORATE EXPLORATION TEAMS

1. P. Robertson and W. Schoonman, "How People Contribute to Growth-Curves," *ResearchGate* (July 2013).

CHAPTER 17: LEADING HIGH-STAKES CONVERSATIONS: GETTING THE SENIOR TEAM ONBOARD

1. The concept of productive tension was introduced to Alex Pett by Todd Holzman from consulting firm Holzman Leadership (www.holzman.com).
2. D. Kantor, *Reading the Room: Group Dynamics for Coachers and Leaders* (Jossey Bass, 2012).

CHAPTER 18: LEADERSHIP MOVEMENT: ENROLLING OTHERS IN THE WORK OF TRANSFORMATION

1. M. Tushman and C. O'Reilly, *Winning Through Innovation* (Harvard Press, 2002).
2. A. Binns, C. O'Reilly, and M. Tushman, *Corporate Explorer: How Corporations Beat Startups at the Innovation Game* (Wiley, 2022).

CHAPTER 19: ORGANIZATIONAL CULTURE: THE SILENT KILLER OF EXPLORATION

1. M. D. Burton and C. O'Reilly, "Management Systems for Exploration and Exploitation," *Research in the Sociology of Organizations* 76 (2021): 53–77.
2. Deloitte Chairman's Survey.
3. "Global Culture Survey 2021: The Link Between Culture and Competitive Advantage," PwC, 2021.
4. J. R. Graham, C. R. Harvey, J. Popadak, and S. Rajgopal, "Corporate Culture: Evidence from the Field," NBER Working Paper 23255, National Bureau of Economic Research, March 2017.

5. N. Goodrich, "Culture Renovation: A Blueprint for Action," Institute for Corporate Productivity, March 21, 2019.
6. C. O'Reilly, "Corporations, Culture and Commitment: Motivation and Social Control in Organizations," *California Management Review* 31 (1989): 9–25.
7. C. O'Reilly and M. Tushman, *Lead and Disrupt: How to Solve the Innovator's Dilemma*, 2nd ed. (Stanford University Press, 2021), Chapter 4.
8. C. O'Reilly, X. Cao, and D. Sull, "CEO Personality: The Cornerstone of Organizational Culture," working paper, Stanford University, 2023.
9. T. White, "Microsoft's Big Layoffs Lays Bare the Dangers of Cultural Change," *Entrepreneur*, July 21, 2014.
10. R. B. Cialdini, *Influence: The Psychology of Persuasion* (New York: HarperCollins, 2007).
11. R. Carlucci, "Microsoft's Chief People Officer: What I've Learned About Leading Culture Change," *Forbes*, October 14, 2019.
12. S. Nadella, presentation at the Stanford Graduate School of Business, 2019. https://www.youtube.com/watch?v=rtgN27z0oi0.
13. Ibid.

ABOUT THE AUTHORS

ELLIE AMIRNASR

Ellie Amirnasr is a director of digital ventures at MANN+HUMMEL. She is responsible for commercializing digital products and services for clean air, clean water, and clean mobility. She is a successful Corporate Explorer, having launched qlair, MANN+HUMMEL's first corporate startup.

ANDREW BINNS

Andrew Binns is a co-founder of Change Logic, a strategic advisory firm, and lead author of *Corporate Explorer* (Wiley, 2021). He is an active keynote speaker on innovation and change.

ANDREAS BRANDSTETTER

Andreas Brandstetter is CEO of UNIQA Insurance Group AG and president of Insurance Europe, an industry group representing European insurance and reinsurance companies.

SARA CARVALHO

Sara Carvalho is a director at Bosch Business Model Innovation Consulting. She was previously a Corporate Explorer at Bosch, developing a business to provide affordable and sustainable hot water to developing nations.

VANESSA CEIA

Dr. Vanessa Ceia is an innovation strategy and management consultant, expert researcher, and policy advisor on responsible tech. She is Global Innovation Lead at Oxfam America and part of Change Logic's extend team. She was formerly a professor at McGill University.

VINCENT DUCRET

Vincent Durcret is an associate principal with Change Logic, and lecturer at the University of St. Gallen and the International Institute in Geneva. He was formerly Head of Design Thinking and Lean Enterprise at Philip Morris International.

YANIV GARTY

Yaniv Garty is a former Intel VP and CEO of Intel Israel. Garty joined Intel as part of the acquisition of Envara and rose through the ranks to serve as the general manager of Intel's Wireless Connectivity Solutions business group.

GEORGE GLACKIN

George Glackin is the founder of the Hatch Innovation Hub, a startup incubator based in Asheville, North Carolina. George founded Hatch following a 35-year career at Procter & Gamble, where he led innovation teams on major brands and led efforts to create new businesses for the company.

JOHN GRECO

John Greco is Director of Market Insight for Automotive segments at Analog Devices. He has worked in product marketing, application engineering, and in strategic planning during his career.

CHRISTINE GRIFFIN

Christine Griffin is a principal at Change Logic. She was previously a founder CEO of a technology startup and management consultant at McKinsey & Company.

SIMON HILL

Simon Hill is the founder and CEO of Wazoku, a B corporation and leader in the global innovation management software sector. Simon is a TEDx speaker, author of *One Smart Crowd*, and a passionate believer in the potential of people aided by technology to drive innovation at scale toward Wazoku's mission to change the world, one idea at a time.

EUGENE IVANOV

Dr. Eugene Ivanov is a technical and business writer and editor. He is interested in open innovation, innovation management, and technology.

UWE KIRSCHNER

Dr. Uwe Kirschner is vice president of Bosch Management Consulting and partner, Business Model Innovation, at Robert Bosch GmbH.

KAIHAN KRIPPENDORFF

Kaihan Krippendorff is the founder and CEO of Outthinker, a think-tank that builds corporate communities and conducts research on business strategy, innovation, and technology. He is a keynote speaker and advisor of leading organizations shaping the future.

ERICH KRUSCHITZ

Erich Kruschitz is the founder and chief exploration officer for SanusX, a corporate startup of UNIQA Insurance Group, and deputy chair of the supervisory board for PremiQaMed Group.

NARENDRA LALJANI

Narendra Laljani is a management educator, consultant, and coach. He has worked at board level with international corporations and has also taught for several leading MBA programs. Narendra is the program director of the Henley Business School Executive Management Program.

MICHAEL NICHOLS

Michael Nichols is a director of corporate ventures for MANN+HUMMEL and honorary practice fellow at Imperial College Business School.

PROFESSOR CHARLES A. O'REILLY, III

Charles O'Reilly is the Frank E. Buck Professor of Management at Stanford Graduate School of Business and co-founder of Change Logic. Charles is the author, with Mike Tushman, of *Lead and Disrupt* (Stanford University Press, 2021) and *Winning Through Innovation* (Harvard Business School Press, 2000).

ALEXANDER PETT

Alex Pett is a leadership coach, advisor, and consultant, with many decades of experience working with C-suite executives and their teams. He was previously head of leadership development at Kingfisher Group and BT Global Services in the UK.

RICHARD ROBERTSON

Richard Robertson is partner and leader for content development at Netherlands-based Human Insight. He also lectures on strategic diversity and organizational ecology.

BEA SCHOFIELD

Bea Schofield is a senior innovation manager at Lloyds Bank Group and former director of customer innovation at Wazoku. Bea works with organizations to build innovation capabilities and increase innovation success. She is a specialist in crowdsourced innovation, putting important problems out to internal or external crowds to capture, evaluate, and implement ideas and solutions.

SARAH SPOTO

Sarah Spoto is head of marketing for General Motors, Europe. She was previously director of brand strategy and innovation at GM Premium Import (The Durant Guild) in Shanghai, China.

PROFESSOR MICHAEL L. TUSHMAN

Michael Tushman is Baker Foundation Professor and Paul R. Lawrence, MBA Class of 1942 Professor Emeritus, at the Harvard Business School, and co-founder of Change Logic. He is the co-author of *Lead and Disrupt* and *Winning Through Innovation*, with Charles O'Reilly, and *Corporate Explorer,* with Andy Binns and Charles O'Reilly.

TONY ULWICK

Tony Ulwick is the pioneer of jobs-to-be-done theory, the inventor of the Outcome-Driven Innovation® (ODI) process, and the founder of the strategy and innovation consulting firm Strategyn.

KRISTIN VON DONOP

Kristin is a principal at Change Logic. She advises senior leadership teams on how to accelerate execution of growth and innovation strategies.

CHARLES VAILLANT

Charles is MANN+HUMMEL chief technology officer and chief digital officer. He is responsible for new technologies, corporate ventures, digital ventures, Big Data analytics, and digital transformation. He is known for creating entrepreneurial cultures that effectively challenge the status quo and building business strategies aimed at reaching optimal growth and profitability.

INDEX

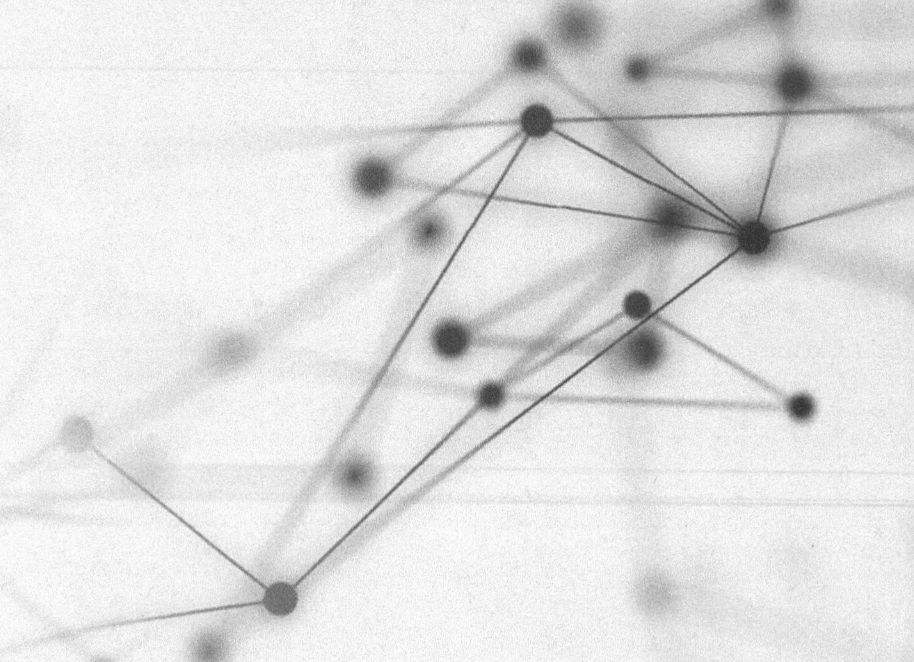